The Lives of the Most Eminent Saints of the Oriental Deserts
by Richard Challoner

Challone

THE
LIVES
OF THE MOST

EMINENT SAINTS
OF THE

ORIENTAL DESERTS,
OR THE

WONDERS OF GOD
IN

THE WILDERNESS.

TO WHICH IS ADDED

AN APPENDIX,

Containing a Collection of remarkable Anecdotes, Aphorisms, &c. of the Eastern Solitaries; compiled from the genuine works of the Holy Fathers, and other Ecclesiastical Writers.

BY BISHOP CHALLONER, V. A. L.

NEW YORK:

J. McLOUGHLIN. PRINTER AND PUBLISHER, 139 Centre Street.
1841.

PREFACE.

THE Lives of the Saints of the Deserts have been always looked upon as the most edifying, as well as entertaining part of ancient church history. The wonders which the grace of God manifested in them, as they have ever engaged the attention of all wellwishers to Christianity, so have they likewise employed the pens of the most eminent eccelsiastical writers and doctors of the church, by which means they immediately produced an extraordinary degree of fervour and piety amongst all ranks of the faithful in every part of Christendom. Neither were these salutary effects confined to the times when the lives and maxims of those servants of God were first published; but as the books wherein they were contained have in every age been carefully preserved in the hands of such as aspired to religious perfection, and since the invention of printing, communicated to all the faithful through innumerable editions, as well in the learned as in the vulgar languages, so they have always continued to produce in the proper soil of well-disposed souls, the happy fruits of grace and life everlasting.

That an attentive perusal of them may prove as benficial to the souls of our countrymen as to those of other nations, is our principal motive in presenting this abstract to the American reader; to whom it may also serve as an Essay upon a part of History which has never appeared collectively in our language, in the compilation whereof we have been careful, first, not to insert any thing for the truth of which we had not the testimony of authors well informed of the facts they deliver; and, in the next place, not to lard our history with our own reflections, but to season it with the words and sentiments of the saints themselves, and the sublime lessons they inculcated to those who came to consult them. Although many of the practices recorded in the lives of those illustrious men, which they were authorised to follow by an extraordinary inspiration, are out of the common road of the other servants of God, and therefore more to be admired than imitated, we may, nevertheless, from the consideration of them, take occasion both to glorify God, who is wonderful in his saints (Ps. lxvii. 36), and animate ourselves to greater fervour and perfection in the discharge of our ordinary christian duties.

By way of Appendix we have added a collection of several of the remarkable sayings, memorable actions, and examples of the ancient religious, from the most authentic records of the ages in which they lived, which we hope will both delight and edify the reader, whose spiritual advantage alone we have in view; dedicating the whole to the greater glory of our common Master, the God of all the Saints, to whom be praise, honour, and glory, for ever and ever.   Amen.

INTRODUCTION.

AMONGST the various departments of reading, none can be more interesting than that which records the actions of men who have rendered themselves illustrious by their wisdom, their heroism, or their eminent virtues. In the Lives of the Saints of the Oriental Deserts, the reader will find an heroism that exceeds the natural powers of man;—a wisdom, in comparison of which that of a Socrates or a Solon is but childishness (for wisdom becomes more or less estimable in proportion to the value of the objects that attract its attention); hence the virtues of the illustrious characters whose memoirs are the subject of the subsequent pages, as far surpass those of the most exalted characters of Pagan antiquity, as man in a state of nature is surpassed by the angelic spirits.

Many traits will be found in their lives that cannot accord with the enervated delicacy of modern ideas and habits, pre-occupied, as they unfortunately are, by the false maxims and vitiated manners of an age that labours to substitute a vain philosophy, the pander of every passion, in lieu of divine revelation, which not only commands and affords the means of their subjugation, but also invites us to erect on their ruins the fabric of evangelical perfection.

The Almighty has at all times inspired his servants with a conduct suitable to the exigencies of the age in which they lived. making them all to all, in order to gain all to himself. Reasonings and exhortations make but a feeble impression on ignorant or brutal men, accustomed to blood and pillage;—men who, as they had been trained up in the fatigues of war, and were always in the har-

1*

ness,—hardened in vicious habits and blinded by heredi-
tary errors, would have esteemed ordinary austerties as to
nothing ; but when they witnessed an absolute contempt
of all earthly comforts in an Antony, a Macarius, &c. the
severe chastisements they inflicted on themselves, and their
alacrity in assuaging the corporal as well as the spiritual
necessities of others, which proceeded to such a length as
even to do penance for them, what could they infer, but
that they loved God and their neighbour with an ardour
at once holy and invincible. With minds therefore deeply
impressed with so edifying an exterior, they became more
docile; and from listening to those whom they so greatly
admired, at length became proselytes to the holy religion
they professed. Thus St. Abraham, by his invincible
patience and meekness under a series of the most cruel
outrages for the space of three years, more than by his
preaching, subdued the blindness and obstinacy of the
Pagans near Edessa, who were at length obliged to acknowledge, "that the God whom he preached must be
the true God, and the religion which taught him so much
patience and charity, the true religion." Thus Theodoret witnessed Simon Stylites from his pillar receiving the
abjuration of multitudes of Iberians, Armenians, Persians,
and Saracens, who, in his presence, with a loud voice renounced their idols, and trampled them under foot. And
thus barbarians and infidels of distant regions frequently
invoked with success, protection amidst the dangers of
the sea, in the name of the God of Theodosius.

But it is not in Pagan or barbarian nations only, that
the lives of these illustrious men have contributed to promote the cause of God and virtue :—St. Chrysostom, who
was no less distinguished for his learning and accom-
plishments, than for being the metropolitan of the Eastern
Empire, recommends (Hom. 8. in Matt. 7. p. 128,) the
reading the life of St. Antony, as replete with instruction
and edification ; and St. Augustin, in the eighth book of
his Confessions, chap, 6, gives a minute detail of the conversion of two courtiers in the emperor's service, who had
renounced the world by accidentally reading the life of

St. Antony; and moreover attributes his own conversion in a great measure to the same cause.

There was a time when the bare testimonies either of St. Chrysostom or St. Augustin, would render any further arguments in favour of a work of this kind unnecessary; but, unfortunately in an age wherein scepticism and infidelity are so prevalent, the most venerable authority or incontestible evidence in support of miraculous or supernaturnl events, whether of an ancient or modern date, will not always satisfy the weak or temporising amongst those who consider themselves of the number of the faithful—who generally listen with indifference, or treat with disdain and derision, the bare mention of a miracle; for stupidity itself will on such occasions assume the office of censor, and aspire to wit, when tinctured by the buffoon philosophy of Voltaire's school.

A distinguished modern, MONTESQUIEU, whose works are supposed to have promoted the French Revolution, imagines the spectres that tempted the otherwise assailed St. Antony and others, to have been metaphorical; whereas such a supposition, if admitted as a truth, would not only invalidate the testimonies of SS. Athanasius, Jerome, Cyril, &c. but even the holy scriptures themselves, Wisd. xvii. where it is said, that during the Egyptian darkness. the infernal spirits increased the terror of the inhabitants by frightful apparitions; of whose existence even the Pagan poet Virgil seems to have had some idea.

> yet be not overbold,
> The slippery God will try to loose his hold;
> And various forms assume to cheat thy sight;
> And with vain images of beasts affright.
> With foamy tusks will seem a bristly boar,
> Or imitate the lion's angry roar;
> Break out in crackling flames to shun thy snare,
> Or hiss a dragon, or a tiger stare;
> Or with a wife thy caution to betray,
> In fleeting streams, attempt to slide away.
>
> Georg. B. iv.

That the Almighty has, at certain periods, granted a limited power to the devil personally to tempt or torment

the sons of men, either with a view to put the virtue of
his chosen servants to a trial, and thereby afford them
opportunities of triumphing over the powers of hell, or
for other reasons best known to his ever just but inscrutable judgments, is evident from the testimonies of the scriptures both of the Old and New Testaments: as in the
cases of Job,——our Saviour in the desert——the young man
possessed by the devil ; and several other instances of the
kind recorded by the Evangelists.   Similar events have
also frequently occurred in every age of the church, in
countries emerging, or struggling to emerge, from Idolatry into Christianity through the missionary labours of
apostolical men;* for when Satan perceives kingdoms
over which he had for so long a time exercised an almost
unlimited control, on the point of being extricated from
his dominion, it is then he exerts the utmost extent of his
power to retain them under his subjection.

   In a word, whatever may appear supernatural to our
readers, in the perusal of the lives of these holy solitaries,
rests on the same credit and authority as the most ordinary and familiar circumstance related of them; nor is
any miraculous interposition of Providence enabling them
to pursue a system of life, impossible to mere human efforts, that has not a parallel in the holy scriptures themselves: for example, if some of them fasted many weeks
without any corporal sustenance [without referring to the
forty days' fast of our Saviour in the desert], did not Elias
and St. John the Baptist also fast in the same rigorous manner?   If St. Paul the first hermit was miraculously fed
by a raven, was not the prophet Elias also fed in a like
miraculous manner?   If a lioness saved the life of St.
Malchus and his companion in a cave, and destroyed their
vengeful pursuers, did not bears also rush from the woods
to devour the wicked children who had derided and insulted the baldness of Elizeus the prophet?   But however
wonderful and interesting the events here recorded of
these venerable solitaries may appear, yet the sublime

---

* See Butler's " Lives of the Saints."   See also " Missiones Orien·
tales," recue et imprime a Londres, ann. 1797.

virtues which they practised are by far more deserving of our frequent contemplation. In profane history we often discover the most splendid actions of worldly heroes tainted by motives of pride, vanity, or self-interest: whereas we invariably find the heroes of the wilderness to have founded their greatness on the most profound humility, and absolute annihilation of their own will, that they might the more implicitly conform in every action and circumstance of their lives to the holy will of God; hereby exemplifying in themselves the character of a monk or anchoret as drawn by the celebrated Abbé Rancé, founder of the Abbey of La Trappe: "When," says he, "a soul relishes God in solitude, she thinks no longer on any thing but heaven—she forgets the earth, on which there is nothing that can please her—she burns with the fire of divine love, and sighing after God alone, regards death as her greatest advantage. Nevertheless, they will find themselves much deceived, who, on forsaking the world, imagine they shall advance towards God by straight paths, or roads sown with lilies and roses; or that they have chosen a state in which they will find no difficulties to encounter that could disturb the tranquillity of their retreat, which the hand of God will not turn aside: on the contrary, they must be persuaded that temptations will every where pursue them; that there is no time nor any place wherein they can be exempt from them; that the peace which God promises is procured in the midst of tribulations, as rosebuds are found among thorns. God has not promised his servants that they should meet with no trials, but that with the temptation he will also give them the grace to overcome it. Heaven is offered us on no other condition: it is a kingdom of conquests, a prize of victory; but, O God! what a prize!!!",

THE
LIVES
OF THE
ANCIENT SAINTS
OF THE
ORIENTAL DESERTS.

———◆———

ST. PAUL THE FIRST HERMIT.

Abridged from his Life written by St. Jerome.

THIS Saint was born in the lower Thebais, a province
of Egypt, in the third century, of Christian parents,
who being wealthy in worldly riches took care to give
him a liberal education, and to train him up both in the
Greek and Egyptian literature; yet without any prejudice to his innocence, or christian piety; for which he
was remarkable from his childhood; being always of a
meek and humble disposition, and greatly fearing and
loving his God. His parents dying when he was
about fifteen years of age, left him their estate; which
he had not long enjoyed, when that bloody persecution
set on foot by the Emperor Decius (who employed all
manner of torments to oblige the Christians to renounce
Jesus Christ, and offer sacrifice to idols) had reached
Egypt and Thebais; where it made many martyrs; and
drove many others into the deserts and mountains;
where great numbers of them perished with hunger or
sickness, or fell a pray to robbers and wild beasts; as
we learn from St. Denys, who was at that very time

bishop of Alexandria, in his epistle to Fabius, bishop of
Antioch. Upon this occasion Paul also withdrew himself to a remote country-house, designing to lie concealed there till the storm blew over: but his sister's husband, who was acquainted with the place of his retreat,
conceived a resolution to betray him to the persecutors
in hopes of possessing himself of his estate. The Saint
being informed of his wicked resolution, quitted his
country-house, and fled into the wilderness, where he
purposed to pass his time till the danger was over.
Here, as he advanced still further and further into the
remoter parts of the desert, he came at last to a rocky
mountain, at the foot of which he found a large den or
cave; and going in, he there discovered a kind of a
spacious porch, open at the top to the heavens, but protected by an old palm-tree, which covered it with its
spreading branches: near which there was a spring
of clear water: and in a hollow part of the mountain, several cells or rooms, which, by the instruments he
found there, appeared to have been formerly occupied by
coiners. This place the Saint judged to be very proper
for his abode; and embraced it as a dwelling assigned
him by divine providence for the remainder of his life.
And thus he who thought only at first to hide himself
for a while in the wilderness from the fury of the persecutors, was by the design of God conducted thither, to
be an inhabitant for life, and the first that should dedicate, and, as it were, consecrate, those deserts to divine
love; by living there for so many years a perfect model
of an entire separation and disengagement from all ties
and affections of this world; for the instruction and encouragement of many thousands, who should, by his example, in following ages, embrace a recluse or eremitical life. Thus the malice of his brother-in-law, by driving him away from his worldly possessions, became the
occasion of his embracing a state of life, in and by
which his soul was daily more and more enriched with

the treasures of divine grace, and placed in the most effectual way to secure to herself immense and everlasting treasures in the eternal possession of her God. Upon which occasion we may admire and adore the wonderful ways of the divine goodness, which generally draws the greatest good, even the sanctification and salvation of our souls, from what we poor mortals apprehend as great evils; more especially from the crosses and sufferings of this life, and the loss of those things which are apt to affect us too much, to the prejudice of that love which we owe to God.

But who shall be able to relate the wonderful manner of life our Saint here led, estranged from all conversation with mortals, perpetually addressing himself to God, by prayer and contemplation, night and day; or the the continual progress he made every day in the love of God, the true science of the Saints, and *that better part which they have chosen with Mary, and which never shall be taken from them?* It may suffice to say, that the perfection which he attained to in divine love, which is the true measure of all sanctity, was so great and superemient in the sight of God, as to exceed by far that of St. Antony, the wonder of all ages for christian and religious perfection: and this, by the testimony of God himself: but yet we are not to suppose that, with all his sanctity, he could be exempted in his solitude, no more than St. Antony was, from the temptations and molestations of the common enemy, who, by the permission of God, is most troublesome to those who oppose him most.; though it all turns in the end to their greater good, and his own confusion. As to the food and raiment of St. Paul, we learn from my author, who had his account from the disciples of St. Antony, and they from their master, that he lived (at least for a good part of the time, till God was pleased to provide for him in a miraculous manner) on those dates which the palm-tree produced; and drank of the water of the spring: and

2

as for his clothing, he made himself a garment of the leaves of the same tree, woven together after the manner of a mat or a basket. And lest this austerity of his life might seem to any one incredible, or a thing impossible, St. Jerome in his relation calls our Lord Jesus and his angels to witness, that he himself saw certain solitaries in that part of the desert of Syria which borders upon the Saracens ; one of whom had lived, shut up for thirty years, upon barley bread alone and muddy water ; and another who had chosen for his mansion an old pit or cistern, where he had no other food to subsist on but five dry figs every day.

Our saint had now lived in his solitude to the age of one hundred and thirteen years ; when St. Antony, who was then about ninety years old, was one day thinking with himself that no one amongst the religious of Egypt had penetrated further into those wildernesses than he had done. Whereupon he was one night admonished in a dream, that there was one still further on in the desert much better than himself ; and that he should make haste to visit him. In compliance with this divine admonition, Antony set out at break of day in quest of this servant of God, with great confidence that he who had sent him forth, would conduct him to the place where he should find him. Thus he spent two whole days, fatigued with the labour of the journey, and broiled by the heat of the sun, which is violent in those sandy deserts, meeting with no creature the whole way, except two in monstrous shape ; the one representing a *centaur*, half man, and half a horse, and the other a *satyr*, made up of a man and a goat : which whether they were phantoms and illusions of the enemy, or monsters bred in those vast wildernesses, is uncertain. The Saint, when he opposed to these frightful figures his usual arms, the shield of faith and sign of the cross, neither of them offered him any harm ; but on the contrary the former, on being asked where the servant of

God dwelt, pointing towards the place, ran swiftly away, and disappeared; and the latter brought him some dates for his food; and being asked, who or what he was? delivered an intelligible answer, (by some supernatural power) with an acknowledgment of God, and of Jesus Christ, his Son; which gave the Saint occasion to glorify our Lord, and to reproach the unbelieving city of Alexandria, which refused to acknowledge the true and living God, whom even beasts adored, and worshipped these very beasts instead of him. At which words of the Saint the monster fled away with incredible speed, and was seen no more.

Antony having spent two nights watching in prayer, at break of day on the third morning, he perceived a wolf at a distance panting for thirst, going into a cavern at the foot of a mountain. Whereupon coming up to the place after the beast was gone, he ventured into the cave, advancing cautiously and silently in the dark, till at length he perceived at some distance a glimmering of light (from the opening from above over the porch of the cell of the Saint,) upon which in hastening forward he stumbled upon a stone, when the noise gave occasion to St. Paul to shut his door, and fasten it within. Antony was now convinced that he found the person whom he sought: and coming up to the door earnestly begged for admittance, with many tears, lying prostrate on the ground from morning till noon, (to teach us the necessity of fervour and perseverance in prayer, if we would obtain what we ask,) till at length the holy old man opened the door to him. Then after falling upon each other's neck, embracing each other, and calling one another by their proper names, as if they had been of long acquaintance, they joined in giving thanks to God. When they had sat down together, Paul said to Antony, behold here the man whom thou hast taken so much pains to seek, and who very speedily must return to dust: tell me, then, if thou pleasest, how mankind

goes on ; what is the present state of the empire ;. are
there any still. remaining that worship devils, &c. ?—
Whilst they were discoursing on these matters, they
perceived a raven alighting upon one of the branches
of the palm-tree, which descending gently, dropped a
loaf of bread before them, and then flew away. Behold, said Paul, how our loving and merciful Lord has
sent us a dinner! There are now sixty years elapsed
since I have daily received from him half a loaf, but upon
thy coming, Christ hath been pleased to send his soldier
a double proportion. Then after praying and thanks-
giving, they sat down by the edge of the spring, to take
the meal which God hath sent them : but not without
an humble contention who should break the loaf; which
they at last decided by breaking it conjointly. After
taking a moderate refreshment, they laid themselves
down to sip at the fountain : and then returned to prayer and the praises of God, in which they spent the
evening, and the whole of the following night.

The next morning Paul thus accosted Antony : "It is
a long time, brother, since I have known of your dwelling in these regions : and the Lord long ago promised me your company. But as my time is now come
to go to rest, (as I have always *desired to be dissolved
and to be with Christ*,) and my race being finished,
the crown of justice waits for me, thou art now sent
by the Lord to cover this body with ground, or rather
to commit earth to earth." Which when Antony
heard, breaking out into sighs and tears, he began to
entreat him not to leave him, but to take him along with
him for his companion in so happy a journey. "Thou
oughtest not," said Paul, " to seek in this thy own interest, but what may be for the good of others. It would
be expedient indeed to thee to lay down this load of
flesh, and to follow the Lamb : but it is necessary to
the rest of the brethren, that thou shouldest continue
here, to instruct them by thy example. Wherefore

go, I beseech thee, if it be not too much trouble, and bring hither the cloak which was given thee, by bishop Athanasius, to wrap up my body for its burial :" which, says St. Jerome, he asked, not that he who for many years had used no other clothing but the leaves of the palm-tree, cared much whether his body was committed to the earth covered or naked, but that Antony being absent when he died, might be less afflicted with his death. To which our church historians add another reason, *viz.* that by his desiring to be buried in the cloak of Athanasius (at that time violently persecuted by the Arians, for the Catholic faith of the Trinity,) he might bear testimony to the cause of God and his truth, and declare to world his communion with this illustrious prelate, who was then, and had been all his lifetime, one of the principal champions of God and his church against the Arian heresy.

Antony being astonished to hear him speak of Athanasius, and of the cloak (of which he could no otherwise have been informed but by revelation,) as if he saw Christ himself in Paul, without making any further reply, kissed his hands with tears, and departing from him, made the best of his way home to his own monastery. Here his two disciples (Amathas and Macarias,) asked him where he had been so long ? To whom he made no answer, but, " wo to me a sinner, who deserve not to bear the name of a religious man ! I have seen Elias : I have seen John in the wilderness : I have seen with truth, Paul in paradise." And thus without explaining himself any further, he went into his cell, striking his breast, and taking up the cloak, instantly hastened away without staying to take any refreshment ; having Paul continually in his mind, and fearing, that which indeed happened, lest Paul should die before he reached his cave. On the second morning, when he had travelled for about three hours, he saw the soul of Paul encompassed in great glory ascending to heaven, attended with an innumerable multitude of angels and saints... At this sight falling down on the ground, he cried out lamenting and mourning : " O Paul, why dost thou leave me ? why dost thou go without letting me salute thee ? too late, alas ! have I come to know thee, and dost thou depart from me so soon ?" Then rising up, he went on the remaining part of the way, notwithstanding his great age, and his having been before greatly fatigued, with such unaccustomed speed, that, as he himself afterwards relates, he seemed rather to fly than walk.

When he arrived and had entered into the cave, he found the body of the Saint in the posture of one at prayer, kneeling with uplifted hands ; so that thinking he might be yet alive, he knelt down to pray with him. But not perceiving him to sigh, as he was accustomed at his prayers, he was convinced he was dead. Wherefore weeping and embracing the dead body, he wrapt it up in the cloak, and carried it out ; singing hymns and psalms according to the christian tradition. But here no small difficulty occurred, how he should bury the body, having no spade or other instrument to dig a grave : so that what to do he knew not : to go back to his monastery, was three days' journey ; to stay where he was, was doing nothing. Whilst he remained in this perplexity, behold two lions, from the remoter part of the wilderness, came running with all speed towards him. At the sight of them Antony was at first surprised ; but presently recollecting himself in God, he shook off all fear, and stood his ground till the beasts coming up to the place, went and laid themselves down at the feet of the deceased saint, and seemed, in their way, to lament his death. Then going a little distance off, they began to scratch up the sandy ground with their claws, and did not cease till they had made a hole big enough to answer the purpose of a grave ; which when they had done, coming to Antony as it were for their wages, wagging their ears and hanging down their heads, they licked his hands and feet.

The Saint conceiving that in their mute way they craved his blessing, took occasion to praise and glorify God, whom all his creatures serve ; and then prayed in this manner : " O Lord, without whose disposition not a leaf falls from the tree, nor a sparrow to the ground, give to them as thou knowest best :" and so making them a sign with his hand he sent them away. Then taking the dead body of St. Paul, he laid it down in the grave which they had made, and covered it with the earth ; and so returned home, carrying with him the garment made of the leaves of the palm-tree, which Paul had worn (which for the remaining years of his life he always put on upon the solemn festivals of Easter and Pentecost,) and related all that he had seen and done to his disciples, from whom St. Jerome had his account.

And here it may not be improper to reflect, with this holy Doctor of the church in the conclusion of his life of this Saint, on the difference between the clothing, eating, drinking, lodging, and, in a word, the whole manner of living of this servant of God, and that of worldings, who never think they have enough, and are always slaves to their own corrupt inclinations. Paul coveted nothing, and wanted nothing ; and therefore was always easy and content : they are always coveting and wanting, and never perfectly easy. Paul with his mean fare enjoyed long life and health, together with a good conscience and interior peace : their intemperances and lusts, their passions, their pride, their ambition, their avarice, their envy, their cares and fears, and the contradictions of their will and humour, to which they are perpetually exposed, rob them of their health, shorten their days, and banish both grace and peace far from their souls. In fine, Paul with all his poverty and mortifications, was happy even here in the experience of the love of his God, in the sense of his divine presence, in the contemplation of his heavenly truths, in the sweets he found in mental prayer, and an inward conversation with our Lord; in the consolations of the Holy Ghost, &c. and by this means he passed his days in good things, (truly such) till he was in an instant put in full possession, by death, of the sovereign and infinite good for eternity: whereas they, after their short deluding dreams of an imaginary happiness, which is ever flying away from them, awake in a moment, and find themselves immersed in the bottomless pit of real, endless, and insupportable miseries.

ST. ANTONY.

From his Life, written by the great St. Athanasius.

St. Antony was born in Egypt about the middle of the third century, of parents noble and wealthy; according to the world, but withal pious and religious. By them he was trained up at home, in great innocence, so as to be a stranger in a manner to the world; and was by his own inclinations, entirely restrained from the company of others of his age, and even from frequenting the schools with them, for fear of his morals being corrupted by their conversation or bad example. His whole desire was bent upon God: he frequented the church in the company of his parents, assisted there with great modesty, gravity, and attention; and endeavoured to follow in his practice the instructions and rules of life which he there learnt. He was not fond, as children usually are, of dainties, or such things as are sweet and agreeable to their appetite, but always took what his parents gave him, and sought nothing more.

He was about eighteen or twenty years old, when his parents dying, left him master of all their wealth, which was considerable, with a little sister that was very young.

But scarce six months were passed after their death, when one day going to church according to his custom, and thinking with himself how the Apostles had left all to follow our Lord, and the primitive Christians (Acts iv.) had sold their possessions, and laid the price at the feet of the Apostles, to be by them distributed to such as were in want, and how great would be the reward in heaven, of them that did in this manner; at his coming into the church he heard the gospel read out of Matt. xix. where our Saviour says to the young man that was rich, v. 21. *If thou wilt be perfect, go sell what thou hast, and give to the poor, and thou shalt have treasure in heaven, and come follow me.* These words he took as addressed by our Lord to himself, and particularly designed for him: and in consequence of this divine call, he presently parted with his whole estate in lands, sold his moveables, which were of great value, and distributed the price to the poor, only reserving a small matter for the use of his sister. Some time after, when he had heard in the church that part of the gospel read (Matt. vi.) where our Lord warns his disciples not to be careful for tomorrow, he concluded to part with his house also, and to distribute all that remained to the poor; and having recommended his young sister to the care of certain devout virgins, to be trained up in their way of life, he quitted the world for good and all, and entered with a strong resolution upon the narrow and arduous path of religious perfection.

There were not very many at that time in Egypt who professed a monastic life; and those that did retired not into the deserts, but only lived in separate cells in the country, at a small distance from their respective villages. One of these, now advanced in years, who from his youth had followed this manner of life, lived in the neighbourhood: him Antony proposed to imitate; and accordingly he began to follow the same kind of life, but in places something more remote from his own village. Accordingly, as often as he could hear of any one that laboured with more diligence than ordinary in the pursuit of virtue and perfection, he was sure to visit him, and to seek in his conversation and method of life, some lessons for his own instruction and edification. In the mean time he laboured with his own hands for his daily food; and all that he gained over and above what was necessary to purchase his pittance of bread, he gave to the poor. He prayed very much, and endeavouring quite to forget the world and all his worldly kindred, he turned all his affections and desires towards the purchasing the hidden treasure of true wisdom, and the precious pearl of divine love. In order to this he gave diligent attention to the word of God, contained in the holy scriptures, which he heard, and by meditating thereon, laid up all these precepts of our Lord in such a manner in his soul, as never to forget any of them; but to have them always written in his memory, as in a book. He envied no one, but had always a great deference for the other servants of God; and was continually studying to remark those virtues, in which each one of them excelled, in order to imitate them; and thus assemble as it were, and unite together in himself the different perfections which he observed in the rest. Thus he quickly outstripped them all: and yet remained always most humble, meek, and full of brotherly love and charity, so as to be ever most dear to them all.

The devil, who was enraged to see so much ardor in the pursuit of virtue in a person so young, employed all his arts and stratagems to divert him from his holy undertaking, and to bring him back agian into the world; and for this end, he strongly represented to his imagination the riches and possessions which he had quitted, the nobility of his family, the glory of this world, the advantages and pleasures of a worldly life; and, on the other hand, the extreme difficulties and labours to be undergone in this way which he had chosen; the weakness of his body, unfit for such extraordinary fatigues; the long time he might have to live under this insupportable burthen, &c. suggesting withal that it was a crime in him to have abandoned, in the manner he did, his little sister, whom he was obliged to have taken care of. By these and such like representations, he strove to induce him, after he had put his hand to the plough, to look back, and to return again to the world. But the Saint overcame all his temptations, by a lively faith in Christ crucified, and by continual and fervent prayer. Wherefore the enemy changed his batteries, and assaulted him in a most violent manner, night and day, sleeping and waking, with carnal suggestions and allurements to lust. But the holy young man, armed with divine grace, which he procured by earnest and constant prayer, conquered also all these temptations, by perpetually opposing to them watchings, fastings, and mortifications of the flesh, together with the faith and remembrance of the judgment to come, of the worm that never dies, and of the eternal flames of hell. By these means he gained so complete a victory over the enemy, that he ceased to molest him any more in this kind. It was in consequence of this victory, that the unclean spirit one day appeared to the Saint in the shape of a most filthy, ugly, black boy; bitterly weeping and lamenting, that after having deceived and seduced so many, he had been overcome by him. On being asked who he was, he answered he was the spirit of impurity, who made it his business to wage a continual war against youth, in which he was commonly successful; and that it was he that had so often attacked him, but had always been repulsed. Upon this the Saint, giving thanks to God, was animated with a new courage against this detestable spirit; and began to sing aloud those words of the Psalmist: *The Lord is my helper, and I will despise my enemies.* (Ps. cxvii. 7.) At which the filthy phantom was put to flight.

These first victories did not render Antony negligent.

as if he might now think himself secure, and on that account might relax in his spiritual exercises; for he very well knew that the devil never sleeps, and that he has a thousand ways of tricking and deceiving unwary souls, especially as he holds a close correspondence with the flesh, our domestic enemy, and with our unhappy self-love and its passions. Wherefore the holy young man resolved to be still more upon his guard, and to make every day, still greater progress in religious perfection. He chastised his body, and brought it under subjection by extraordinary austerities; which how difficult sover in themselves, became sweet and agreeable to him, by reason of that ardent affection wherewith he embraced them. He frequently watched whole nights in prayer;—he eat but once in the four and twenty hours, and that not till after sun-set. His food was nothing but bread and salt, his drink nothing but water, which he drank in a small quantity : he sometimes fasted two days, or more, without taking any food whatever. His bed was a sort of mat made of bulrushes, with a covering of hair cloth : and sometimes only the bare ground. His application to God in prayer was without intermission, like the Apostles (Philip iii. 13, 14.) *forgetting the things that were behind*, that is, all that he had already done, he was continually *stretching forth himself to the things that were before ; and pressing*, with all his power *towards the mark, to the prize of the high calling of God in Christ Jesus :* ever considering himself as if he was just beginning, and thinking of no more than of the present day.

All this not being sufficient to satisfy his hunger and thirst after perfection, he chose for himself a dwelling amongst the tombs or monuments of the dead. In one of these he shut himself up, and received from time to time his necessary sustenance from a religious man who came to visit him. The devil, foreseing the consequences he had to apprehend from this new kind of enterprise, and fearing lest by degrees this young man should draw many by his example into the desert, to the prejudice of his usurped empire, was resolved not to suffer him to go on thus; and therefore (God so permitting for the greater merit and glory of his Saint,) Satan gathering together his infernal spirits, attacked him one night with the utmost fury, inflicting upon him many stripes and grievous wounds, till he left him stretched out like one dead, without either speech or motion. In this condition his friend found him the next morning, and carried him back to the village on his shoulders, where a great multitude of his kindred and neighbours were assembled about him to perform his funeral obsequies; when, behold, towards midnight, coming to himself, like one awakened from a deep sleep, and looking about him, he perceived his friend there watching by him (for the rest were all asleep) and he made a sign to him to carry him back again to his monument, without waking any of the company. He did so, and Antony being now alone, but not as yet able to support himself on his feet, by reason of his late treatment, performed his devotions, as well as he could, lying prostrate on the floor. At the end of his prayer, lifting up his voice in defiance of the spirits of darkness, he cried out with a lively faith and confidence in his God, " Lo, here am I: here is Antony, ready to encounter with you all; I shall not run away; do your worst; none of you shall be able to separate me from the love of Christ." Then he began to sing with the Psalmist: *If whole armies should stand together against me, my heart shall not fear.* Ps. xxvi. 3.

The enemy not enduring to be thus outbraved, re-assembled his hellish fiends, and returned to the charge with greater violence than before, and raising a sudden violent tempest, which shook the very foundations of the place, he laid it open on all sides; and entering in with all his wicked ones, in the shape of wild beasts and serpents of sundry kinds, he not only sought to terrify the Saint with their hideous yelling, roaring, howling, hissing, &c. but

3

also made him feel their fury in a most sensible manner, by the fresh wounds they inflicted upon him. But his courage and constancy was proof against all their attempts; so that notwithstanding the excessive pains he felt in his wounded body, he mocked at all their vain efforts, reproached them with their weakness and cowardice, and with those forms of brutes, to which they were now reduced, who had formerly proudly aspired to be like unto God. At length Jesus Christ was pleased to come in a visible manner to the assistance of his servant in the midst of this conflict; for lifting up his eyes, he saw the top of the place open, and a bright ray of divine light to enter in, which instantly dissipated those infernal spirits, and released him from all his pains. The Saint understanding that his Lord was present, thus addressed him: " Where wast thou my good Jesus, all this while? Where wast thou? Why didst thou not come before to heal my wounds? The Lord answered, I was here Antony; but I waited to see thy combat. And now because thou hast fought so bravely, and not yielded, I will always assist thee, and make thy name famous over the whole earth." Antony having heard these words, raised himself up to pray, and found that our Lord had now given him greater strength than he had before. At the time when this happened to him he was about thirty-five years old.

After this, being desirous of advancing still more in christian perfection, he took a resolution of retiring into the desert, and of withdrawing himself altogether from the conversation of men. This resolution he communicated to the old monk his friend, of whom we spoke above, proposing that he should accompany him; but the old man excused himself, alleging his advanced age, and the novelty of such an enterprise. Antony, however, no way discouraged, set out upon his journey towards the heart of the wilderness, at that time utterly uninhabited, and lying at a very great distance from any town or village. As he walked along, he saw a large dish of silver with which the enemy sought to interrupt his journey, lying on the ground ; but he easily discovered the artifice, and cried : " This is a trick of thine, Satan ; thou shalt not divert me from my resolution ; keep thy silver to thyself, and let it perish with thee." At which words the dish was immediately dissolved into smoke. Afterwards a large lump of true gold was flung in his way ; but this was no more capable of interrupting his journey, than the glittering appearance of the silver dish : for as soon as he perceived it, he flew from it with as much speed, as if he were flying from a devouring fire ; and proceeded on his way until he came to a mountain, where he found an old desolate castle, full of serpents and venemous creatures, which had taken up their abode therein by reason of the length of time it had remained uninhabited. This place he made choice of for his dwelling ; taking in with him his provisions of bread, which with a little water, according to his scanty allowance, might suffice him for six months.

At his coming to take possession of this castle, all its old inhabitants, the serpents and other venemous creatures, having fled away, he shut up the entrance with stones, and during the twenty years that he dwelt therein, he neither went out at any time himself, nor suffered any one to enter, not even those who brought him, at the end of every half year, a fresh provision of bread : which they conveyed to him by getting up to the roof and letting it drop down. They that came thither, as many did in process of time, out of a desire of seeing him, or learning what was become of him, sometimes remained the whole night at the door ; and were frequently surprised at hearing the noises wherewith the devils sought to molest him, and the voices, as it were, of many persons contending with him and saying : " Why camest thou into our habitation ? What hast thou to do in the desert ? Depart from these coasts which belong not to thee ; never think to be able remain here, or to resist our attacks."

When those that were without, heard these or such like words, they at first imagined some men had found means to get into his habitation, and were there contending with him; but looking through the chinks, and seeing him all alone, they understood that the voices they had heard proceeded from the evil spirits, seeking to drive him thence; and being upon this occasion very much frightened, they called to Antony, begging his assistance, whilst, he comforted and encouraged them from within, bidding them to arm themselves with the sign of the cross, and not to be alarmed at these vain terrors. At other times when they came, and scarcely expected to find him alive, they heard him cheerfully singing within, and repeating those words of the 67th Pslam: *Let God arise, and let his enemies be scattered: and let them that hate him flee from before his face; as smoke vanisheth, so let them vanish away: as wax melteth before the fire, so let the wicked perish at the presence of God.*

At the end of the twenty years he had spent with God in this solitude, Antony, yielding to the importunity of the multitude that resorted to him, and were even ready to force their way into his habitation, more especially as many of them desired to learn and imitate his manner of life, came forth, as it were out of a heavenly sanctuary, with so serene a countenance, and such animation, strength and vigour in his whole person, as attracted the admiration of all who saw him. And here God was pleased to work many miracles by him, in casting out devils from such as were possessed, and healing various diseases. The Saint took occasion, at the same time, to make powerful exhortations to those that addressed themselves to him: he comforted the afflicted;—instructed the ignorant;—reconciled such as were at variance, and earnestly exhorted all to look to the welfare of their souls, and to prefer nothing before the love of Christ. He set before the eyes of his auditory the greatness of the good things to come in a happy eternity—the infinite

...... and mercy of God—the benefits he has con-
.... and the love he bears towards mankind, particularly manifested in not sparing, but delivering up his own
Son to death for the salvation of us all. By these and
such like discourses, the Saint brought over a great number of his hearers to a contempt of all those things that
pass away with time, and to an effectual resolution of
dedicating the short remainder of the days of their mortality to the love and service of God, in a solitary and
religious life. Thus, by degrees, the deserts and mountains began to be peopled with a number of holy souls
(all acknowledging Antony for their father, founder, and
master,) who, by the purity and sanctity of their lives,
seemed to resemble so many angels in human bodies.
They renounced all the honours, riches, and pleasures of
this world : or rather, exchanged them for others by far
more great and solid even in this life, and for such as shall
never end hereafter. They watched and prayed without
ceasing ;—they meditated frequently on the word of God ;
—they sung his praises day and night ;—they kept, in a
manner, a continual fast ;—they laboured with their hands
for their own support, and to have wherewith to supply
the necessities of their indigent neighbours : in fine, they
all lived in a holy union and perfect charity, without
murmurs or detractions. and felt no other ambition or
strife, but who should excel his neighbour in all kind of
christian virtues : so that to behold this multitude of holy
solitaries separated at a distance, both in place and manners, from the children of the world; in those vast deserts, and leading there such angelical lives, was enough
to make any one cry out with Balaam, Numb. xxiv.
*How beautiful are thy pavilions, O Jacob, and thy tents,
O Israel, as vallies overshaded with woods, as well watered gardens near the rivers : as tabernacles which the Lord
hath pitched,* &c.

St. Athanasius sets down at large an excellent discourse which Antony delivered one day, by the desire,

and for the instruction of his disciples, in which, (after earnestly exhorting them to such an unwearied fervour and constancy in pursuit of their holy undertaking, as never to slacken their pace, but daily to renew their resolutions as if they were just now beginning, and to strive to advance by great strides towards religious perfection,) he puts them in mind, first of the shortness of the time of this mortal life, of the length of eternity, and how trivial those services are which God requires of us for the purchasing of eternal life :—that all the labours and sufferings of this life shall shortly have an end, but that our reward shall continue for ever.   Secondly, he would therefore not have them imagine they had made any great sacrifice to God in parting with their estates, houses, or money, from which they must, whether they will or not, be in a short time separated by death : since what they were to receive in exchange from our Lord, would infinitely surpass in value the possession of the whole earth, and be theirs for all eternity.   Thirdly, he inculcates to them, that a Christian ought never to fix his affection, or bestow his care upon any of those things which he cannot take along with him when he dies, but only on such as may help him on his way to heaven, and there remain with him during eternity : such as true wisdom—purity of soul and body—christian justice—fortitude—charity, and tranquillity of soul, by a victory over our passions: for these are the real goods of a christian, which are alone worthy of his love.   Fourthly, he puts them in mind, that they are strictly obliged, in consequence of their *creation*, to dedicate their whole lives to the service of that Lord who *made them* for this very end, *that they should be his servants ;* and who, by all manner of titles, has an indisputable right to their service ; and that neither their past, nor present labours can exempt them from continuing therein till death ; so that if they would not lose their crown, they must resolve to labour to the end, relying always on the assistance of their good God, who never forsakes those who do not first forsake him. Fifthly, he recommends to them the remembrance of death; the certainty thereof, as well as the uncertainty of the hour in which we shall be called from hence—of the judgment that is to follow after death, and of the eternity to come, as so many powerful restraints to preserve them from sin; and as sovereign means to cure their sloth—spur them on to the practices of virtue—wean their affections from transitory things, and teach them to tread under their feet the riches and pleasures of a world which we must so suddenly part with. Sixthly, he tells them that the Greeks took great pains, and travelled into distant countries, in order to meet with masters from whom they might learn vain and empty sciences, such as were of no service to their souls in order to eternity: but that the christian, in order to acquire *true wisdom* and the *science of the saints*, which conducts to eternal life, needed to go no farther than into his own soul: where he should, if he sought him by a spirit of recollection and prayer, find his true master, the kingdom of God, and with it all good. Seventhly, he exhorts them to fight in a particular manner against the *tyranny*, as he calls it, of the passion *of anger*, as a mortal evil and capital enemy of the justice of God; and therefore he would have them to keep a constant guard upon their own hearts: the more so, because of the enemies that are continually waging war with Christians, but more especially against religious men and women: and who employ a thousand tricks and artifices to deceive the unwary. And here, as one that had long experience in this kind of warfare, he acquaints them with the different stratagems and manifold temptations by which these wicked spirits labour, without ceasing, to withdraw religious souls from the service of God, and bring them back to the broad road of the world, and the ways of iniquity and sin: but for their comfort and encouragement, he assures them, that these enemies have no power over such as heartily resist and despise their

suggestions : that Christ has triumphed over them by his
death : and that a lively faith—a purity and sincerity in
seeking him—a diligence in the spiritual exercises of
watching, praying, fasting, &c. together with the virtues
of meekness, voluntary poverty, humility, contempt of
vain-glory, and especially an ardent devotion to Christ
crucified, are weapons which all the powers of hell cannot withstand.   By such lessons as these, but more especially by the great example of their master, the disciples
of Antony were encouraged and spurred on to a daily
progress in the ways of christian perfection.

When the persecution, which had been first set on
foot by Diocletian, and carried on with great fury by
Maximinian Galerius, raged exceedingly in Egypt, where
it crowned innumerable martyrs, many were led to Alexandria out of the country to be put to death for Christ.
On this occasion Antony quitted his cell, to follow these
that were going to become the victims of Christ : saying to his disciples, " let us go to the glorious triumphs
of our brethren, that we may either share with them in
the fight, or at least be spectators of their conflict." He
was in hopes of obtaining for himself the crown of mar-
tyrdom ; but could not deliver himself up, nor obtain
permission to associate himself with the glorious confessors that were condemned to the mines or confined in
the prisons.   However, whenever any were brought before the judge, he accompanied them into the court, and
with great liberty and diligence exhorted them to constancy and perseverance ; and when they were sentenced
to die, he rejoiced as much in their victory as if it had been
his own, and failed not to accompany them to the place
of execution, to be a witness of their happy triumph.
The judge seeing the courage and zeal of Antony and
his companions, published an order prohibiting any of
the monks to be present in court during the trials of the
christians, and enjoining them all to depart from the city.
Upon these orders the others absconded for that day ; but

Antony, fearing nothing, washed his garments, and took the next opportunity to present himself in a more eminent place in sight of the judge, desiring nothing more than to suffer for Christ. But God was pleased to accept of his good-will, and to reserve his servant for the benefit of innumerable souls. However, he continued assisting and encouraging the confessors of Christ upon all occasions till the storm of the persecution was blown over, and then returned with new fervour to his former solitude, where he redoubled his watchings and fastings, wearing always a garment of hair-cloth next to his skin, and never washing his body; insomuch, that no one ever saw Antony naked during his life.

And now he began again to shut himself up for a time in his cell, without admitting any one to come in to him. But still he could not prevent many from resorting to his door, nor even from remaining there the whole night, in order to seek a cure for their different maladies, through the experience they had of the miracles that God frequently wrought by him; so that partly to avoid the distractions occasioned by this concourse of people, and partly to fly the danger of vain-glory, he took the resolution to fly as far as the higher Thebais, where no man might know him. Wherefore, taking some bread with him, he went to the banks of the Nile, and there sat down, waiting for some boat that might pass that way. And here he heard a voice, saying to him, "Antony, whither art thou going? and to what end?" He, as one accustomed to such colloquies, answered without fear: "Because the people will not suffer me to remain quiet, but require things of me that are out of the reach of my weakness, I have thought it best to go away to the higher Thebais." "If thou goest," said the voice, "to the place thou proposest, thou shalt endure a greater, yea, a double labour; but if thou desirest to be quiet indeed, go thy way now to such a place," naming a mountain in the heart of the wilderness. "But who," said Antony, "shall shew me the way? for there are no tracks or paths that lead thither, and I know nothing of the country." He that spoke with him replied, that there were some Saracens or Arabians at hand, who were come into Egypt to trade, and that they would shew him the way. Antony followed this heavenly direction, and going up to the Saracens, desired they would take him along with them in their journey through the desert: and after having travelled with him three days and three nights, he arrived at a very high mountain, the place appointed him by heaven, at the foot of which there was a spring of clear water, and in the adjacent field a few wild palm-trees. Here then he resolved to fix his abode, where he might live quite separated from the conversation of men. As to his food, he contented himself with a little bread (which the Saracens, admiring his virtue, gave him at parting, or bestowed upon him afterwards when they passed that way), and with the small provision of wild dates which the palms afforded him, till his brethren, having found out the place of his retreat, brought him necessaries from time to time. Antony, desirous to ease them of that trouble, having procured by their means some wheat, and a proper instrument for the purpose, found a little spot of ground wherein he sowed the wheat, which brought him a crop sufficient for his use, to his great satisfaction at being thus enabled to live by the labour of his hands, without becoming troublesome to any one. He also cultivated a little garden with herbs, in order to entertain his wearied brethren after their journey, when they came to visit him through the burning deserts. This spot of ground lay exposed to the beasts which resorted thither for the sake of the spring, who did no small damage to Antony, by feeding upon his herbs and corn: wherefore having caught one of them, he said to them all: " Why do you this wrong to me, who do none to you? Get ye gone: and, in the name of the Lord, never come hither

any more." From which time they were never after seen
to come near that place.

Whilst Antony remained here entertaining himself with
God, the devils, his unwearied enemies, ceased not to
wage perpetual war against him; but he despised all
their efforts, and always triumphed over them, by his
usual arms of a lively faith and fervent prayer. His disciples who came to visit him, and were sometimes witnesses of his conflicts relate, how they heard the tumultu-
ous noise and voices of a numerous people, with the rat-
tling of arms, and had seen the whole mountain covered
by a multitude of devils, with Antony fighting against
them, and putting them all to flight by his prayers. "It
is indeed, worthy of admiration," says St. Athanasius,
"that in so vast a wilderness one man alone should have
stood his ground so long, without either apprehending the
daily encounters he met with from wicked spirits, or yielding to the fury of so many wild beasts and serpents as
swarm in these deserts. But it was with good reason that
David sung, Psalm cxxiv. *They that trust in the Lord
shall be as mount Sion: they shall not be moved for ever:*
for so Antony, by keeping his mind firm, quiet, and immovable in God, put all the devils to flight, and had *even
the beasts of the earth at peace with him,*" (Job v. 23.)
and subject to him. One night whilst he was watching
in prayer, the devil brought such a multitude of wild beasts
together about him, that it seemed as if there were none
left behind in the whole desert, all of whom, encompass-
ing him on every side, with open jaws, threatened to tear
him in pieces. The Saint understanding the artifice of
the malignant spirit, said, unconcernedly: "If the Lord
has given you any power over me, make use of it in devouring me; but if you are brought hither by devils, depart instantly, for I am a servant of Christ." No sooner had he spoke these words but the whole multitude of
wild beasts fled away, and left him alone to continue his
devotion. One day whilst he was at work, according to

his custom, making baskets, to exchange them for the provisions which the brethren brought him, a monster presented itself before him, in the shape of half a man and half an ass; having on this occasion made the sign of the cross, and said: "I am a servant of Christ—if thou art sent to me, here am I;—I don't run away." At these words the monster instantly fled, and falling down in the midst of its flight, burst and was destroyed: to shew how all the attempts of Satan against Antony should in the end perish, and come to nothing.

After some time the brethren prevailed on the man of God to come down from his mountain, in order to visit their monasteries. Now in their way homeward through those burning deserts, the provision of water quite failed them; and as none could be found, and the weather being violently hot, they were all in danger of perishing. Antony on this occasion had recourse to prayer; when, after withdrawing himself at a little distance from the company, and falling upon his knees, he had implored, with his hands stretched forth to heaven, the mercy of the Lord, behold the tears which he then shed presently brought forth a spring of water out of the earth, with which they both refreshed their own thirst, saved the life of their camel, and filled their vessels for the remainder of their journey. The Saint who was received with great joy by all the religious, as their common father, conceived no less joy within himself, to see the fervour and resolution with which they all applied themselves to their spiritual exercises. And that he might not seem to come to them from his mountain empty handed, he made them excellent exhortations in order to their spiritual progress. He had also the comfort to hear the agreeable news, that his sister, whom he had left so young in the world, was now grown old in the profession of virginity, and was become mistress and superior of other holy virgins in a religious state of life.

After some days, Antony returned again to his mountain, where he again received more frequent visits, as well from his own religious as from others, who, being possessed or obsessed by evil spirits, or afflicted with various infirmities, had recourse to his prayers for their delivery; on which occasion God wrought many miracles by him; favouring him also with prophetic light, and other extraordinary graces and gifts. He exhorted all that came to see him to have a strong faith in Jesus Christ :—to love him with their whole hearts ;—to keep their minds pure from all evil thoughts, and their bodies uncontaminated from all uncleanness ;—not to suffer themselves to be imposed upon by gluttony ;—to hate vain-glory ;—to pray very often ;—to sing psalms to the divine praise every morning, noon, and night ;—to meditate on the precepts of the word of God ;—to have the great example of the saints always before their eyes, in order to spur themselves on to the practice of all virtues ;—*not to let the sun set upon their anger*, Eph. iv. which precept of the apostles he applied to all other sins; recommending to all to call themselves to a strict account by a daily examination of conscience, and to repent and amend without delay whensoever they found themselves to have failed in any thing. He added, that if they did not discover any guilt in themselves, they must not therefore be puffed up with self-conceit, or presume to justify themselves, and despise others; but rather fear, least self-love should blind and deceive them ; remembering that an all-seeing God is to be their judge ;—that his judgments are very different from those of men ;—and that *there is,* according to the wise man, Prov. xiv. 16. *a way that seemeth right to man ; and that the latter end thereof leadeth to d eath.*"

One day, about the ninth hour, viz. about three of the clock in the afternoon, when he had begun his prayers before the taking of his meal, he was seized with a rapt or ecstacy in which he saw himself in spirit carried up aloft by angels, whilst the demons of the air, opposing his passage, alledged against him the sins of his younger days, even from his very childhood ; and when the an-

'gels replied, that these sins, by the mercy of Christ, had been forgiven, they bid them to charge him, if they could, with any material sin he had committed since he had consecrated himself to God in a religious state of life. Accordingly these lying spirits having forged many false accusations against him which they could not prove, they were therefore forced to leave the passage free for him. Upon this Antony returned to himself, but so greatly affected with what he had seen, as well as with the dreadful and dangerous conflict a poor soul has to pass through with these princes of darkness, that he forgot his food, and spent the remainder of the day, as well as the whole night, in sighs and lamentations, at considering the dangers from these wicked spirits, that threaten the souls of men both in life and death, which thoughtless mortals nevertheless so little apprehend. One night, whilst his disciples had been questioning him concerning the state of souls immediately after death, he was called upon by a voice saying : " Antony arise, go out, and see." He arose, and went out, and looking up towards heaven, he saw a spectre of a monstrous height and dreadful aspect, whose head reached the clouds : he saw also persons with wings that sought to fly up to heaven, and he perceived that the monster, with outstretched hands, strove to stop them in their passage : some of whom he caught and cast down to the earth, but could not prevent the rest from flying above his reach, or of mounting up to heaven. By this vision he was given to understand, that the devil had power to stop the flight of those departing souls who were in sin, but that he had no power over pure and holy souls, nor could prevent their flying up to heaven. These visions Antony related to his disciples : not out of ostentation or vain-glory, being always averse to attributing any thing to himself, or suffering any thing to be ascribed to him, but merely for their instruction and edification.

As to the rest, no one could be more meek, patient,

or humble than Antony. He entertained a particular respect and veneration for all the clergy; giving even to the lowest clerk in minor orders, the preference before himself, and even bowing down his head before bishops and priests, to crave their benediction. Although he had so great a mastery over himself in spirituals, and was so divinely taught, yet he was never ashamed to seek instruction, not only from the clerks that came to visit him, but even from his own disciples; and whatsoever good he heard from any one, he humbly and thankfully acknowledged himself assisted thereby. Among other gifts with which he was favoured by our Lord, he was particularly remarkable for an admirable grace that shewed itself in his countenance, which distinguished him in such a manner from all the rest of the holy inhabitants of the deserts, that any stranger who came to visit him, though he happened to be in the company of a multitude of other monks, leaving all others would be sure to run up to him: as if the purity of his soul had shone forth from his very face, which was always modestly cheerful and amiable, and never altered either by prosperity or adversity. However he would have no communication with schismatics or heretics; but exhorted all that came near him, to fly their dangerous conversation and impious doctrines. He had a particular horror for the blasphemies of the Arians, whom he considered as the forerunners of Antichrist. He even quitted for a while his solitude, at the desire of Athanasius and the catholic bishops, to go to Alexandria to confute their wicked assertions; where, by his doctrine and miracles, he not only effectually confuted the heretics, and confirmed the catholics in their faith, but also brought over a great number of infidels to the christian religion. The heathen philosophers also came often to dispute with him about religion, imagining they could easily entangle a man so entirely illiterate, and an utter stranger to all human sciences as Antony was known to be, with their captious reasoning and learned sophistry; but they were surprised beyond conception to find with what depth of wisdom he answered all their objections, and proved the truth of the christian religion in a manner to which they knew not what reply to make, and even confirm it with miracles wrought in their presence.

The reputation of Antony's sanctity and heavenly wisdom was not confined to Egypt: it spread itself far and near through a great part of the then known world: it even reached the imperial court, insomuch that the emperor Constantine the Great, and his sons Constan and Constantious, wrote several times to him, and begged that he would favour them with an answer. As to his part, he made very little account of this honour, and told his disciples that they were not to think it much that an emperor, who was no more than a mortal man, should write to him; but rather ought to admire and bear always in mind, that the eternal God had been so good as not only to write his law for man, but to send down his only Son to deliver his word to them. However, at the desire of all the brethren, he returned them an answer, in which, after congratulating with them for their believing in and worshipping Christ, he gave them wholesome instructions for the welfare of their souls; advising them not to make any great account of their wordly grandeur and power, nor of any of those things that pass away with time, and never to forget that they were mortals, who must quickly appear before another judge. He also put them in mind of their obligation of shewing clemency to their subjects, of rendering them justice, and of succouring the poor and distressed; and they must remember that the true and everlasting king of all ages is Jesus Christ alone.

After Antony had finished the business that brought him to Alexandria, he hastened back to his cell on the mountain, and to his usual exercises and austerities. For he used to say, that a religious man conversing with seculars out of his monastery was like a fish out of water, which is in danger of perishing, except it quickly be restored again to its element; and therefore, as to his part, he would never come out of his solitude, but when some work of great charity obliged him. However, he willingly received those seculars that came to him, and entertained them with heavenly discourses; exhorting them to look beyond this world, and to labour for a happiness that shall have no end: and such was the unction and efficacy which God gave to his words, that many were moved by his exhortations to give up their honours, their riches, and all their wordly expectations, in order to dedicate themselves eternally to the same happy service in which they saw him engaged. He seemed to have been given to the land of Egypt by our Lord, as an excellent physician to heal all their spiritual diseases: for whoever came to him in his troubles and temptations found a sensible benefit in his conversation;—if he came with sorrow, he returned with joy;—if he came with rancour in his heart against his neighbour, he returned with dispositions of peace and charity;—if he came oppressed with the sense of his poverty and distress, he returned with the contempt of this world,—a willingness to take up the cross, and to wear the livery of Jesus Christ. The lukewarm learnt from him to be fervent in the service of God; nay, the very libertines returned from him with a desire of embracing a chaste and penitential life: for such was the gift he had of discerning spirits; that he seemed to read in the faces of all, the interior dispositions and state of their souls, and accordingly accommodated his instructions and prescriptions to the nature and quality of their disorders. Nor was this benefit confined to Egypt alone: for as the fame of Antony had reached all parts of the world, so men came from all parts to see him, and no one visited him without fruit: no one ever complained that he had lost his labour in coming to see him, how long or difficult soever his journey might have been.

The multitude who went to see him did not interrupt

his interior attention to God any more than his daily
labours, which he sanctified with mental prayer. Oftentimes whilst he was walking or sitting with his visitors, he was ravished out of himself, so as to remain for
a long time insensible ; at which time many secrets were
revealed to him. Once in particular he beheld a vision
in his ecstacy, by which he was admonished two years
before it happened of the cruel havoc the Arians would
make in the church of Alexandria : which, when he returned to himself, he related with many sighs and tears
to those that were with him ; but then added for their
comfort, that this storm would quickly blow over, and
that the church should again be restored to her former
lustre. This persecution was raised against the church
of Alexandria, when the Arians, having procured the
banishment of St. Athanasius, introduced one Gregory,
a man of their faction, to be the bishop in his place : upon which occasion Balacius, an Arian, the commander of
the troops, particularly exerted himself in persecuting the
faithful ; which he did with so much rigour, that he ordered even the sacred virgins, and the religious men to be
publicly scourged, as if they had been the vilest male-
factors. St. Antony wrote a letter to him to deter him
from this cruelty, to this effect : " I see the wrath of God
coming upon thee : cease to persecute the Christians, lest
that wrath should overtake thee which already threatens
thee with approaching destruction." The unhappy man
slighted the warning of the Saint, and spitting upon the
letter, flung it down upon the ground ; then after having
abused the persons that brought it, bid them go tell Antony, that he should serve him also in the same manner
as he had done these monks for whom he interested
himself. But not many days passed before the venge-
ance of God overtook the wretch, when, as he was riding out to a place in the neighbourhood, in the company
of Nestorious the governor, one of his own horses, who
was before remarkably gentle and quiet, with a sudden

bite brought him down to the ground, and standing over him, knawed and tore his thighs in so terrible a manner, that he died within three days.

And now the time drew near when Antony, now about one hundred and five years of age, should exchange his mortal pilgrimage for a happy immortality. He went, according to his custom, to visit his brethren that dwelt in the nearer desert, signifying to them that his dissolution was at hand, and that this was the last time they should see him. These words drew tears from their eyes : they all embraced him as their parent about to depart from them into another world. They would have detained him with them, desiring to be present at his death. To this he would not consent; but after having given them his last instructions, he strongly exhorted them to fervour and perseverance in their holy institute, and to constancy in the catholic faith ; showing the utmost joy that he was now shortly to depart from this place of banishment to his true and everlasting home ; and taking his last farewell of them he hastened back to his mountain. A few months afterwards, finding his death to draw near, he called the two disciples, (who for the last fifteen years of his life had their cells in his neighbourhood) and said to them : " My children, I am now going, according to the expression of the scripture, the way of my fathers : for now the Lord calls for me : I long now to see the heavenly mansions. But as for you, my dearly beloved, I admonish you to beware lest you lose on a sudden the labour of so long a time ; but every day consider yourselves if you had but that day entered upon a religious life, and the strength of your purpose shall daily increase. You know the various artifices of the devils ; you have also seen their furious assaults, and how weak and cowardly they are. Retain an ardent love for Jesus , let the faith of his name be strongly fixed in your mind ; a strong faith in Jesus will put all the devils to flight. Remember also the lessons I have given you, and the uncertain

condition of this mortal life, which may be cut off any
day; and make no doubt but the heavenly mansions shall
be your portion.   Avoid the poison of schismatics and
heretics, and follow my example in keeping them at a distance, because they are enemies of Christ.   Make it your
principal care to keep the commandments of the Lord,
that so after your death the saints of God may receive
you as their friends and acquaintance into the eternal tabernacles."   He added, as his last request, that they
should bury his body privately, and let no man know the
place; lest the Egyptians, according to their custom,
should take it up to embalm it, and keep it as they did
their mummies.   "As to my garments, (said he) give
my sheep-skin, and this old cloak which I lie upon, to
bishop Athanasius, who brought it me new; let bishop
Serapion, another generous defender of the faith, have
my other sheep skin; and keep my garment of hair-cloth
for yourselves: so fare you well, my children, for Antony
is departing, and shall remain no longer with you in this
world."

When he had made an end of speaking, as his disciples where kissing him, he drew up his feet a little, and
met death with a joyful countenance, (anno 356) breath-
ing out his pure soul into the hands of the angels, who
were there ready to receive him, and carry him to the happy regions of eternal blss. His disciples buried him privately, as he had desired: " And his legatee, says St. Athanasius, (speaking of himself) "who had the happiness to
receive by the orders of blessed Antony, his old cloak
and his sheep-skin, embraces Antony, in his gifts, as if
he had been enriched by him with a large inheritance;
he rejoices in the garments, which present before the
eyes of his soul the image of his sanctity."   The same
holy doctor of the Church and champion of the faith,
wrote the life of St. Antony, from his own knowledge
of him, and from the testimonies of his disciples, which
we have here abridged, and which was then and has been

ever since received, embraced, and admired in all parts of the world, by every well-wisher to christian piety, for the important lessons it contains. The share it had in bringing the conversion of the great St. Augustine to a happy conclusion, is too remarkable to be passed over in silence.

The Saint relates in his Confessions (lib. 8. ch. 6.) how, whilst he was yet struggling under the load of those wicked habits, which he could not resolve effectually to cast off, he was one day visited by Pontitianus, one that belonged to the emperor's court, but a good Christian, who introduced a discourse " concerning Antony, a monk of Egypt, whose name, says St. Augustine, speaking to God, was exceeding illustrious among thy servants, but to that hour unknown to us : which he perceiving dwelt the longer upon that subject, informing us of the life of so great a man, and wondering that we had heard nothing of him. We were astonished (speaking of himself and his friend Alipius) to hear of thy miracles so very well attested, done so lately, and almost in our days, in the true faith, and in the catholic church : and indeed we all wondered ;—we, that they were so great, and he, that they were unknown to us. Thence he changed his discourse to the societies of monasteries and to their manner of life, yielding a sweet odour to thee, and to the fruitful breasts of those barren deserts ; of all which we had heard nothing, although there was then without the walls of Milan a convent full of good brothers, under the care of Ambrose, and yet we knew it not. He proceeded in his discourse, to which we listened with a silent attention, and related how upon a certain time, whilst the court was at Triers, and the emperor was one afternoon entertained with the sports of the Circus, he and three of his companions went out a walking among the gardens, near the walls of the city, and there, as it happened, going two and two together, one with him took one way, and the other two another ; and that these two, as they were wandering about, lighted upon a certain cottage, where some servants of thine dwelt, *poor in spirit, of whom is the kingdom of heaven,* (Matt. v.) and there they found a book, containing the life of Antony, which one of them began to read, to admire, and be inflamed with : and whilst he was reading, he began to think of embracing the same kind of life, and of quitting his worldly office in the emperor's court to become thy servant. Then being suddenly filled with divine love, a wholesome shame, and anger at himself, he cast his eyes upon his friend, and said : Tell me, I beseech thee, with all the pains we take in this world, whither would our ambition aspire to ? what do we seek ? what is it we propose to ourselves in this employment ? can we ever hope for any greater honour at court than to arrive at the friendship and favour of the emperor ? and there—what is to be found there, that is not brittle and full of dangers ? and through how many dangers must we ascend to this greater danger ? and how long will this continue ? But the friend and favourite of God, I may, if I please, become now presently, and remain so for ever. Having said this, and labouring as it were in travail of a new life, he again cast his eyes on the book, and continuing to read, was changed where thou sawest, and his mind totally stripped of the world, as soon appeared : for whilst he was reading, the waves of his heart, rolling to and fro, cast forth some sighs and groans, till at length he concluded and resolved upon better things ; and being now wholly thine, he said to his friend : Now I have entirely bid adieu to our former hope, and am fully resolved on being a servant of God, and upon beginning to be so from this hour and in this place. If thou be not willing to do the same, do not at least offer to oppose my resolution. The other replied : That he would stick by him as a companion in the service of so great a Master, and for such immense wages. By this time Pontitianus and his companion, who were seeking after them, came to the same place ; and having found them, reminded them of returning home, because the day was far spent. But they acquainting them with their determination, as well as with the manner in which they had taken this resolution, and were confirmed in it, requested that if they did not choose to join with them, they would at least give them no disturbance. Whereupon being nothing altered from what they were before, they nevertheless bewailed themselves, and after piously congratulating them, and recommending themselves to their prayers, with hearts weighed downwards towards the earth, they returned to the palace, whilst the other two, with hearts elevated to heaven, continued in the cottage: both of them were contracted to young ladies, who as soon as they heard their resolution, consecrated in like manner their virginity to thee. These things were related to us by Pontitianus," concludes St. Augustine, who declares in the following chapter, the wonderful effects this discourse had upon him; and how, as soon as Pontitianus was gone, he set upon Alipius, and exclaimed: " What is this we suffer? what is this thou hast been hearing? the unlettered rise up and seize heaven by force: and whilst with all our learning we, remaining without courage or heart, still wallow in the flesh and blood. Are we ashamed to follow them, because they have got the start, and are gone before us? But ought we not to be still more ashamed, if we do not so much as follow?" With these words he hurried himself away into the garden, where, after a strong conflict, he was at length fully converted, by taking up, by the admonition of a voice from heaven, the epistles of St. Paul, and reading there the sentence that first occurred, Rom. xiii. 13, 14. *Not in rioting and drunkenness, not in chambering and impurities, not in strife and envy; but put ye on the Lord Jesus Christ, and make not provision for the flesh in its concupiscences.*

ST. HILARION.

From his Life written by St. Jerome.

HILARION was born at a village called Thabatha, five miles from the city of Gaza in Palestine, of infidel parents, who sent him, when very young, to study at Alexandria, where he gave proofs of an excellent genius for his age, and of his good dispositions to virtue. Here he embraced the faith of Christ, and young as he was, could find no pleasure either in theatrical shows, incentives to lust, or any other wordly diversions, but delighted only in frequenting the church, and in religious exercises. Hearing of the fame of St. Antony, he went to visit him in the desert, and put off his secular habit, in order to embrace the same institute. He remained with the Saint about two months, making it his study to observe and learn perfectly the whole order and method of his life;—his continual prayer—his humility—his charity—his mortification—and all his other virtues. Then returning into his own country with some other religious men, and finding that his parents were dead, he distributed his whole substance between his brethren and the poor, without reserving any thing for himself, bearing in mind that saying of our Lord: *He that doth not renounce all that he possesseth, cannot be my disciple,* Luke xiv. 33. Thus stript of the world, and armed with Christ, being only in his sixteenth year, he took the resolution of retiring into the wilderness (which lies on the left of the road that leads from Gaza into Egypt), without apprehending the dangers which his worldly friends objected, from the robberies and murders for which that place was infamous; but rather despising a temporal death, that he might escape that which is eternal; nor regarding the tenderness of his own constitution, which made him very sensible of cold, heat, and other injuries of the weather, and of the hardships and austerities that are incident to that kind of life which he was going to undertake.

On going into the desert, he took on other clothing with him than the frock of a peasant, a sackcloth and hair-cloth, with a leathern habit to wear over it, which St. Antony had given him. Here he built himself a little hut, covered with sedges and rushes, to modify the inclemency of the weather, which served him from the sixteenth to the twentieth year of his age, and afterwards in a cell, which, according to St. Jerome's account, who had seen it, was but four feet wide, five feet high, and in length but a little longer than his body, so that as he could not stand in it upright, it seemed rather a tomb for a dead corpse, than a dwelling for a living man. Here his diet was suitable to his lodging; his food for the first years being but fifteen dry figs in the day, and that not till after sunset. Afterwards, from the twenty-first to the twenty seventh year of his age, he took only about eight or ten ounces of lentiles, steeped in cold water, or a little dry bread, with salt and water. For the space of three or four years more, he lived upon nothing but the wild herbs, or roots of the shrubs of the wilderness. From the thirty-first till the thirty-fifth year of his age he confined himself to six ounces of barley bread per day, and a few pot-herbs without oil; which rule he continued to observe to his sixty-third year, when he began to allow himself a little oil with his herbs, but tasted nothing else, either of fruit or of pulse, or of any other kind of food. From that time, as he now supposed that by course of nature he could not have long to live, instead of relaxing in his austerities, he redoubled them; so that from the sixty-fourth year of his age till his death, that is, till he was eighty years old, he totally abstained from bread, and eat nothing, during the four and twenty hours, but a kind of mess composed of meal and herbs,

5

which served him both for meat and drink: and this in
so small a quantity, that his whole daily sustenance did
not weigh above five ounces.   Such was his austerity,
with respect to his food, that, throughout these different
periods of his life, he ever observed it as a constant rule,
never to eat or drink till after sun-set, how weak soever
his health might be, not even on the greatest solemnities.

Hilarion had no sooner, in imitation of his great model
and master St. Antony, entered upon this course of life
in a vast and frightful desert, where no man before had
ventured to dwell, and, like him, applied himself incessantly to God in prayer, than the devil, not bearing to
see himself thus trodden under foot by a young man,
began to assault him with violent temptations of the
flesh, filling his mind with impure imaginations, and in-
citing him by sensual allurements, to carnal pleasures, of
which before he had no conception.   The chaste youth
perfectly abhorred himself, when he perceived these
abominable emotions to lust in his body and mind.   He
struck his breast, as if he meant by this exterior violence
to put those lewd suggestions to flight : he condemned
himself to longer, and still more rigorous fasts and hard
labour, saying thus to himself: " thou little jack-ass, I
will teach thee to kick ; instead of corn thou shalt feed
only on straw ;—I will tame thy courage with hunger
and thirst : I will lay heavy burthens upon thee :—I
will make thee work both in summer and winter, that
instead of wanton pleasures thou mayest think of thy
meat."   The Saint was steadfast in his resolution : fasting without intermission, sometimes for three or four
days together, and then taking only a little juice of herbs
and a few figs for his meal : incessantly praying, singing psalms, and working at the same time, either in
digging the earth or in making baskets, till at length,
by these exercises, he reduced his body to a mere skeleton.
Wherefore the enemy perceiving he could not prevail this
way, began to trouble him with fantastic apparitions

and other temptations. One night he was on a sudden surprised with hearing the crying as it were of children, the bleating of sheep, the bellowing of oxen, the lamentations of women, the roaring of lions, and the confused noise of an army of barbarians, with strange and frightful voices. Suspecting them to be nothing but diabolical illusions, he armed himself with the sign of the cross, and with a lively faith, cast himself down upon the ground, to be the better enabled, in this humble posture, to encounter the proud enemy. Then looking forward, it being a clear moon-light night, he perceived, as it were, a coach, drawn by furious horses, coming with a violent gallop towards him: at the sight of which he called upon the name of Jesus, when behold on a sudden the whole fantastic scene sunk down into the earth before his eyes: upon which he burst forth the praises of his Deliverer. At several other times this indefatigable enemy sought various ways, both by day and night, to molest him : either by exhibiting naked figures to excite him to concupiscence, or by seeking to interrupt his devotion and distract him at prayer by a variety of either comic or tragic scenes : but none of these, or any other of his attempts, were able to shake the resolution of the servant of God, or prevent his perpetual application to the love and service of his Maker. One day whilst he was praying with his head fixed on the ground, it happened that his mind wandered on some other thoughts, the watchful enemy, taking advantage of this distraction, jumped upon his back, as if to ride upon him ; and whipping and spurring, cried out: " What, art thou asleep ? Thou a saint! come shall I give thee some provender ?" But this, like the rest of his vain efforts, only served to excite the Saint to still more vigilance and fervour.

About the eighteenth year of his age the robbers that frequented the desert, took it in their heads to pay him a visit ; expecting either to find something in his hut to take away, or looking upon it as a rash attempt in a single boy to venture to dwell alone in their dominions, and not be afraid of them. They therefore began their search after him in the evening, and continued it till the sun-rising, without being able to find his lodging: but meeting him at day-light, they asked him as it were in jest, " what he would do if he were visited by robbers ?" " Oh !" said he, " he that has nothing to lose fears no robbers." " But," said they, " perhaps they may kill thee." " True," said he, " but I do not dread death : and therefore am not afraid of them, because I am prepared to die." Amazed at his constancy and faith, they acknowledged that having sought him during the night, they were so blinded as not to be able to find him ; and so deeply were they affected with his words, that they promised to amend their lives.

Hilarion had now spent twenty-two years in perfect solitude in the wilderness, conversing only with God and his angels, and only known to the world by the fame of his sanctity, which was spread over all Palestine, when a certain woman of the city of Eleutheropolis, who had lived fifteen years in the state of wedlock without bearing a child, finding herself despised by her husband on account of her barrenness, ventured to break in upon his solitude ; and coming unexpectedly upon him, cast herself upon her knees before him, saying : " Pardon my boldness ; pity my distress : why do you turn away your eyes from me ? Why do you flee from your petitioner ? Do not look at me as a woman, but as a distressed fellow-creature. Remember that a woman brought forth the Saviour of the world, those that are well stand not in need of a physician, but they that are ill." At these words he stood still ; and having learnt of her, the first woman he had seen since his retiring into the desert, the cause of her grief, he lifted up his eyes towards heaven, bid her be of good heart, and weeping for her, sent her away ; but he said, within a twelvemonth she returned, bringing her son with her to visit him. This, his first miracle, was followed by a greater. When Aristeneta, the wife of Elpidius, a Christian nobleman (who was afterwards advanced to one of the first posts in the empire), was on her return from Egypt, where she had been, with her husband and her three sons, to see St. Antony, she stopped at Gaza on account of the illness of her children, who were all seized by a semitertian fever, and brought so low that their lives were despaired of by the physicians. The disconsolate mother, hearing of the sanctity of Hilarion, whose wilderness was not far distant from Gaza, went in haste to visit him, accompanied by some of her servants, and thus addressed herself to him : " I beg of thee for God's sake : for the sake of Jesus our most merciful God ; through his cross and his blood ; that thou wouldst vouchsafe to come and restore health to my three sons, that the name of the Lord our Saviour may be glorified in that pagan city : that when his servant comes into Gaza, Marnas (the idol which they there worship) may fall to the ground." The man of God excused himself, alledging, that he never went out of his cell, not so much as into any village, much less into a populous city ; but she, casting herself down upon the ground, ceased not to importune him with many tears ; often crying out, " O Hilarion ! thou blessed servant of God, restore to me my sons : Antony has laid his hands upon them in Egypt, but do thou save their lives in Syria." Her earnest entreaties at length obliged him to promise her that he would come to Gaza after sun-set. No sooner had he arrived at their lodgings, and seen them confined to their beds in burning fevers, bereft of sense, than he called upon our Lord Jesus, when immediately a copious sweat, issuing as it were from three fountains, followed his prayer, and in the space of an hour they took their meat, knew their mournful mother, blessed God, and kissed the hands of the Saint.

No sooner was this miracle published abroad, than multitudes of the inhabitants of both Syria and Egypt began to visit him. Many infidels were by his means converted to the faith of Christ, and many also, by his example, embraced a monastic life; for, before his time, there were neither monks nor monasteries in Palestine or Syria: he must therefore be considered the father, founder, and first teacher of the monastic institute in those provinces. And now it was that he began to be joined by many disciples, whom he trained up to religious perfection, who were witnesses of the wonderful miracles that God wrought by him. St. Jerome, as one perfectly well informed, has recorded several of the most remarkable, with all their circumstances. A woman of the neighbourhood of Rhinocorura, (a city on the confines of Egypt,) who had been blind for ten years, was brought to the Saint to be healed: after having told him that she had expended her whole substance on physicians, " you had done better (said he) if you had given it to the poor; you would then have given it to Jesus Christ, the true physician, who would have healed you." She earnestly begged that he would have pity on her; and he, with spitting on her eyes, restored her to her sight. A charioteer of Gaza was also brought to him on his bed, struck in such a manner by the devil, that he could not stir any of the members of his body except his tongue, with which he besought the servant of God to heal him. The Saint told him, that if he desired to be healed, he must first believe in Jesus Christ, and promise to renounce a profession which exposed him to the immediate occasion of sin. To these conditions he agreed, and having received his cure, he returned home, rejoicing more for the health of his soul, than for that of his body.

Marsitas, a young man of the territory of Jerusalem of an extraordinary bulk and strength, who had been possessed by an evil spirit, and done much mischief to many, was dragged by ropes to the cell of the servant of

God, like a mad bull bound in chains. The brethren at
the very sight of him were affrighted, but the saint bid
the people bring him up and let him loose; which when
they had done, he commanded him to bend down his
head and come to him. The poor man trembling bent
his neck, when laying aside all his fierceness, and falling
down he licked the feet of the man of God; and after
seven days' exorcisms was entirely cured. Another man,
named Orion, a principal citizen of Aila, a city near the
Red Sea, who was possessed by a whole legion of devils,
was brought in like manner loaded with chains to the
Saint, who happened at that time to be walking with
his disciples, and interpreting to them some passages of
the Scripture: when behold the possessed man broke
loose from those that held him, and running up to the
man of God, whose back was turned towards him, lifted
him up from the ground on high in his arms: at which
all that were present cried out, apprehending that he
would do the Saint some mischief; but Hilarion said
smiling, " suffer me to wrestle with my antagonist."
Then putting back his hand, he laid hold on the hair of
Orion, and bringing him before his feet, kept him down
howling, and turning back his neck, so as to touch the
ground with the top of his head. Then praying, he
said: " O Lord Jesus, I am a poor wretch; do thou re-
lease this captive; thou canst as easily overcome many
as one." On this occasion they were all astonished to
hear so many different voices issuing from the mouth of
the possessed person, and a confused out-cry, as it were
of a whole people: but their wonder ceased when they
saw the multitude of wicked spirits that was expelled
from him by the prayers of the humble servant of God.
Orion came shortly afterwards with his wife and children
to return thanks to the Saint, and brought him large
presents out of gratitude, which he absolutely refused to
accept: but when he besought him with tears to take
at least what he had brought, and to give it to the poor,

he answered; " thou canst better distribute thyself what thou wouldst have to be given to the poor; for thou frequentest cities, and knowest the poor; why should I, who have left my own, covet the goods of others? Many have been imposed upon by avarice, under the name of the poor. Do not make thyself uneasy; it is for both thy sake and mine I refuse thy presents: for if I should accept of them, I should offend God, and the legion of devils would return to thee."

One Italicus, a Christian of Maiuma, the haven of Gaza, who bred horses for the public races that were to be exhibited at Gaza, came to the Saint to beg his prayers against the enchantments wherewith his pagan antagonist, one of the magistrates of the city, had bewitched his horses. Hilarion, who disliked all these public games, was unwilling to employ his prayers on so vain an occasion. But the other representing to him that it was not by his own choice, but by his office, he was obliged to do what he did; and that the honour of God and religion was here at stake, because the men of Gaza, who, for the most part, were infidels, would take occasion, from his being worsted, to insult, not so much over him as over the church of Christ: the Saint, at the request of the brethren, ordered his earthen pot, in which he used to drink, to be filled with water, and given to him. Italicus took the water, and with it sprinkled his stable, his horses, his chariot, and his drivers, in the sight of the pagans, who made a jest of it, whilst the Christians, confiding in the prayers of the Saint, made no doubt of success. Wherefore, as soon as the signal was given, the horses of Italicus sprung forth with incredible speed, whilst those of his adversary were presently distanced, and could scarce keep within sight of them that were gone before. Upon this a loud cry of all the people was immediately raised, and even the very adversaries cried out, that *Marnas, the God of Gaza, was worsted by Christ.* This miracle gave occasion to the conversion of many.

There was also in the same town of Maiuma, a virgin dedicated to God, with whom a young man in the neighbourhood was vehemently in love. After having employed, without success, flattering speeches, idle jokes, and other freedoms, which too often pave the way to greater crimes, he went to Memphis in Egypt, to seek a remedy for his wound from the priests of Esculapius. They furnished him with certain magical spells and monstrous figures, graven upon a plate of copper, which he buried under the threshold of the house where the maid dwelt, when behold immediately (in punishment of her having laid herself too open to the enemy, by not flying, as she ought, or not resisting former freedoms) the maid ran mad with love, tearing off her head clothes, whirling about her hair, gnashing with her teeth, and calling upon the name of the young man. Her parents, therefore, took her to St. Hilarion, when presently it appeared how the case stood; for the devil began to howl within her, and to cry out: " I was forced in hither; I was brought from Memphis against my will: where I succeeded well, in deluding men with dreams. But, oh! what torments dost thou make me suffer here! Thou compellest me to depart, but behold I am bound fast, and kept in by the thread and plate that lie under the threshold. I cannot go out till the young man who keeps me here, lets me go." " Thou art very strong indeed!" said the Saint, " if thou art held by a thread and a plate. But tell me, how didst thou dare to enter into a maid dedicated to God!" " It was," said he, " to preserve her virginity." " What! thou preserve her virginity," said the Saint, " who art the mortal enemy of chastity. Why didst thou not rather enter into him that sent thee?" " Oh," said the devil, " there was no necessity for my entering into him, who was already possessed by my comrade, the demon of wanton love." The Saint would hear no more, nor send for the young man, not order the things mentioned to be taken

away, to shew the little regard that is to be had to the
devil's speeches or signs, but instantly delivered the
maid from her wicked guest, and sent her away perfectly cured, after severely reprehending her for admitting of those liberties which had given the devil the
power to possess her.

It would be endless to recount all the other miracles
that God wrought by this Saint, which rendered his
name illustrious, even in the most remote provinces. St.
Antony himself, hearing of his life and conversation,
wrote to him, and gladly received letters from him; and
when any diseased came to him for their cure from any
part of Syria, he blamed them for giving themselves the
trouble to come so far, since you have, said he, in those
parts my son Hilarion. His bright example attracted great
numbers to the service of God, so that now there were
innumerable monasteries, or cells of religious, throughout
Palestine, who all looked upon him as their father, and
resorted to him for their direction. These he exhorted
to attend to their spiritual progress; ever reminding
them, " that the figure of this world passeth away, and
that eternal life can only be purchased by parting with
the pleasures and affections of this life." He visited all
their monasteries once a year for their instruction and edification : and such was his diligence and charity on these
occasions, that he would not pass by the cell of the least or
meanest of the brethren without calling in to instruct and
console him, insomuch that he went as far as the desert of
Kadesh, on purpose to visit one single monk who dwelt
there. In this journey he was accompanied by a great
number of his disciples into the city of Elusa, on the
confines of the Saracens, on a festival day, when the
people were all assembled in the temple of Venus, who
was there worshipped by the Saracens on account of the
star that bears her name. No sooner had they heard that
Hilarion, of whose sanctity and miracles they had been
previously informed by several of their nation whom he had

delivered from evil spirits, was passing by, but all the men, women, and children ran out in crowds to meet him and to beg his blessing. The Saint received them all with the utmost tenderness and humility, and begged that they would henceforth worship the living God, rather than stocks and stones: shedding at the same time many tears, and looking up towards heaven, he promised, if they would believe in Christ, that he would frequently come to see them. So wonderful was the grace that accompanied the words and prayers of the man of God, that they would not suffer him to quit their city, till he had first marked out a plot of ground for the building of a church; nay, their very priest had received the sign of the cross of Christ, in order to his baptism.

Another year, when the Saint was making his visitation, a little before the time of the vintage, he came with all his companions to the monastery of one of the brethren, who was remarkable for being a niggardly miser. This man had a vineyard, and apprehending lest the multitude of the monks that accompanied the Saint should eat up his grapes, he set several men to keep them off with stones and clods in slings, and would not so much as let them taste of them. The servant of God smiled at the treatment they had met with, but taking no notice of it to the niggard, he went on the next day to another monastery, where he and his whole company were kindly received by a monk named Sabas, who kindly invited them (it being the Lord's day,) to go and feast themselves in his vineyard. The •Saint ordered that they should first take the food of their souls, by applying themselves to their religious exercises of prayer, singing psalms, and paying their duty to God: and then after giving them his blessing, he sent the whole multitude of his disciples to the vineyard to take their corporal refection. The blessing of the man of God was attended with so miraculous an effect, that whereas the vineyard of Sabas was not before thought capable of yielding more than a hundred gallons of wine, it yielded that year three hundred, whilst the vineyard of the niggard yielded much less than usual, and the little that it produced turned into vinegar, a circumstance which the man of God had foretold. Hilarion could never endure in religious men any thing that looked like covetousness, or too great an affection to any of those things that pass away with this transitory world : he was moreover endowed by God with the gift of discovering who were addicted to this, that, or any other kind of vice, by the stench that proceeded from their bodies or garments.

And now the Saint, seeing that his hermitage was converted into a great monastery; and that the wilderness about him was continually crowded with the people who resorted thither, bringing their diseased, or such as were possessed with unclean spirits, and that not only the common sort of people from all the neighbouring provinces, but even the gentry,—ladies of the first rank,—clerks, monks, priests, and bishops, were daily visiting him, and interrupting his devotions, he bitterly regretted the loss of his former solitude, perpetually lamenting, weeping, and saying, that since he had returned back into the world, he apprehended he should have his reward in this life, because all Palestine and the neighbouring provinces took him to be somebody, &c. nor did he cease to mourn and bewail his condition, till he took a fixed resolution to quit his monastery, and retire into some place where he might be unknown, and more freely enjoy his God without the interruption of so many visits. In the mean time, whilst he was meditating upon his flight, the lady Aristeneta, whose three sons he had cured, came to see him, acquainting him with her design of returning into Egypt, to make a second visit to St. Antony. He replied, with tears in his eyes, that he could have wished to have taken the same journey, if he were not kept prisoner in his monastery, but that it was now too late to find Antony alive ; for, said he, two days ago the world was deprived of so great a father. Having believed him, she did not proceed in her journey, and, behold, after some days the news of his death was brought from Egypt. When it was known abroad that the man of God was upon the point of quitting Palestine, the whole province took the alarm, and no less than ten thousand people, of all degrees and conditions, were gathered together, in order to stop and detain him. But his resolution was not to be altered; and as he had learnt by revelation the havock that the infidels of Gaza were about to make in his monastery, and all through that neighbourhood, under the reign of Julian the Apostate, he gave them broad hints of this his fore-knowledge, saying, that he could not call in question the truth of what God had said; nor could he endure to see the churches destroyed, the altars of Christ trodden under foot, and his children massacred. In short, he assured them he would neither eat nor drink till they let him go. And thus, after he had fasted seven days, they were contented at last to suffer him depart, accompanied by about forty of his monks. With these he made the best of his way to Pelusium, (now called Damietta) in Egypt, and after visiting the holy solitaries who lived in the neighbouring deserts, he waited upon Dracontius and Philo; two illustrious confessors of Christ, of the number of those catholic prelates who had been banished from their sees by the fury of the Arians, under the emperor Constantius. After paying these visits, he hastened to keep the anniversary day of the happy decease of St. Antony in the place where he died : and being conducted by the deacon Baisanes upon dromedaries, three days' journey through that vast and dreary wilderness, he arrived at length at the mountain of the Saint. Here he found his two disciples, who showed him all the places where their master had been accustomed to sing psalms— to pray—to work—and sit down to rest himself, after being wearied with his labour; as also the garden he had cultivated—the trees he had planted—the instrument with which he had dug the earth—the private cells to which he often retired towards the top of the mountain, &c. and then agreeably entertained him with divers particulars of the acts of the latter part of St. Antony's life. Hilarion was much moved to devotion with the sight and recital of all this ; and after watching in prayer the whole night of the anniversary of the Saint, he returned the same way he came, through the dreary wilderness to the neighbourhood of the town called Aphroditon. Here in an adjoining desert, with two of his disciples whom he kept with him, he led so abstemious, abstracted, and silent a life, that on feeling the fervour he now found within himself, he seemed never to have before begun to serve Christ in earnest.

He had not been above two years in this wilderness, when the fame of his sanctity brought all the people of the neighbouring country to him, to beg his prayers for rain. For from the time of the death of St. Antony, no rain had fallen upon their land, for the space of three whole years, so that being afflicted with a great famine, they resorted to him, whom they considered as the successor of St. Antony, for a redress of their misery. Moved to pity by the sight of their distress, he lifted up his hands and eyes to heaven to pray for them, and his prayer was immediately followed by plentiful rains. But the rains, whilst they fertilized the earth, having, in falling on the dry hot sand, also produced an incredible multitude of venomous reptiles and insects, with which innumerable persons were struck, they were again forced to have recourse to the Saint, who gave them some oil which he had blessed, with which they were cured. But now finding himself after these miracles greatly honoured, he would stay no longer in this place, but departed in order to go and hide himself in the desert of Oasis. In his way thither he passed through Alexandria : and as he made it a rule never to lodge in any city, he went on to a place in the neighbourhood, called Bruchium, where there was a monastery of the servants of God. From hence, when night drew on, he hastened away. telling the brethren, who were greatly afflicted, that they should soon know the reason of his sudden departure. Accordingly, on the next day their monastery was searched by the Gazites, accompanied by officers sent from the governor of Alexandria to apprehend Hilarion, of whose arrival there they had received intelligence. For the infidels of Gaza, who bore a mortal hatred to the Saint, as soon as Julian came to the empire, destroyed his monastery, and obtained an edict from the tyrant, that both he, and his disciple Hesychius, should be sought for and put to death wherever they were found. Of this the Saint had a fore-knowledge by prophetic light, and thereupon withdrew himself: so that the infidels, who had thought themselves certain of seizing their priest, finding he was gone, departed, saying to each other, that now they were sure he was a magician, and had a foresight of things to come.

He had not been a year in the wilderness of Oasis, before he found that fame had also followed him thither; and therefore now despairing to be able to conceal himself upon the continent, he formed a resolution of seeking out a place in some of the islands of the Mediterranean, where he might hide himself. In order to this he embarked, with one only disciple, at Paretonium, a haven on the coast of Lybia, on board a vessel bound for Sicily; hoping that henceforward no one should know him, or become troublesome to him in his retirement. When, behold, in the midst of the voyage the son of the master of the ship, or rather the devil by his mouth, cried out : " Hilarion, thou servant of God, let me alone, at least till we come to land; how comes it to pass, that even at sea thou art still persecuting us." The Saint would have disguised the grace which God had given him, fearing lest the sailors and passengers should publish his fame when they came to land, and

therefore mildly replied : " If my God permits thee to
stay, stay if thou wilt ; but if he cast thee out, what hast
thou to do to complain of me, who am but a poor beggar and a sinful man." However, upon the solemn
promise of the father, and of all the rest, that they would
not discover him, he cast the devil out of the boy. When
they arrived at Pachynum (now Capo Passaro), he
would have paid for the passage of himself and his companion, by giving the captain the book of the gospels,
which was all his wealth, but he, seeing their poverty,
would not receive it. Wherefore the Saint leaving the
sea-coast, withdrew himself into a little kind of wilderness, about twenty miles within the land, and there fixed
his abode ; living upon what little he could get, by making up faggots, which his companion carried to a neighbouring village, bringing from thence in exchange what
they stood need of for their food.

But the Saint could not long lie concealed here ; for
soon after his arrival, a man possessed with an evil spirit,
being under the exorcisms of the church at St. Peter's in
Rome, the devil cried out thus by his mouth : " Hilarion,
the servant of Christ, is some days since come into Sicily,
where no man knows him, and he thinks himself secret :
but I will go and discover him." This man therefore
taking some of his servants with him, and going on board
a ship sailed immediately for Sicily ; and after coming to
shore, being conducted by the devil, he went straight to
the hut of the servant of God, and there casting himself at his feet, was perfectly cured. This being noised
abroad, great multitudes, who laboured under various
corporeal diseases, resorted to him to obtain their cure ;
whilst numbers also of devout and religious people applied to him for their spiritual profit. Amongst the rest, he
cured upon the spot one of the principal men of the island,
who was swollen up with the dropsy, and who on the
same day, returned home in perfect health. This man
offered to make him considerable presents, which the Saint

absolutely refused, alledging the precept of our Saviour, Matt. x. 8. *Freely have you received, freely give :* which rule he invariably observed in all the other innumerable miracles which he wrought, whether in Sicily or elsewhere, for, he never would receive any thing, no not so much as a morsel of bread from any one of those on whom he had wrought those miracles.

And now his beloved disciple Hesychius, after having sought after him in vain through many different regions came at length to Sicily, upon the report he had heard at Modon in Greece, from a Jewish pedlar, that a christain prophet had appeared in Sicily, who wrought all kinds of wonderful miracles. No sooner had he found him than the Saint gave him to understand, that he wanted to depart from Sicily into some strange country where he might be utterly unknown. Wherefore, in compliance with his desire, he conveyed him away by a ship to the coast of Dalmatia, where for a short time he led a solitary life, not far from the city of Epidaurus, now called Ragusa. But neither here could he remain long concealed, his miracles every where betraying him. There was at that time, in the neighbourhood of Epidaurus, a monstrous serpent, of that species named *boas*, which did great mischief in destroying both men and cattle ; the Saint, to put a stop to this calamity ordered the country people to heap up a pile of wood, and after addressing a prayer to Christ he called the serpent out of his den, and commanded him to go on the top of the pile of wood, and then setting fire to it, he burnt the monster in sight of a great multitude of people. This miracle was followed by another still greater. About this time, viz. the second year of the reign of Valentinian the first, there happened so remarkable an earthquake that, according to Amianus, a cotemporary historian, its like was never recorded, either in authentic or fabulous history. On this occasion, the swelling seas, in several places, broke in and overflowed the land in such a manner as to threaten

the earth with a second deluge, and in some places
the waves ran so high as to carry the ships along with
them, and leave them hanging on the cliffs. The Epi-
daurians perceiving the danger in which their city as well
as many others were in of being destroyed, had recourse
to Hilarion, and opposed him to the mountains of water
that were just upon the point of overwhelming them.
No sooner had the Saint made three crosses on the sand,
and lifted up his arms to heaven, than the swelling waves,
though they raged, foamed, and rose up to an incredible
height, not able to advance, gradually returned back again
and subsided. This wonder, says St. Jerome, who was
then a boy in the same province, the city of Epidaurus,
as well as the whole country, recount to this day—the
mothers relate it to their children, in order to transmit
the memory of it to posterity.

The applause that followed these miracles would not
suffer the humble servant of Christ to remain any longer
in Dalmatia; therefore taking boat privately by night he
fled away, and within two days found a ship departing
for Cyprus, on which he embarked. In this voyage his
ship being pursued by some pirates in two light vessels,
there appeared no hopes of escaping them. The ship's
crew being in the utmost consternation, the Saint turning to his disciples said: " Why are you afraid, O ye
of little faith ?" And when the pirates were now come
within a stone's cast of the ship, he stood on the fore-
deck, and stretching out his hand to them, he said:
" *You have come far enough ;*" when behold immediately
their vessels fell back, and the more they tugged and
rowed, in order to push forward towards their expected
prey, the more rapidly were they carried away from it.
The Saint landed at Paphos, a noted city of Cyprus,
and chose himself a dwelling place about two miles
from thence; being now wonderfully pleased that he had
found rest, at least for a short time, in this solitude; but
scarcely had twenty days elapsed when the devils in dif-

ferent parts of the island published his arrival by the mouths of those that were possessed; and several of these, both men and women, hastened to him and were delivered. Here he remained about two years meditating upon some private place of retirement. In the mean time he sent Hesychius into Palestine, to salute the brethren there, and to visit the ashes of his monastery; and upon his return proposed that they should sail into Egypt, and advance a great way into the country, to some place inhabited only by pagans. But Hesychius opposed this; and after a long search, discovered a place in the island about twelve miles distant from the sea, amongst mountains and woods that were almost inaccessible, which proved quite to his mind. In this solitude, to which no one could arrive in several places but by creeping on hands and knees, they found springs of water on the sides of the hills,—a little garden within, with several fruit trees, of which however the Saint would never eat, and near the garden the ruins of an ancient temple, from whence, as both he and his disciples related, were often heard, both night and day, a great noise, like the voices of a whole army of devils. In this solitary abode the man of God dwelt for the last five years of his mortal life, seldom visited by any one but Hesychius, on account of the difficulty of coming at his dwelling, as also because the people were persuaded that the neighbourhood was haunted with a multitude of demons. However, there were some that ventured to come to him for the cure of their maladies; their necessities overcoming all difficulties, especially after it was known, that he had cured upon the spot, the bailiff of the place of a palsy, which had deprived him of the use of his limbs, by only stretching out his hand to him, and lifting him up with these words: *In the name of the Lord Jesus Christ, rise up and walk.*

But now the time arrived which was to put a period to all the labours of his mortal pilgrimage, and unite him eternally to his God, when being now eighty years old he was seized with his last illness. Although Hesychius was then absent, he nevertheless bequeathed to him by will all he had, viz. his book of the gospels, his sackcloth, cowl, and habit. Many religious men from Paphos came to attend him in his sickness, who had heard of his having said, " that he was now going to our Lord;" and with them a holy woman named Constantia, whose daughter and son-in-law he had delivered from death by anointing them with oil. And now he was drawing near his end, when in the very agony of death he distinctly spoke these words : " Go forth my soul : what art thou afraid of ? Go forth, why art thou at a stand ? Thou hast served Christ almost seventy years, and art thou afraid to die?" and with these words he gave up the ghost. He was immediately buried as he had desired, in the same place : where the devout lady Constantia frequently passed whole nights in prayer at his sepulchre, speaking with him as if he were alive, and desiring the assistance of his prayers. His disciple Hesychius, after ten months, privately conveyed his body away to Palestine, where it was solemnly interred in his own monastery; at which time it was found entirely incorrupt, and sending forth a most fragrant odure. Many great miracles were daily wrought through his intercession, even to the time when St. Jerome published his life, as well at his sepulchre in Palestine, as at the place where he was first buried in Cyprus.

ST. MALCHUS.

Abridged from St. Jerome.

WHILST St. Jerome in his younger days made some stay at Maronia, a village of Syria, about thirty miles distant from Antioch, he learnt that there dwelt in that neighbourhood a religious man, now advanced in years, whose name was Malchus, and near him a decrepit old woman, both eminent servants of God, constant in the church, and wholly addicted to the exercises of religion: of whom the neighbours published wonderful things and extolled their sanctity to the skies, which gave occasion to St. Jerome, in order to his own justification, to visit that holy man, and to learn from his own mouth the particulars of his history; which he afterwards published to the world in a small book, of which the following is an abstract.

Malchus was a native of the territory of Nisibis, a city of Mesopotamia, upon the confines of the Roman and Persian empires. Being the only child of his parents they looked upon him as the heir and support of their family, and therefore, when he was grown up, they pressed him to marry; but declaring himself quite averse to this state of life, he made known to them his desire of entering into religion, and of wholly dedicating himself to God. But as they ceased not still to importune him, both with flatteries and threats to part with the treasure of his virginal purity, which he valued above all the possessions of the world, in order to rid himself of their importunities, and to secure his treasure, he took a resolution to withdraw himself entirely from house and home, parents and country. Accordingly, taking a trifling matter with him for his journey, he travelled westward, till at length he arrived at the desert of Chalcis in Syria. Here he found some servants of God leading a monastic life, and put himself under their direction, following the same institute as they did, living by the labour of his hands, and restraining the rebellions of flesh by rigorous fasting. In this course of life he continued for many years, till the common enemy, envying the progress he made in virtue, suggested to him, under specious pretexts, to leave the monastery, and to return to his own country to see whether his mother were yet alive (for he had heard of his father's death), and if she were, to comfort her in her widowhood, and after her decease to sell the estate, distribute part of the money to the poor, employ another part in building a monastery, and to reserve what remained for his own use; a design which he afterwards lamented, as a grievous transgression, and infidelity to his religious engagements.

His Abbot was no sooner informed of his purposes, than he remonstrated to him, in the strongest terms, that the whole was a temptation of the devil, who, by such plausible pretences as these, had oftentimes imposed upon religious men, and drawn them back again into the world; alledging also several examples from Scripture, of the wiles and impostures of this wicked old serpent. When the abbot saw that his remonstrances were not hearkened to, he even cast himself down upon his knees, and earnestly entreated his disciple not to abandon him, nor fling himself away, nor to look back after setting his hand to the plough. But all in vain : Malchus imagined that his superior, in seeking to detain him, had more an eye to his own comfort and satisfaction, than to his advantage, and therefore would not be diverted from his design. When he set out upon his journey, his abbot followed him out of the monastery, bewailing him, as if he had been following his corpse to the grave ; and at their last parting told him plainly, that the sheep which had left the fold must expect nothing but to fall an immediate prey to the wolves.

In his journey he was to go from Beroea to Edessa, by a road which borders upon an extensive wilderness, much infested by parties of the Saracens or Arabians, who robbed or carried off all they met with. This obliged the travellers who passed that way, to travel in large companies for their mutual defence; and it happened that there were at this time no less than about three-score and ten persons in company with Malchus, young and old, men and women. But this precaution could not secure the fugitive, who was running away from his Lord, from being overtaken, or from meeting with captivity and slavery, instead of the possessions to which he imagined himself returning. For behold a party of armed Saracens, some on horseback, others upon camels rushed suddenly upon them; made them prisoners, and then, by lot, divided their captives amongst them. Malchus happened to fall into the hands of the same master with a married woman, one of the company, whose husband fell to the lot of another : and both he, and the rest of the prisoners, now slaves, being set upon camels, were carried for many days through an immense wilderness, living in the mean time upon meat half raw and camels' milk ; till having passed over a great river, they came into the heart of the country. Here Malchus and his fellow captive were brought in, and being presented to their master's wife, were obliged according to the manner of the custom of the country, to prostrate themselves and do reverence to their new mistress and her children. And now, instead of his monastic habit, or any other clothing, Malchus is obliged to go naked, as well on account of his condition of a slave, as by the violent heat reflected by the sun-beams on those Arabian sands, which would not suffer him to wear any other covering than what modesty indispensably required. His office was to tend his master's sheep in the wilderness ; in which it was his comfort to be generally alone, seldom seeing either his master, or any of his fellow-servants. He pleased himself also with the thought, that in his way of life he resembled some of the ancient Saints who had in like manner fed sheep in the wilderness. In the mean time his whole diet was new cheese and milk, and his whole employment continual prayer and singing of the psalms which he had learnt by heart in the monastery. He now became delighted with his captivity, and gave thanks to God for the wonderful dispositions of his merciful providence, in conducting him to find the monk again in the land of his slavery, which he was going to loose for ever in his own country.

The devil, who could not endure to be a witness to the great advantages our captive made of his present condition, by the help of his solitude, recollection, and continual prayer, contrived a dangerous stratagem for the robbing him at once both of his chastity and all his other virtues, which he sought to bring about in the following manner. The Saracen, finding that his flock encreased under the hands of Malchus, that he served him honestly and with fidelity, took it into his head, doubtless by the suggestion of the enemy, to reward him, and as it were, to fix him for ever in his service, by giving him the same married woman for a wife who was taken captive with him :—this he proposed as an act of friendship, or a favour which he was desirous to confer on him. But when Malchus replied that this could not be, because he was a Christian, and therefore could not, by the law of God, marry a woman whose husband was still living, the barbarian, in a rage, drew his sword, and would have instantly killed him upon the spot, had he not hastened to take his fellow captive by the arm, which his master mistook for a token of his consent to the marriage. When night arrived they went both together with a heavy heart into a ruinous cave, which served Malchus for his lodging, neither of them knowing the dispositions of the other. Here

Malchus casting himself upon the ground, grievously lamented his wretched condition, that after having in his younger days forsaken all his worldly pretensions, together with his country, parents, and estate, purely to preserve his virginity, he should now in a more advanced age, lose it in so illegal and wicked a manner : accusing himself withal of his sins, especially of his crime in quitting his monastery to return to his own country, to which he imputed his being now caught in this labyrinth, out of which he knew not how to extricate himself but by death : and this he was strongly inclined to choose, as the only means remaining, as he thought, to preserve his virtue. His fellow-captive, perceiving the excessive trouble and agitation of mind under which he lay, and hearing him talk of making himself *a martyr of chastity*. cast herself at his feet, and begged, for the sake of Jesus Christ, that he would not think of doing himself any harm ; that, for her part, she abhorred the proposed marriage as much as himself, and would rather suffer death than consent to any unchastity : but why may we not live together, said she, as brother and sister, in perfect purity, whilst our master and mistress take us for man and wife? These words calmed the soul of Malchus, and made him esteem and admire the virtue of the woman, and love her the more ; but, according to God, with a holy friendship, cemented by heavenly charity.

Pursuant to this proposal, they lived a long time together, in perfect chastity of mind and body, and were beloved by their master and mistress, who entertained not the least suspicion, either of their not being married, nor of any danger of their making their escape : so that Malchus was accustomed to be absent with his flock for a whole month together in the wilderness, at a great distance from his master's house. One day, whilst he was sitting alone, he began to consider the great advantages of a spiritual life that are found in well or-

7

dered religious communities: remembering in particular the helps and directions he had received from the good abbot, his ghostly father, and regretted his leaving him: when behold, in the midst of his meditation, he perceives at a little distance a hillock of ants (a creature proposed to us by the wise man as a pattern of industry and wisdom), and was pleased to see the order and harmony which they observed in their labours—that mutual help which they gave to each other, and how they ran to the assistance of such as fell under their burthens. This seemed to him a lively representation of a regular community; and joined to his foregoing considerations made him begin to be weary of his captivity, and long to return to his abbot and his monastery. When he came home at night, the woman perceived him to be pensive and melancholy, and having learnt the reason, persuaded him to set off, offering at the same time to accompany him. Having concluded upon so doing, and watching a proper opportunity, he killed two large goats of his flock, made vessels of their skins, and prepared part of the meat to support them during their journey. On the next evening they set out, making the best of their way to a river about ten miles distant, which they crossed by the help of the vessels they had made of the skins of the goats. In crossing the river they lost some part of the meat they had carried with them, so that what remained was scarce sufficient to support them for three days, and as to drink, they took plenty of water, not knowing when they should meet with more.

They made what haste they possibly could through the sandy deserts, looking back from time to time, with fear and trembling, to see if any one were in pursuit of them, travelling mostly by night, as well to avoid the meeting with any of the Saracen rovers, as on account of the excessive heat. They had been now three days upon their journey, when looking behind them, they saw at a distance two men riding on camels, and hastening towards them, one of whom they concluded to be their master, who had discovered the way they had gone by their tracks in the sands, and now they expected nothing but certain death. There happening to be a den or cave at hand that reached a considerable way under ground, they ran thither for shelter; but fearing the serpents and other venomous creatures that usually resort to such places in order to avoid the heat of the sun, they would not venture to penetrate to the further end, lest in flying from death in one shape, they should meet it in another. Wherefore discovering within, near the entrance of the den, a hole on their left hand, into which they had no sooner trusted themselves, when behold their master, with one of their fellow servants, tracing them by their footsteps, quickly came up to the mouth of the cavern. The master having sent his servant in to drag them out, stood without, holding the camels, and waiting for them with his drawn sword. The servant passed by the hole where they lay concealed, without being able to see them, on account of his being just come out of the light, and advancing forward made a great uproar, crying aloud : " Come forward, ye villains and receive your wages : come out, your master calls for you : come out, and die." Malchus and his companion saw him pass by them, and looking after him, perceived a lioness, roused by the noise, flying at him, and strangling him, and then drawing his bloody body further into the den. The master, ignorant of what had happened, finding that the servant did not come out, supposed that they, being two, might make resistance against one. He came therefore in a great rage to the entrance of the cave, with his sword in his hand, and raving at the cowardice of his servant, began to enter in; but before he had passed the lurking hole where Malchus lay, he was suddenly seized by the breast before their eyes, and served in the same manner as his servant had been. Thus by an extraordinary providence were these servants of God delivered from the hands of those that sought their life : but they remained still in dread lest they should meet with no less cruel death from the furious beast that was so near them. In this fear they remained close, without making the least motion or noise, having no other means of defence or dependence but the providence of God, and a good conscience in point of chastity, which is respected even by lions. But it was not long before the lioness, finding herself discovered, and disturbed in her den, taking up her whelp (for she had but one), carried it out with her teeth, in order to go and seek for another lodging, and thus abandoned the whole cave to themselves. The apprehension, however, of meeting with the beast, kept them close prisoners till the evening, when they ventured out, and found the two camels (who were of the kind which for their great swiftness are called dromedaries), and with them fresh provisions, of which they were in great need : and thus, after refreshing themselves with food, they mounted upon the camels, and continued their journey through the desert, and on the tenth day arrived at the Roman camp, on the confines of the empire. The commanding officer, after having heard their history, sent them to Sabinianus, the governor of Mesopotamia, who gave them the price of their camels, and so dismissed them.

And now Malchus would have returned to his good father, the abbot of his monastery, in the desert of Chalsis : but being informed that he was gone to sleep in the Lord, he turned his course towards Maronia, and there associated himself with the monks of that place ; and as to his companion, he committed her to the care of the nuns that were there ; ever *loving her as if she had been his sister*, as he told St. Jerome, *yet never trusting himself to her as a sister*, or exposing himself to danger by any familiarity with her. Here, as St. Jerome concludes his narration, we cannot pretend to add any further particulars of the acts of this servant of God, only that he continued to the end the saintly life he had begun, and crowned it with a happy death; so that he has deserved to have his name recorded amongst the Saints of the the Roman Martyrology, October 21.

SS. PACHOMIUS AND PALEMON.

Abridged from the Life of St. Pachomius, by an ancient writer, who had his information from the companions and disciples of of the Saint.

St. Pachomius was born in Thebais, or the higher Egypt, about the year 292, of infidel parents, who carried him, when as yet a child, to the temples of their idols, to make him a partaker of their impious sacrifices; but as a presage of what he was one day to be, when they gave him a little of the wine of the devil's libations, or drink offerings, to taste, he presently cast it up again; and when upon another solemn occasion he had accompanied them to celebrate the festival of an idol that was worshipped upon the banks of the Nile, the devil was restrained, by his presence, from returning answers, and deluding the people with his usual tricks, till by the mouth of the priest he had ordered Pachomius to be sent away as an enemy of the gods. Yet all this while he was totally ignorant of the christian religion, but otherwise led a very moral life, and was always modest, temperate, and chaste.

When about twenty years old, Constantine being then emperor, he was, with many other of his countrymen, impressed for the service, on account of a war just then breaking out. The young recruits were put on ship board, in order to pass down the Nile, and so to be carried to the army. In their way they arrived at a certain city, where they found the inhabitants remarkably officious in administering all the comfort and assistance in their power to some young men, who were kept close confined by their officers, and in great distress. Pachomius enquired who these men were that shewed so much humanity and benevolence to the afflicted and distressed? On benig told they were Christians, a set of men who made it their business to do good to all men, and especially to strangers in distress, he further enquired what was meant by the name of Christians, and what were their tenets? They told him they were godly and religious people who believed in Jesus Christ, the only Son of God, and exercised themselves in all the virtues and works of charity, in expectation of an eternal reward from God in another life. Pachominus was touched with this account, and being visited by the divine grace, withdrew himself into a corner, and lifting up his hands and heart to heaven, he called upon the great God, who made heaven and earth, to enlighten his soul with the knowledge of the true and perfect rule of life which he would have him to follow; and promised, if he would deliver him from his present bondage, that he would yield himself up to his divine service during the remainder of his life, and quit all worldly hopes, to adhere to him alone. The emperor having shortly afterwards obtained a complete victory over his enemies, and put an end to the war, ordered the new raised troops to be discharged. Pachomius having now recovered his wished-for liberty, returned to his own country, and presently enrolled himself in the number of those that were under instructions in order to receive baptism, and being baptised shortly afterwards in the church of the town of Chinoboscium, he was on the following night favoured with a heavenly vision, which strongly moved him to consecrate the residue of his life to divine love.

In obedience to this call, he repaired immediately to

Palemon, a holy anchoret, who led a recluse life in a neighbouring desert, with a desire of putting himself under his conduct and direction, and of spending the remainder of his life with him. This servant of God, who led a very austere life, at first refused him admittance, alleging, that several others had in like manner pretended to put themselves under his discipline, but became quickly tired of his way of life. Pachomius requested that he would at least put him to the trial, for that he trusted God would enable him to execute all that he should require of him. " My son," said Palemon, " the way of life that I follow is not the easiest. I eat nothing but bread and salt, and wholly refrain from oil and wine. I watch one half the night; employing that time in solemn prayer, and in meditating on the word of God; and sometimes I pass the whole night without sleep. " Pachomius replied, that he hoped the grace of our Lord Jesus Christ, with the help of his prayers, would inspire him with the necessary courage to embrace, and patience to suffer all this rigour, even to the end of his life. Palemon perceiving the lively faith and steadfast resolution of the young man, was content to receive him, and clothe him with the monastic habit; and Pachomius, on his part, from the very beginning, embraced the exercises of a religious life with so much ardour; and advanced with such large steps, day by day, in the paths of virtue and perfection, as to give unspeakable satisfaction and joy to his master, who continually returned thanks to Christ for the wonders of his grace which he discovered in his disciple. In the mean time they lived together in the same cell, preformed the same practices of abstinence and prayer, and laboured together in the same manual exercises, that they might not only support themselves without being burthensome to others, but also to have wherewith to entertain and relieve their indigent brethren. After the labours of the day, they watched and prayed together for the best part of the night; and if, upon these occasions, Palemon observed that Pachomius was in danger of falling asleep, he led him out of the cell, and employed him in carrying loads of sand from one place to another, in order to overcome his drowsiness; telling him, that if he hoped to persevere to the end in his holy undertaking, he must not by any means suffer himself to relax in watching and prayer. Besides these exercises, Pachomius, in a more particular manner, applied himself to the cultivating and purifying his interior. In order to this, whilst he was reading the holy scriptures, and committing them to his memory, which was a part of his daily occupation, he paused in silent and deep meditation upon each of the heavenly precepts, suffering them to sink deep into his soul, and studying to reduce each of them to practice; but the favourite virtues in which he particularly laboured to excel, were, a profound humility, unweared patience, and unbounded charity and love both for God and his neighbour.

When Easter arrived, Palemon ordered Pachomius to prepare them a dinner for that great festival. The latter readily obeyed, and, in consideration of the solemnity of the feast, mingled a little oil and salt together to be eaten with the wild herbs which he had gathered. But when, after having prayed together, Palemon came to table, and saw the sallad prepared for him, instead of eating it, he wept bitterly, saying : " my Lord was crucified, and' shall I indulge myself in eating oil!" Neither would he at any rate be induced to take any other food but his bread and salt as usual, blessing it with the sign of the cross before he eat thereof, and returning humble thanks to our Lord afterwards.

One day, whilst Palemon and Pachomius were watching together by a fire they had kindled in their cell, another religious man coming to them, desired admittance, whom they courteously received. After some discourse the stranger proposed to them, " that if they had as much faith as he had, they would shew it, by standing with their bare feet over the burning coals, which himself was ready to do, whilst they repeated at leisure the Lord's prayer." The servants of God were shocked at the arrogance of their guest; and Palemon besought him to desist from so mad an attempt. But instead of hearkening to him, being puffed up with pride and presumption, he went and stood upon the coals, and by the help of the enemy, God so permitting, in punishment of his pride, received no injury whatsoever. The next morning at departing, he added to his pride the insolence of insulting' the two saints, by reproaching them with their want of faith. But it was not long before his arrogance was most dreadfully punished: for the devil perceiving that his self-conceit had already stripped him of divine grace, and left him in a condition to become an easy prey to lust, came one day to his cell, in the shape of a most beautiful woman, pretending to be in the utmost distress, and being admitted, enkindled in his heart the fire of concupisence. The unhappy man readily yielded to these wicked suggestions, and attempting to put them in execution, was so unmercifully handled by the evil spirit, as to be left extended upon the floor, without speech or sense. Having however, after some time, come to himself, he, as soon as he was able to walk, went to the cell of St. Palemon telling what had happened, and acknowledging that he had drawn all this evil upon himself by his pride, and begging their prayers, that the devil might not tear him in pieces, or otherwise destroy him. The Saints lamented his case, and wept for him; but the enemy to whom he had made himself a slave, would not suffer him to remain with them; for all on a sudden he jumped out of the cell, and after running about the wilderness like a mad man, he went to the neighbouring city of Panopolis, and there, having flung himself into the furnace of the hot baths, he perished in the flames—a deplorable example of the dreadful consequences of pride and presumption.

Pachomius, from hearing the direful exit of this unhappy man, took occasion of being still more humble, mortified, and fervent in prayer; and as he had an extraordinary love for solitude, he often withdrew from his cell into lonely places, spending his whole time in prayer; earnestly begging of the divine Majesty to deliver him from all the deceits and snares of the wicked one. There was also in the neighbourhood a wild place full of thorns, to which he often went to procure wood for their use. Upon these occasions it was his custom to walk bare-foot among the thorns, pleasing himself with the pricks and wounds that he received in his feet, by the meditation of the piercing of the feet of our Saviour upon the cross. One day, going to a greater distance than ordinary from his cell, he came to a place called Tabenna, at that time altogether uninhabited, where having, according to custom, remained a considerable time in prayer, it was revealed to him, that he should there build a monastery, to which many should resort, and put themselves under his conduct; for whose instruction and direction he should receive a rule from heaven; a sketch of which was then presented him by an angel. When he returned back to Palemon, he acquainted him with this revelation, and prevailed on him to accompany him to Tabenna, where they built a small cell, and for some time remained together, performing their accustomed exercises, till at length Palemon, seeing the extraordinary grace that God had conferred on Pachomius, went back again, and left him sole possessor of this new cell, upon condition, that, as long as they lived, they should frequently visit each other for their mutual comfort and spiritual assistance.

And now the time drew near which was to crown the labours of St. Palemon with an eternal recompense in the land of the living. Previous to his death, he was seized with a grievous and most painful illness, which the brethren who came to visit him, attributed to his austere and penitential manner of life, and therefore prevailed upon him to admit of some, little comfort, in point of eating and drinking, in consideration of his age and weakness. But he quickly returned again to his former manner of diet, alleging, that the change had only contributed to increase his pains, and that if the martyrs had bravely suffered so many cruel torments for the love of Christ, and thereby purchased a happy eternity, it would be shameful in him to forfeit the eternal reward prepared for patient suffering, by a cowardly murmuring under his light and momentary pains. After he had continued about a month, suffering with invincible courage and constancy, his soul, sufficiently purified in the furnace of tribulation, took her happy flight, accompanied by angels to the heavenly mansions. His name stands recorded amongst the Saints in the Roman Martyrology, on the eleventh of January.

After Pachomius had buried his holy father, and was returned to his cell at Tabenna, God was pleased to send him his own brother for a companion, who, having heard of his wonderful life, came to visit him, which was the first time the Saint had seen any of his relations since his conversion, and proposed to live with him. Pachomius having joyfully received him, found in his brother all the dispositions that could be desired in a perfect religious man. The two brothers continued together, meditating incessantly on the law of God both by day and night, with all the affection of their souls, ever tending towards him, and totally disengaged from the least affection towards the things of the earth. They laboured with their hands for their daily food, and never reserved any thing for to-morrow; but whatever they earned above the necessary sustenance of the day they gave to the poor. Pachomius to his former austerities added that of humbling his soul and body, by wearing hair-cloth; and during the space of fifteen years, notwithstanding his hard labours, long watchings, and continual fastings, never allowed himself to lie down at night to take his rest; but whatever sleep he admitted of, he took sitting in the midst of his cell, without having any thing at his back to support himself, or to lean against for his ease.

In the mean time, the Saint being a second time admonished from heaven concerning the religious congregation he was to institute, and the rules he was to give them, began to enlarge the place of their habitation, and to build several additional cells for the reception of those whom he expected would come in good time to join him in the service of so great a Master. His brother, whose spirit inclined rather to the life of an anchoret, in a more perfect solitude, after some time blamed his proceedings, and being the elder brother, took upon him to bid him desist from so useless a labour. The Saint, although he could not help being troubled at this opposition, yet bore it with meekness and humility, without making the least reply. But the following night, prostrating himself alone in prayer in the new building, he remained till morning in this humble posture, lamenting his misery, and imploring the divine mercy for having suffered any emotions of impatience or resentment on this occasion to take place in his soul, begging the grace of God to guard and protect him from sin, and so powerfully to assist him for the future, that he might acquire a perfect mastery over all his passions, and serve him with all perfection all the days of his life. So numerous were the tears he shed that night, so great the fervour of his prayer, and the weather so violently hot, that what with his weeping and sweat, the place on which he lay prostrate became as wet as if water had been cast upon it. At other times, during his devotions by night, he used to excite himself to watching and fervour in prayer, by stretching out his arms, keeping his body as immovable as if he were fastened to the cross, and remaining for several hours in this painful posture. On all occasions Pachomius behaved himself with such humility, meekness, and condescension towards his brother, that they lived together in the most perfect harmony and peace, till God was pleased to take the brother to himself. Pachomius took care for his burial, and spent the whole night in singing pashns and hymns over his body, and recommending his soul to God.

And now Pachomius, as if all he had hitherto done had been nothing, *forgetting* with the Apostle, *the things that were behind, stretched forth himself to the things that were before*, by a new fervour in the study and practice of religious perfection, having the congregation which he was to establish in that place always before his eyes. This drew upon him the inveterate envy and malice of the wicked enemy, by whom he was incessantly plied with temptations of every kind, and frequently with fantastical apparitions; who sought either to puff him up with pride and vain-glory, by the honours he pretended to pay him, or to allure him to lust, by placing the figures of impudent women with bare bosoms before him, or by interrupting and distracting him in his devotions, by a variety of illusions and ludicrous scenes; sometimes also assaulting him with open violence, and even laying many blows and stripes upon him. But the Saint, armed with a lively faith and strong confidence in Jesus Christ, whom he called to his assistance by fervent prayer, ever came off victorious in all these conflicts, and even with a great increase of virtue, to the utter confusion of all the powers of hell: so that being now enabled by the gift of God, to tread under his feet serpents and scorpions, the very crocodiles obeyed him. In the mean time he would have willingly debarred himself even of the short time he was obliged to allow to necessary sleep, which he would have gladly spent in prayer, and earnestly prayed that the Lord would enable him to live without it, that he might be wholly intent on his divine

8

love, which, in some measure, as far as his mortal condition could bear was granted to him. Now the great subject of his prayer, both night and day, was *that the will of God might be ever accomplished in all things.*

Shortly afterwards he was again visited by an angel, who told him that it was the will of God that he should not only serve him himself, with all purity and perfection, but also that he should assemble a great multitude of religious men together, and train them up, and dedicate them to his divine service, according to the method and rule which had been shewn him before. So that now he began to receive all such as came to him, that were desirous to fly from the contagion of the world, and, by penance, present themselves as humble suitors to the mercy of God. After having made them pass through a long and severe noviceship, he admitted them to the monastic profession, incessantly inculcating to them the strict obligation of their institute, as well with respect to flying from all the allurements of the world, as of diligently exercising themselves in the ways of virtue and holiness : adding, that a monk, according to the directions of the gospel, ought *first* to renounce the world in general : *secondly*, all disorderly affections of flesh and blood to his nearest kindred and worldly friends ; and, in the *last place*, the most difficult of all, he ought to renounce and deny himself, take up his cross and follow Christ.

As the number of those that resorted to him increased every day, he distributed them into different classes and and monasteries, appointing to each of them their regular exercises and different employments, according to their several abilities and dispositions, and making himself all to all, not only by a general solicitude for their spiritual progress, but also by his readiness to serve even the least of them in the meanest offices, so as to make himself, on every occasion, their cook—their gardener —their porter—and especially their *infirmarian*, by the tender care he always showed to *the sick*, on whom he attended both night and day.

He delivered to all his monks the rules he had received from heaven, appointing for them a very moderate food, a mean habit, and no more sleep than necessity required. He laboured to inspire them with a well-grounded *humility*, as the necessary foundation of all virtue, without which the spiritual edifice of a religious life is sure to fall to the ground. To exclude all ambition, or desire of preferment and superiority, he would not even allow his monks to be promoted to the priestly dignity, choosing that they should rather remain in the humble condition of laics ; and therefore, till God sent him some priests, who desired to be admitted to his congregation (for such as these he did not refuse, but received with great respect), he was forced to have recourse to some neighbouring clergymen, requesting them to come and say mass, and administer the holy communion to the religious in his monasteries. But above all things he recommended a ready and perfect *obedience*, as the very soul of religion, and the shortest way to religious perfection, by divesting them of their own will, and making them securely find, and faithfully follow, in all things, the blessed will of God.

He had the bowels of a tender parent towards all his children, but a more particular affection and compassion for the aged and sick, as also for young boys, serving them, and exercising the works of mercy towards them with his own hands, and feeling a more than ordinary solicitude for their comfort and instruction. Nothing could equal the respect he retained for the clergy in general, more particularly the bishops of God's church, or the zeal he had for the purity of the catholic faith, which made him conceive a horror against the Arians and other heretics, as enemies of God's truth : and, as at that time the writings of Origen, who had unhappily blended the errors of the Platonic philosophers with the

Christian doctrine, were very much handed about among
the Egyptian monks, to the great prejudice of their
souls, Pachomius declared open war against them, and
prohibited all his monks the reading of them.

Being likewise animated by an extraordinary zeal for
the salvation of the souls, not only of his own religious,
but also of all others whom he saw in want of spiritual
assistance, and observing in that part of the country
many of the meaner sort of people employed in the care
of the cattle, who had for want of having a church at
hand to which they might resort, lived in great igno-
rance, deprived of the use of the sacraments ; to remedy so
great an evil, he applied to the bishop of Tentyra, and
procured that a church should be built for them in the
neighbouring village ; and as it was some time before
they were provided with clergymen, he went himself
with his monks, on Sundays and holidays, and read lessons out of the divine Scriptures, proper for their instruction, in so edifying a manner, with such a saintly air of
devotion, and so serene and heavenly a countenance, as
made his auditory receive him, and attend to him, not
as to a man, but as to an angel sent them from heaven.
Numbers upon this occasion were brought over by his
instructions from the gulf of infidelity and error to the
christian faith ; and the more so, because he, on his part,
employed not only the words of exhortation and doctrine
in their behalf, but also the more effectual arms of fervent prayer for their conversion, accompained with many
sighs and tears.

About this time the great St. Athanasius, bishop of
Alexandria, in visiting the churches of Egypt, which
were all under his jurisdiction, came also to Tabenna,
where our Saint had established his monasteries. Pachomius, who had venerated this holy patriarch, as the great
pillar of the church of God, and respected him much
more for his sanctity than for his dignity, caused all his
monks to go out to meet him, singing psalms and hymns,

and to receive him with great reverence and joy; yet so that he himself would not appear at their head, nor any way distinguish himself amongst them, but hid himself in the crowd, to avoid being particularly taken notice of by that great prelate, who, as he feared, would promote him against his will to the priestly dignity, at the recommendation of the bishop of Tentyra his diocesan, who very much desired to have him ordained priest.

Whilst Pachomius was thus happily employed in conducting a great number of holy souls in the ways of eternal life, and directing them to perfection, both by word and example, his sister, hearing the fame of his sanctity, came one day to his monastery, desiring to see him. The Saint, who never admitted any woman into his monastery, sent her word by the porter that he was alive and well, and requested she would return home in peace, and not make herself uneasy on account of her not seeing him in this transitory life; but added, that if she desired to follow the same kind of life as he did, in order find mercy with God, and secure to her soul a happy eternity, she should think seriously of it; and if this should be her fixed resolution, he would give orders for building a proper mansion for her at a distance from his monastery, where she might serve the Lord, under regular discipline, in all purity of soul and body, and in time engage many others, by her example, to dedicate themselves in like manner to the love and service of Christ in a religious life: for, to expect to find, said he, any solid rest, content, or happiness, but in works of godliness, as long as we carry this body of death about us, is a thing utterly impossible. His sister hearing this, shed a flood of tears; and being at the same time touched with a powerful grace, determined upon the spot to choose that better part which he had so strenuously recommended to her; and accordingly, as soon as the monstery which he ordered to be built for her, was in readiness, she entered into it, and there served our Lord with such sanctity and

8*

perfection, as to attract many others of her sex to join in her holy undertaking, and consecrate themselves to Christ under her direction. This was the origin of the nuns of the order of St. Pachomius, to whom the Saint gave the same rules as to his monks: and took the strictest care imaginable, that the one should have little or no communication with the other, so that he might cut off all occasions of temptation.

Among the disciples of St. Pachomius, the most illustrious imitator of his virtues, and his successor in sanctity, was St. Theodore, whose history is briefly as follows: He was born of noble and wealthy christian parents, according to the world. His father dying when he was very young, left him heir to a plentiful estate, under the care of a tender and affectionate mother. But he had a better Father in heaven, who showed his great care and tender love for him by an early weaning of his heart from the love of the world and its vanities; and sweetly invititing him to his divine service in a very extraordinary manner, when he was as yet scarcely twelve years old. His conversion happened upon a solemn occasion of public mirth, whilst a great feast was preparing in his house, which abounded in rich furniture and all kind of worldly wealth, when behold he was suddenly visited with a heavenly light in his interior, which clearly convinced him of the nothingness of transitory things, accompanied with a strong call to give up all to follow Christ. "Alas! what would it profit thee, O unhappy Theodore," said he to himself on this occasion, "if thou shouldest even gain the whole world, and enjoy all the temporal delights the world can give, shouldst thou lose by these means the eternal goods and immortal joys of heaven? for there is no pretending to pass thy life here in these vain pleasures and delights, and yet expect to merit everlasting rewards hereafter." With these sentiments he withdrew himself into a private closet, and there prostrating himself on the floor, with many sighs and tears he prayed thus to our

Lord: "O Almighty God, who knowest all the secrets of hearts, thou knowest there is not any thing in this world that I prefer before the love of thee. Wherefore I implore thy mercy, that thou wouldst direct me to accomplish thy holy will, enlightening my poor soul, that she may never sleep in the darkness of sin and eternal death, but being redeemed by thy grace, may be brought to praise and glorify thee for ever." Whilst he was praying to this effect his mother came in, and finding him all in tears, asked him who had given him any trouble or offence, that he should grieve in such a manner, and separate himself at dinner time from the company?—that they had been seeking him every where, and were greatly concerned about him. He begged of her to make herself quite easy, and to go to table, but desired withal to be excused from bearing her company. From this time he accustomed himself, in going to school, to fast every day till the evening, and frequently, to eat nothing for two days; and for two whole years, whilst he remained in the world, he totally refrained from all delicacies, contenting himself with the meanest and coarsest kind of food. After some time he quitted all that he seemed to possess in the world, and entered into a monastery: where he had not been long before he heard of St. Pachomius, and was inspired with a desire of putting himself under his discipline. Having followed the call, he went to Tabenna, was cordially received by the Saint, and, in a short time, by the great fervour with which he applied himself to watching, fasting, and prayer, and to all good works, made a very considerable progress in all virtues.

Whilst Theodore was climbing up the hill of christian perfection, by a constant attention to please God, and omit nothing which he conceived would promote his spiritual advancement, his mother having heard where he was, attempted to bring him back again into the world. Wherefore having obtained letters of recommendation from some bishops, to whom the new Pachomius could refuse nothing, she went to the monastery of the nuns, and wrote from thence to the holy abbot, desiring that she might see her son. Pachomius called for Theodore, and told him how the case stood; and that to satisfy his mother's desire, and in consideration of the holy prelates whose letters she had brought, he thought he might go and see her. And will you assure me, reverend father, said Theodore, that after receiving such great lights and calls from God, as I have received, and leaving both my mother and all things else in the world, for the love of Christ, I shall have nothing to answer to our Lord, at the last day, if I should go now and see my mother to gratify flesh and blood, and give this disedification to my brethren? Nay, said Pachomius, if you don't judge it expedient for your soul, I don't wish to compel you: for it is far more becoming a true monk whose profession it is to renounce the whole world, and himself also, to shun all manner of unprofitable worldly visits and vain conversation, and to admit of no other company, but of those, from whose godly discourse he may be edified in the ways of God. This refusal, however disagreeable it might be at first to the mother of Theodore, turned to her great advantage, in order to the salvation of her soul; for in hopes of meeting with some opportunity, sooner or later, of seeing her son amongst the other religious, she resolved to continue with the nuns, and to follow the same holy way of life. And as to Theodore, his whole life from this time was so perfect and saint-like in every regard, that after his death he was enrolled amongst the saints. His name occurs in the Roman Martyrology on the twenty-eighth of December.

But to return to St. Pachomius. As he had received unspeakable joy and comfort on occasion of the fervour of Theodore and many others of his monks, whom he saw advancing rapidly in the way of religious perfection, so he was exceedingly afflicted when he met any one, who, under the habit of religion, had nothing of the spirit of religion, but lived rather according to the flesh, not having as yet put off the old man of their former worldly conversation.   With such as these he spared no pains, but employed every means, such as admonitions—exhortations—corrections—fervent prayers to God, and tears poured forth in their behalf, in order to obtain for them the grace of a perfect conversion : and did not desist till they were either brought to a sense of their duty, and reclaimed from their evil ways, or else, if they proved incorrigible, entirely cut off from his congregation.   A young man, named Silvanus, who had been an actor upon the stage, quitting his sinful profession, came to put himself under the discipline of the Saint, and was received in his monastery.   But whilst he was here, he led for some time a careless life, breaking through the rules of the congregation, and spending his time in entertaining himself and others with his former ridiculous buffooneries, to the great scandal of his brethren, who desired the holy abbot to dismiss him.   The man of God, who was very unwilling to send back again into the world any of his children, employed, besides his charitable remonstrances and exhortations, which were without effect, his more potent arm of continual prayer, sighs and tears, for this poor soul ; and then taking him aside, represented to him, in so strong and powerful a manner, the truths of eternity, the dreadful judgments that threaten impenitent sinners, with the rest of the motives that are most proper to excite in souls both the fear and love of God : that the grace of God entering into the heart of Silvanus, he was immediately touched with so lively a sense of his sins, and such deep compunction for them, as not only entirely to refrain for the time to come from his former faults, and begin to lead a new life of great edification to the rest of his brethren, but also in every place, and in all his occupations to be continually weeping and lamenting so bitterly for his past crimes, that he could not refrain from sobbing and mourning, even whilst he was taking his meal with the other religious.   When his brethren desired him not to afflict himself to such an excessive degree, since it became even troublesome to them, but rather to restrain these outward tokens of grief which were no way necessary even to the most perfect compunction, the true seat of which dwelt within the heart, he answered, that he would gladly obey them, and accordingly made all the efforts he could to refrain from them; but he found a certain flame burning within his breast, that would not suffer him to be quiet.   But, said they, what subject or occasion is there for all these flood of tears? "Ah!" said he, "how can I help weeping, when I see so many holy brethren, the dust of whose feet I ought to venerate, so charitable as to take notice of me?   When I see a wretch that is come from the playhouse, quite laden with sins, receive so many good offices!   Alas! I have reason to fear, lest the earth should open under my feet, and swallow me down, as it did Dathan and Abiron, in punishment of my having profaned all that was sacred, after so clear a knowledge and experience of divine grace, by leading so slothful and wicked a life. Wonder not at my weeping.   Oh? my brethren, I have just reason to labour to expiate my innumerable sins with ever flowing fountains of tears; and if I could even pour forth this wretched soul of mine in mourning, it would be all too little to punish my crimes.".   With these sentiments of humility and contrition he made so rapid a progress in virtue and sanctity, as to be admired by the holy abbot himself, who proposed him to the rest of his monks, as a singular pattern of humility, and assured them that neither Theodore himself, nor any of the rest of them, whose lives had been the most innocent, and who seemed, by their good works, to have already trodden Satan under their feet, were near so much out of danger of this enemy rising up against them, and overthrowing them by pride, as Silvanus was, whose perpetual contrition and humility kept the devil at so great a distance, that he could lay no manner of hold on him. This glorious penitent, after eight years spent in thus continually offering to God the sacrifice of a contrite and humble heart, put a happy end to his penitential course of life, by dying the death of the saints : and St. Pachomius gave testimony, that at the hour of his death a multitude of heavenly spirits conveyed his soul along with them, with great joy, and presented it as a choice sacrifice to Christ our Lord.

There was another also of the religious whose sanctity was much esteemed by Pachomius, whom he likewise proposed as an extraordinary pattern of virtue and perfection to the rest of his monks. His name was Zacheus; who, after he had for a long time served the Lord with great diligence and fervour in a religious state, fell ill of the jaundice, which forsook him not till his death. On this occasion he had a cell appointed him, in which he lived separated from the rest of the religious; yet he omitted none of the regular exercises of the community, but was always with the rest at all the hours of prayer. He never allowed himself in his illness any sleep in the day; and every night, before he laid himself down to rest, he employed himself for a considerable time in meditating on some passages of the holy Scriptures, and then signing his whole body with the sign of the cross, and glorifying God, he took his short repose. About midnight he rose again, and continued praising God till the time of the morning prayers. His entire food was only bread and salt, and the whole time that was vacant from other duties, he spent in making mats, and working with his hands. In twisting the palm-leaves which he made use of in his work, though his hands became so much galled and wounded thereby as oftentimes to shed blood, yet he never interrupted his work, nor betrayed the least emotion to impatience. One of the brethren, on seeing his hands grievously wounded, and all bloody whilst at work, entreated him to consider his illness, and to spare himself; for that God, who knew what he suffered, and how much he was otherwise afflicted by his disease, would not impute it to him for sin, nor charge him with sloth, if he did not work; and as to the community, they expected it not from him; but as they willingly exercised hospitality to the greatest strangers, and to all that were in want, they would, no doubt, take a much greater pleasure in serving him. Zacheus answered that he could not possibly think of living without working. Well, said the other, if you are fixed in your resolution of continuing to work, at least anoint your hands with oil, to prevent the loss of so much blood. Zacheus followed his advice; but instead of finding any ease by the application of the oil to his wounded hands, the pain increased to such a degree as to become quite insupportable. St. Pachomius came to visit him on this occasion, and treating him as one that stood not in need of milk, but was capable of digesting the strongest diet, reprehended him for having sought this assuagement of his pains, which God had sent him for his profit, and not having resigned himself wholly to him, but rather trusted in this visible medicine than in the living God. Zacheus made no apology for himself, but meekly answered: "Forgive me, reverend father, and pray to the Lord for me, that he may vouchsafe in his mercy to remit me this sin also, together with all my other sins." My author adds, from the testimony of many of the brethren, that he bewailed himself for a whole twelvemonth on this occasion, and observed during that time so strict a fast, as to eat but once in two days, and that in a small quantity. Pachomius used to direct such as were afflicted, or oppressed with sadness, to this holy man, for he had a wonderful talent of administering comfort to all that were in trouble or affliction of mind. He continued his labours and conflicts to the end ; when in a good old age he passed from temporal sorrows to eternal joys.

St. Pachomius was invited by Varus, the holy bishop of Panopolis, to come into his diocese, in order to establish some monasteries of his institute. In his way he visited divers religious houses included in the number of those that were under his direction. On entering into one of these houses, he met the brethren carrying out the corpse of one of the religious, accompanied by his worldly friends and relations, in order to be buried with a solemn office in an honourable manner. At the sight of the Saint they all stood still, desiring him to pray both for themselves and the deceased brother. Having finished his prayer, understanding in spirit the wretched state of his soul, (for the man had led a very careless and indolent life), he forbid them to proceed in their psalms, and ordered them to strip off the fine garments with which they had clad him, and to bury him without any solemnity or tokens of honour, which, as the holy abbot assured them, would be rather prejudicial than beneficial to his unhappy soul ; which proceeding of the Saint was designed as a warning to all his disciples not to rely so much on wearing the habit, as in leading the life of a religious. After remaining here two days, teaching and instructing his monks, and arming them against the deceits of Satan, a message was brought him from the monastery of Chenoboscium, that one of the religious there, who was near his end, desired to see him, and to have his last blessing before he died. Thither he hastened with the utmost speed : but when he came within two or three miles of the monastery, he heard a heavenly melody in the air, and looking up beheld the soul of the servant of God carried up by angels to heaven, who died at the very instant of time, as the companions of the Saint, to whom he related what he had heard and seen, found when they returned to the monastery.

Pachomius was received with great honour by the bishop, who assigned proper places to him and his monks for the building of their monasteries, which, whilst they were rising up, some wicked men, by the instigation of Satan, pulled down in the night what they had built during the day. On this occasion the Saint preached patience to his people; but God took his cause in hand for one night, whilst these wretches were intent upon their wickedness, they were suddenly consumed by fire, and seen no more. On several other occasions God was pleased to work miracles in favour of the faith and sanctity of his servant Pachomius, of which the following instances may suffice. A woman, who had laboured for a long time under an issue of blood, was suddenly cured, by coming behind him, and only touching his habit whilst he was sitting in the church of Tentyra, with Denys the priest. Many others were healed of divers diseases, and delivered from the possession of wicked spirits, by his prayers. A man came to him one day, desiring him to cast the devil out of his daughter. The Saint told him that he and his religious never spoke to women, but that he should send him in any garment that belonged to his daughter, which he would bless in the name of the Lord; and that he trusted in Christ she would be rescued from the power of the enemy. The father accordingly brought him one of her garments, which when the holy abbot beheld, he presently understood in spirit the case of the young woman, viz. that she was guilty of sins of impurity, by which she had violated the vow of chastity she had made to God, and that upon this account the devil had permission to take possession of her. He returned therefore the garment to the father, telling him how the case stood, and that if he desired his daughter should be delivered from the devil, she must first repent, be converted from her sins, promise not to be guilty of them any more, and that then she should find mercy. Her father took her to task, and at length she acknowledged her guilt, with great signs of repentance, and promised, in the most solemn manner, to refrain from committing the like sins for the future. Upon which the man of God gave the father some oil which he had blessed, by the use of which she was presently cured, and never ceased to glorify God, who had delivered her at once, both from the possession of the devil, and from her sinful habit. The Saint on his part was never puffed up with pride or vain glory on account of any of the miraculous cures that God wrought by him; but continuing always in the fear of God, and in a perfect sense of his own nothingness, he kept his soul always even, so as neither to be elevated by good success, nor depressed with evil; and if at any time God did not grant the things for which he petitioned, he was perfectly resigned to the divine will, knowing that to be best, both for himself and for all others, which God ordained, and saw to be most fitting.

One of the religious, who was a diligent imitator of the virtues of the holy abbot, standing one day in prayer, was struck in the foot by a scorpion, and though the torment he suffered on that occasion was extreme, and the pain, together with the poison, had spread itself even to the heart, and threatened him with present death, yet he would by no means interrupt his devotions, nor stir from his place, till he had finished his prayer; and then Pachomius prayed to our Lord in his behalf, and he was presently healed. On the other hand Theodore, being afflicted with a violent pain in the head, desired the man of God to pray for his cure: but he answered, that it was far better for him to bear the pain, which God had sent for his profit, with perfect resignation, patience, and humility, how long soever it might continue to afflict him, and to thank his divine Majesty for it, as for a great favour; saying, that a religious man might merit more, and please God better, by patience and conformity to his divine will in sufferings and sickness, than by the most rigorous abstinence, or long continued prayers in the time of health.

And now after our Saint had established his congregation upon a solid foundation, and assembled together a multitude of holy souls, serving God in great perfection, many of whom he had sent before him to heaven, he himself was seized with his last illness a little after Easter, anno 348. In his sickness he preserved always a serene and cheerful countenance: and after having called together the brethren, and made an excellent exhortation to them, begging of them to ever remember all the lessons he had given, to avoid the conversation of heretics, and to be ever vigilant in prayer and all other exercises of virtue, he recommended to them the choice of a successor: and after two days, arming himself with the sign of the cross, and looking with a cheerful aspect on an angel of light, who was sent to conduct him to heaven, he breathed out his holy soul, to take her flight to her heavenly country, upon the ninth of May. His name stands recorded among the Saints in the Roman Martyrology, on the fourteenth of May; and in the Menologies of the Greeks on the fifteenth; where also they affirm that the number of his monks, before his death, amounted to one thousand four hundred. But Palladius, afterwards bishop of Helenopolis, who has given an abstract of the life of St. Pachomius, in his *Historia Lausiaca*, chap. 38, and who had visited in person the holy inhabitants of the deserts of Egypt, some years after the death of this Saint, affirms that the whole number of the monks, whom St. Pachomius had under his care in all his monasteries, amounted to seven thousand; and that in his own monastery of Tabenna alone, there were no less than one thousand four hundred monks, who maintained themselves by the labour of of their own hands, without being troublesome to any one, and who, at the same time, by their frugal way of living, were enabled also to exercise hospitality, and to give liberal charities to the poor.

ST. AMMON, *ABBOT*.

From St. Athanasius, in his Life of St. Antony, chap. 32. Rufinus and Palladius, in their History of the Holy Fathers of the Deserts of Egypt.

ST. AMMON, or Amon, the first founder of the monasteries of Nitria, and as some authors affirm, the first author of a cenobitical or conventual life, was born of noble and wealthy Egyptian parents in the third century. From his youth he embraced a saintly life, desiring to serve God in perfect purity both of soul and body; but when he arrived at the age of twenty-two, his relations compelled him to marry a christian virgin animated by the like virtuous dispositions as himself, as appeared shortly after; for as soon as they were left alone on their wedding night, Ammon represented to his spouse how much happier and more pleasing to God the state of virginity was, than that of the use of matrimony, strengthening his arguments with the authority of holy Scripture, and at the same time so powerfully exhorting her to preserve the treasure of her virginal purity, and instructing her in the manner of life she should lead to please Christ, the true spouse of virgins, that she willing agreed that they should live like brother and sister in the same house, in perfect continence, lying in different beds, and only united with the bonds of the spirit, in charity and prayer. After this manner they lived together in the world for the space of eighteen years; Ammon dividing his time in such manner as to dedicate the best part of it to labour, by working in his garden and balm-yard, and the rest to his exercises of prayer and devotion, usually fasting till the evening. At the expiration of this time, their parents and friends, who

9*

had obliged them to marry, being now dead, they mutually agreed to live assunder, and each of them to embrace a monastic life.   Ammon, therefore, left her in possession of the house, which, in process of time, she converted into a nunnery : many devout virgins resorting to her, and putting themselves under her direction, whilst he retired into the wilderness of mount Nitria, forty miles distant from Alexandria, where he built two cells, and laid the foundations of that admirable religious institute, which was afterwards followed by no less than five thousand religious, who, although dwelling in about fifty different habitations, yet all meeting to their public devotions in one large church, served by eight priests.

As to the particulars of the acts of St. Ammon, after his retiring to mount Nitria, as none of his contemporaries have given us his life at large, we must content ourselves with briefly inserting what is incidently related of him in the life of St. Antony, chap. 32. Here we are informed by St. Athanasius, *first*, that St. Ammon, who was united with St. Antony in the bands of a most holy friendship, frequently visited him ;—*secondly*, that from his childhood to an advanced age, he always lived the life of a saint ;—*thirdly*, that he was greatly renowned for signs, wonders, and miraculous graces ;—and *fourthly*, that at the instant of his death, his happy soul was seen by St. Antony, then at the distance of thirteen day's journey from Nitria, taking her flight to heaven, escorted by a multitude of celestial spirits.   As an instance of his great favour with God, and how great a lover he was of modesty and purity, St. Athanasius relates, that upon a certain occasion, when he was obliged, together with his disciple Theodore, a man also of great sanctity to pass over the river Lycus, then swelled by sudden rains, he desired Theodore to retire, and keep at a distance whilst he put off his garments, that they might not behold each other naked ; but whilst he was thinking to strip, he felt a great repugnance to divest himself, through modesty and shame of seeing his own naked flesh, when behold, being on a sudden seized with an extacy or trance, he found himself on the other side of the river, without knowing how he came thither. Theodore coming up, was surprised to find he had been so expeditious in passing the river, and the more so, as he could perceive no marks of moisture either on his feet or garments, and did not cease to importune him to let him know how it happened, which he refused, till after he had promised to keep the matter a secret as long as Ammon should live. Though this Theodore be different from St. Theodore, the disciple of St. Pachomius, yet he has deserved no less than he, by his extraordinary virtues, a place amongst the saints, with whom his name stands enrolled in the Roman Martyrology on the 7th of January.

Rufinus, in his Lives of the Fathers, chap. 30, and Palladius, in his *Historia Lausiaca*, chap. 3, relate several other instances of the grace, miracles, and prophetic spirit of St. Ammon. Whilst he lived retired in the wilderness, a youth, who had been bit by a mad dog, was brought to him bound in chains in a frantic condition. His parents, who accompanied him, begged that the Saint, who at this time was renowned for miracles, would cure him. " You demand that of me which far exceeds my merits ; but thus much," said he, " I will tell you, if you restore the poor widow the ox you have privately stolen, your son shall be healed." They were frightened as well as astonished, when they heard him speak of the theft, which they were sensible he could not know but by revelation. However, having made the restitution which was required, the young man, at the prayer of the servant of God, was perfectly cured.

On another occasion, when two men, who had come to visit him in his solitude, found that he stood in need of a large vessel to keep water for the use of such as re-

ported to him, they promised to bring him a vessel sufficiently capacious for that purpose ; the one being master
of a camel, the other of an ass. The former, after his
return home, repented of his promise, and told his companion that he would not risk the life of his camel by
loading him with so heavy a burthen. Well, said the
latter, rather than be worse than my word, I will venture
to lay upon my ass the load which you say would kill
your camel ; trusting that the merits of the man of God
will make that possible which appears impossible. Having done as he said, the ass carried the vessel with as
much ease as if he felt no burthen whatever. When he
came to the cell, the Saint commended his faith, and told
him that his neighbour had in the mean while lost his
camel by death : and accordingly, on his return home,
he found that whilst he was on his way to the Saint, the
camel had been worried and killed by wolves.

As to the disciples of St. Ammon, as well as the
monks his successors in the congregation of mount Nitria, they were for a long time after so renowned for
their regular discipline, hospitality and charity, that Rufinus and Palladius, from their own experience, who had
been some time among them, hesitate not to bestow on
them the highest encomiums. St. Jerome also, as we
learn from his apology against Rufinus, made a journey
on purpose to visit them. "I went," says he, " to Egypt
to "survey the monasteries of Nitria, and plainly perceived some asps lurking amongst the choirs of the saints,"
alluding to the errors of Origen, which had crept in
amongst some of the religious. We also learn from the
authors above-named, that as soon as they and their companions were come within sight of the monasteries, the
religious, according to their custom, came out to meet
them, bringing loaves of bread and pitchers of water to
refresh them, after the fatigue of their journey over those
burning sands ; that then they conducted them to the
church, singing psalms, where, after washing and wip-

ing their feet, they contended which of them should introduce them into their cells, and there entertain them not only with all offices of humanity and charity in their power with regard to their corporal refreshment, but also with excellent lessons of spirituality for the benefit of their souls; in which they particularly inculcated the practice of their favourite virtues of humility and meekness, in which they themselves singularly excelled.

For the entertainment of strangers and foreigners, they had built a large hospital near to the church, where all that came were welcome to stay as long as they pleased, although it were for two or three years; yet so, that after the first seven days they were employed in some kind of work, as all the monks were; or at least if they were persons of note, in reading such good books as they put in their hands. They were also to have no conversation together, but to keep silence at least till noon. As to the afternoon, about the ninth hour, " one might stand," says Palladius, chap. 7, " and hear in every one of the monasteries the religious ' singing hymns and psalms to Christ, and joining prayers with their hymns in so sweet and molodious a manner, that one would be apt to think himself elevated on high, and translated into a heavenly paradise."

About ten miles from Nitria, further on in the wilderness, there was a place named *Cellia*, from the multitude of *cells* that lay every where dispersed up and down. Here such of the Nitrian monks as aspired after greater solitude and perfection made themselves cells, in which they lived as anchorets, at a good distance from each other; never conversing together, or seeing one another, but when they met twice a week at church, unless the case of sickness, or some office of charity, required that any one should visit the cell of another, or break in upon his silence and solitude. In this place, charity, piety, and sanctity, were seen to reign in the utmost perfection.

St. Ammon passed to a better life on the fourth of October, on which day he is commemorated in the Menologies of the Greeks, about the middle of the fourth century.

ST. PAUL THE SIMPLE.

From Rufinus, chap. 31, and Palladius, chap. 28.

PAUL, surnamed *the Simple*, from his innocent simplicity, was, by his education, a plain honest husbandman, who had led a blameless life to the age of sixty, in a married state, when, upon a certain occasion, having caught his wife in adultery, he resolved to forsake both her and the world ; and after travelling eight days into the wilderness, addressed himself to St. Antony, requesting he would receive him into the number of his disciples, and teach him the way to save his soul. St. Antony told him he was now too old to think of becoming a monk, and that he could never be able to support the difficulties and austerities of a monastic life, especially in his eremitical way : " but go," said he, " into the village, and there employ yourself in working for your bread, and praising God :" and having said this, he went in and shut his cell. Paul nevertheless, continued fasting and praying at the door during three days and three nights, till Antony, at length seeing his faith and perseverance, came out and told him, that the way to salvation was obedience, and that if he would be his disciple, he must do all that he said to him ; to which Paul readily gave his assent, and made good his word, by complying to a tittle with every injunction of the Saint, how difficult or irrational soever it seemed to be.

Antony, in order to try him, imposed upon him a variety of labours, mortifications, and humiliations, till at length he found him to be a man entirely humble, simple, and quite according to his own heart. He gave him therefore a rule of life which he should follow, and after some time appointed him a cell, at the distance of three miles from his own, where he frequently visited him; teaching him to spend his solitary hours in such a manner, as that whilst his hands were at work, his heart should be in heaven: and as to his corporal sustenance, he directed him never to eat or drink till evening, and even then with such moderation as never to satisfy his appetite, especially in his drink, though his beverage was nothing but water.

By following these rules, but more particularly by a constant and fervent application of his soul to God in mental prayer, Paul quickly arrived at great perfection in all virtues; amongst which his obedience, as well as his humility, were particularly remarkable. One day, when many religious were assembled with St. Antony, conferring about spiritual matters, on making frequent mention of the prophets, Paul, who was one of the company, according to his simplicity, asked whether the prophets lived before or since the time of our Saviour? St. Antony, by way of reproving his putting such an absurd question, made a nod to him, saying: *Go, hold your peace.* Paul, who had previously resolved to obey every word that Antony said to him, as if it had been an oracle from God himself, immediately departed to his cell, and kept there so strict a silence, that he would not upon any occasion utter so much as a single word; till Antony hearing of it, desired him to speak, and asked him the meaning of his long silence? "Why father," said he, "it was in obedience to you: for you bid me go, and hold by peace." St. Antony took occasion from hence to say to the rest of his disciples: "This man condemns us all; for whereas we are so often wanting in our obedience to our great Master, who speaks to us from heaven; he always scrupulously observes every single word, of what kind soever he hears from my mouth."

By these large steps of obedience and humility, Paul advanced rapidly towards God, and was rewarded by him with such admirable gifts and graces, as to work even more and greater miracles than St. Antony himself; insomuch that this holy abbot used to send such possessed persons to Paul as he himself could not cure. An instance of which is thus recorded by Palladius. A young man, posessed by a most furious and obstinate devil, being brought to Antony, he told the people, that this evil spirit was one of the principal demons, and that the power of casting them out was not as yet given to him, but to the humble and simple Paul. Having therefore himself conducted him to Paul, he said: "Here cast out the devil from this man, that he may return home and glorify God." "Why don't you do it yourself?" said Paul. "I have something else to do," replied Antony, and so hastened back to his cell. Paul fell prostrate in prayer, and then rising up, said to the devil, in his innocent way, "Get thee gone out of the man: father Antony says thou must go out." The devil called him a foolish old man, and told him he would not: and when he urged him a second time, repeating again that Antony said he must out, he abused both him and Antony, calling them by contemptuous names, and still refused to depart. "If thou wilt not go out," said Paul, "I will go and tell Jesus Christ, and it shall be worse for thee." The devil broke out into blasphemies against Christ, and obstinately kept his hold. The holy man therefore went out of his cell, in the broiling heat of the sun at noon-day (which, in Egypt, says my author, is not unlike the Babylonian furnace), and standing upon a rock, addressed his prayer to Jesus Christ crucified, protesting in his simplicity, that he would neither come down from the rock, nor eat or drink, till he was pleased to hear him, and to force the devil out of the man; when, behold, whilst he was at prayer, the devil roared out, " I go, I go, I suffer violence, this is an intolerable tyranny ; I am departing from the man, never, never more to return. It is Paul's humility and simplicity casts me out : I know not whither I must go." With these words the man was presently delivered ; and as a token of the devil's departure, a serpent of an unusual length was seen at the same time to crawl towards the red sea.

Many other still greater miracles were wrought by the prayers of this Saint ; but what is related of him in an antient author, published by Rosweydus, in the 7th book of the Lives of the Fathers, c. 23. is still more admirable ; viz. that he had received the gift from God, of reading in the countenances of the brethren their very thoughts, and the whole state of their souls. Thus, one day, whilst the religious were entering into the church, he saw all of them go in with a great serenity and brightness on their countenance, attended by their good angels full of joy, except one who appeared black and gloomy, having on either side of him a devil, who held him with a bridle, whilst his good angel followed behind at a distance, and appeared sad and sorrowful. The man of God, on seeing this, spent the whole time they were at church in weeping and lamenting for his soul, which he understood to be in the deplorable state of mortal sin ; but on looking at him when they came out again, he found him quite changed,—his countenance now bright and beautiful,—his good angel rejoicing, and the devils standing at a distance, grieving for having lost their prey. At the sight of this wonderful change, the Saint could not contain his joy, but broke out into the praises of God, extolling aloud the wonders of his mercy, manifested in behalf of poor sinners. Having related what he had seen, he earnestly entreated the converted monk, for the glory of God, and the edification of his brethren, to declare what change he had experienced in his interior, which could occasion the sudden and wonderful alterration he had remarked in his exteriour. In compliance with the request of the Saint, he publicly confessed, that his soul had been, through a habit of impurity, in a most wretched condition, but that upon hearing those words, of God, by the prophet Isaias, read in the church, (*Be clean, take away the evil of your devices from my eyes, cease to do perversely, learn to do well,—and then if your sins are red as scarlet, they shall be made white as snow.—If you be willing, and will hearken to me, you shall eat the good things of the land ; but if you will not, and will provoke me to wrath, the sword shall devour you, because the mouth of the Lord hath spoken it*), he found himself not only strongly affected with a sense of the heinousness of his sins, had a horror and compunction for them, joined with a great love of the infinite goodness and mercy of God, but had also firmly resolved on the spot to renounce his evil ways, and dedicate himself henceforward in good earnest to the love and service of so good a God; and that this had been the subject of his thoughts and prayers during the whole time he was in church. Upon this declaration of their penitent brother, all the monks that were present magnified the mercies of God, who so readily forgives the greatest sinners, when, like the prodigal son, they return to him with a contrite and humble heart. Whilst this whole passage, as recorded by our author, is an instance of the wonderful efficacy of a perfect contrition, in the speedy reconciliation it effects between the sinner and God, it shows at the same time the wonderful efficacy of the prayers and tears of our Saint, which procured for this sinner the effectual grace of a perfect contrition.

St. Paul the Simple is registered amongst the saints in the Roman Martyrology on the seventh of March.

ST. MACARIUS THE ELDER.

From Rufinus, chap. 28. Palladius, chap. 19, 20. and other ancient Records.

THE lustre of the sancity and miracles of this Saint shine forth in an extraordina y manner in the history of the primitive religious of the deserts of Egypt. Besides one of the same name who attended on St. Antony the last fifteen years of his mortal life, supposed to be one of the two disciples that buried him, of whom we know few other particulars, there were also two others greatly celebrated by antiquity for their sanctity and miracles, each of them cotemporaries with, if not also disciples of St. Antony, and both honoured with the priestly character: the *elder*, by some authors sirnamed *the Egyptian* and the *younger*, *the Alexandrian*, from the former being a native of Egypt, and the latter of Alexandria.

Macarius *the Elder* or *the Egyptian*, was born about the year 300. Being as yet a youth, he retired into a cell near his village, where he began to serve God with such perfection as to be held in the highest estimation by the whole neighbourhood, and thought worthy to be promoted by his bishop to the minor orders. But his humility, seeking to decline the office and ministry of a clerk, induced him to retire to a distant solitude, where he might be at liberty, without let or hinderance, to practice an anchoretical life ; working with his hands for his subsistence, whilst his heart was in the mean time conversing with God. Here a certain secular, of a religious disposition, observing the penitential life he led, came in order to minister to him, and assist him in selling his baskets. But as great trials, in one shape or other, are commonly the attendants or forerunners of the most eminent sanctity,

Macarius met with a very severe one, upon the following occasion.

A young woman in the neighbouring village was unhappily seduced and corrupted by a fellow of the neighbourhood. On being found with child by her parents and friends, and interrogated concerning the person that had corrupted her, she by the suggestion of the devil, said it was by that hermit who passed for a Saint, meaning Macarius. Upon this the whole town was in an uproar, and going out, they dragged the servant of God out of his cell into the village, where, hanging pots and pans about his neck, they led him through all the highways, crying aloud to all they met : " This hermit is the villian that has seduced our girl ;" beating him at the same time in so unmerciful a manner, that it was expected he would have died under their hands; nor did they desist, till at the remonstrances of an old man whom they met, they consented to let him go, provided any responsible person would become a surety for his maintaining the girl and her child. His friend who had followed him all the way, and been insulted on his account, for having given testimony before to his sanctity, undertook to be responsible for him ; and having delivered him out of their hands, brought him back to his cell, where he was now obliged to redouble his labours night and day in making baskets, in order to have wherewithal not only to procure food for himself, but also to furnish a maintainance for the unhappy woman by whom he had been thus basely calumniated. He bore this heavy cross with wonderful cheerfulness till the time the young woman fell in labour, and suffered such extraordinary pains for several days, without being able to be delivered, as brought her to a sense of her crime, when she acknowledged the wrong to Macarius, and declared who was the real father of the child. This gladsome news having presently come to the ears of the good man, the friend of the Saint, he ran with great joy to announce to him the joyful tidings, adding, that all the people were coming out to beg his pardon for the wrong they had done him. Macarius, on hearing this, being more afraid of honour than of humiliations and disgrace, would not wait for their coming, but presently withdrew himself into the desert of Scete, or Scithi, being then about thirty years of age.

This desert, in which no man had dwelt before, was of a vast extent, but so destitute of all the necessaries of life, that it was hard to meet with even a drop of water among the burning sands, and the little that could be found, was of so very disagreeable a taste and smell, as to render it unfit for use. Hither Macarius went, by divine inspiration, to seek a solitude, to which no way nor path conducted ; and here he began to lay the foundation of that sublime perfection to which God afterwards raised him, and to which many others were raised by his means, who, in process of time, followed him into this frightful wilderness, and put themselves under his discipline, whose number, in a short time, became very considerable, and amongst whom were several eminent saints ; for such was the general character of the solitaries of Scete, for the austerity and sanctity of their lives, that they were looked upon by all the rest as models of religious perfection. Macarius had been about ten years in this desert, when the number of the brethren increasing, it was thought necessary that a priest should be ordained for them, to feed them both with the word of God and the holy sacraments ; on which occasion the Saint was obliged to accept of the priestly order and to execute its functions amongst his religious; being already so far favoured by divine grace, as to have received from God the power of casting out evil spirits, and of working other wonderful miracles, together with the spirit of prophecy, and a foreknowledge of future events.

, As an instance of his prophetic spirit, Palladius relates how he often forewarned his disciple John against

10*

the spirit of covetousness, telling him, that if he did not mortify his unhappy inclination to worldly pelf, as he laboured under the vice of Giezi, so he should incur the punishment of Giezi. Which happened accordingly, when fifteen or twenty years after the Saint's death, appropriating to himself what should have been given to the poor, he was struck with the leprosy in so terrible a manner, that there was not one sound place to be discovered in his body. The same author relates also several instances of his power over evil spirits, in casting them out, and destroying their magical operations by his prayers, as in the case of a woman that was bewitched in so strange a manner as to appear to herself and friends metamorphosed into a mare, but was delivered by the Saint's pouring upon her head some holy water which he had blessed. The Saint, on sending her home, admonished her never to neglect the public worship of the church, nor the frequentation of the sacraments; for that the enemy could not have had this power over her, had she not, for five weeks, kept away from the sacred mysteries.

Many were the miracles whereby God evinced the sanctity of his servant Macarius, and some of them of the first magnitude. It happened that a murder was committed in one of the places bordering upon the wilderness wherein the man of God dwelt, and that an innocent man was accused thereof, who fled for refuge to the cell of the Saint. The people having pursued him, and found him, were for binding him, and carrying him off, in order to deliver him up to justice. The man strongly pleaded his own innocence, protesting by all that was sacred, that he knew nothing of the murder; whilst they, on the contrary, insisted upon taking him away, alleging, that they should be called to an account themselves if they let him escape. Macarius having enquired where they had buried the murdered man, accompanied them to the place, when kneeling down by the grave, and invoking the name of Jesus Christ, he said to the standers by; "The Lord will now show whether this man be guilty or not." Then raising his voice, he called on the dead man by his name, and conjured him, in the name of Christ, to tell whether this was the man that had murdered him; when behold, a tremendous loud voice was heard to issue from the grave, declaring that he was not the man. Upon this all the by-standers, struck with dread and astonishment, fell prostrate on the ground, at the feet of the man of God, earnestly requesting that he would put one question more to the deceased, to learn from him by whom it was that he had been murdered. "No," replied the Saint, "it is enough for me to clear the innocent; it is not my business to detect the guilty; for who knows, if he be suffered to live longer, but he may have the grace to do penance for his crime?"

A certain heretic of the sect called *Hieracites*, a branch of the *Manichean heresy*, coming into the wilderness, endeavoured not only to corrupt the brethren, with his captious arguments, but had the temerity also to attack Macarius upon the score of his faith in the presence of many of the religious, and to oppose to the solidity of the Saint's reasonings from the Scripture, delivered with his usual meekness and simplicity, a number of such frothy words and sophisms as are but too apt to impose upon the weak and ignorant. Wherefore the man of God, apprehending lest the faith of the by-standers should be endangered on this occasion, proposed instead of *contending with words, which would be to no profit but to the subverting of the hearers*, 2 Tim. ii. that they should go out to the burying place of the religious, and put the cause upon this issue, viz. that he who could raise a dead man to life should be acknowledged to be the teacher of God's truth, and consequently that his faith should be followed. This proposal being universally applauded, the heretic consented, provided that Macarius should be the first to make the trial. When therefore they had arrived at the cemetry, the Saint prostrating himself on one of the graves, employed some time in silent prayer ; and then lifting up his eyes to heaven, he said : " Be pleased, O Lord, to make it manifest to all here present, which of us two holds the right faith, by restoring this dead man to life." With this having called the brother that had been last buried by name, he presently answered ; and upon opening the grave, by removing all the earth that was laid upon him, was taken out alive and presented to the man of God, to the great astonishment as well as confusion to the heretic, who immediately fled away, and never durst shew his face any more in Scete.

But let us pass from the miracles of Macarius to his virtues. We find the eminent sanctity for which he has been so justly admired by all succeeding ages, was built upon its true foundation, *viz.* a knowledge and contempt of himself, united with a profound humility, which was always apparent by his ever joyfully embracing humiliations, and flying from honours and applause. Those were always his most welcome guests who abused or ridiculed him most ; to such he more freely opened himself, whereas he was ever silent and reserved with those who came, as many did, to hear him speak of the things of God, or showed him any particular marks of honour or esteem : this was so generally known and observed that at length such as came with a desire to hear his heavenly lessons, would on purpose, begin their conversation, by telling him the many ridiculous or wicked things of which they had heard him to have been guilty in his youth, and then they were sure to please him best. The devil himself was obliged to acknowlege that it was the humility of the Saint, and not his extraordinary austerities, that had kept him hitherto out of his reach. Having appeared to him one day, as he was returning to his cell, laden with palm-leaves for his work he endeavoured, but was not able, to strike him with a sharp scythe which he held in his hand. Upon which he cried out : " It is a hard case, O Macarius, that I should suffer so much from thee, and yet not to be able to hurt thee: whereas in point of fasting and watching, I do a great deal more than thou dost ; for though thou fastest and watchest often, yet sometimes thou eatest and sleepest ; but as to me, I never eat, nor close my eyes to sleep. Nevertheless, I acknowledge there is one thing in which thou overcomest me." What is it ?" said the Saint. " Thy humility," replied the devil : " Oh ! there is nothing else conquers me." Whereupon the Saint, having stretched forth his hand to heaven in prayer, the enemy presently vanished.

The humility of the Saint was ever accompanied with an extraordinary meekness : as these two sister-virtues generally walk hand in hand. By this his extraordinary meekness he wrought greater wonders, in conducting souls to God, than by any of his other miracles. An instance hereof appears in the case of a pagan priest, who having been incited to fury, by the contemptuous treatment he had met with from one of the religious, was not only appeased, but gained over on the spot to Jesus Christ, by the mildness and sweetness wherewith he was treated by St. Macarius : insomuch, that he immediately quitted the world to become a religious man, and gave occasion, by his example, to the conversion of many other pagans.

The humility of Macarius was also accompanied with a wholesome fear of the divine justice, together with a deep sense of, and an extraordinary compunction for his sins, which continued with him even to the end of his life. In proof whereof, we read, that shortly before his death, when the monks of Nitria invited him to come over to their mountain that they might receive his blessing before he departed to the Lord, declaring, that otherwise they would all come in a body to visit him ; he complied indeed with their request ; but when the multitude of the brethren were assembled about him, expecting to hear the word of God from his mouth, instead of a sermon, he entertained them with a flood of tears, saying : " Let us weep, my brethren, let us weep whilst we have time. Let torrents of tears flow from our eyes to wash away the stains of our sins, before we depart hence into another world, where out tears will come too late, and only serve to nourish the flames of our torments." At these words, accompanied by the tears of the Saint, all the congregation wept, and cast themselves down on the ground, to beg the assistance of his prayers.

A certain brother desiring to know from the Saint how he might secure the salvation of his soul : " Fly," said the man of God, " from the company of men—keep close to thy cell, and there weep continually for thy sins ; and as the best penance for them, be equally careful to mortify thy tongue by keeping silence, as thy belly, by fasting and abstinence." To the like effect he said one day to the brethren as they were coming out of church after mass : " Fly, my brethren, fly." " Whither, O father," said one of them, " wouldst thou have us fly ? can we go farther from the world than we are at present in this vast solitude ?" The Saint put his finger to his tongue, and said, I mean that we should fly from this ; and saying no more, he entered into his cell, and there remained in silence and recollection.

The prayers of St. Macarius were in a manner incessant, particularly in the mental and contemplative way. He is said to have been often almost in an extacy, ravished as it were out of himself, and for the greatest part of his time entertaining himself with God in so absolute a state of insensibihty, as to forget every created objeet. That he might apply himself with more freedom to God in prayer, he had made a passage under ground from his cell, to a certain cave at about half a furlong distance, to which he frequently retired, and there kept himself con-

cealed from all other company, to the end he might be
alone with God, free from the interruption of the visits
of the many strangers who resorted to him on account of
the great reputation of his sanctity. He had, during
five years, been pressed by frequent thoughts to proceed
further into the desert to try what he should there discover; but as it was his maxim to do nothing rashly, he
examined well these suggestions, lest they should prove
to be temptations. The inclination, however, still continuing, he concluded it to be God's holy will, and accordingly following the call, he penetrated into the remote parts of the wilderness, where he found a lake of
water, and in it a small island, inhabited by two solitaries, who had dwelt there for the space of forty years,
quite secluded from the conversation of mortals, and in
so great a state of perfection, that Macarius, after having
seen and conversed with them, according to his humble
way of thinking of himself, professed to the religious of
Nitria, who had some time after requested he would deliver a discourse of edification in the monastery of Abbot
Pambo, " that for his part he was not worthy to be
called a *monk*, but that he had seen *monks* indeed : and
that the lesson he had learnt of them was, that to be a
monk indeed, a man must absolutely renounce every
thing in this world, and that if he thought himself too
weak to practice this renunciation, in the manner they
did, he should return back to his cell, there to sit and
bewail his sins."

The zeal that Macarius had for his own spiritual
advancement, carried him also another time a fifteen
day's journey from the desert of Scete, to visit St. Antony,
then residing on his mountain. When he arrived with
his strength quite exhausted by the fatigue of his long
travelling through those burning sands, he knocked at
the door of the Saint's cell : Antony coming forth,
asked him who he was? and upon his answering that he
was Macarius, he went in again, and shut the door ; for

although he had a great desire for a long time to see
him, knowing his extraordinary sanctity, yet he was
willing to make this trial of his patience and humility.
Macarius remained at the door till Antony, thinking he
had now sufficiently put his patience to a trial, opened it
to him; and having lovingly embraced him, entertained
him with the best that his cell could afford.   In the
evening, Antony prepared a certain quanity of the leaves
of palm-trees for himself to work on at making of mats;
Macarius, was ever a lover of manual labour, and hated
idleness, desired to be employed in the same manner; and
thus having sat down together, whilst they worked with
their hands, they entertained each other with heavenly
discourses and the praises of their great Master.   In the
morning Antony was surprised to behold the quanity of
matting that Macarius had made during the night; and
taking his hands he kissed them, affirming, that there
was much virtue in them.   I know not whether it was
upon this, or some other occasion, that he saw the Holy
Spirit descend upon Macarius; for I find it recorded of
St. Antony, that he himself declared he had seen the
Holy Ghost decend upon three eminent servants of God,
who in their lives appeared to be in an extraordinary
manner replenished with his graces, and that these three
were, St. Athanasius, St. Pachomius, and St. Macarius.
As to the penitential exercises practised by St. Macarius and his disciples the solitaries of Scete, they appear
more the objects of our admiration than of our imitation,
especially in the point of fasting; for we read in some
ancient writers, that it was their custom to eat but once
in the week; but as to St. Macarius himself, he told his
disciple Evargius upon occasion of his complaining of a
violent thirst which he felt in the excessive noonday
heat of the Eygptian climate, that for his own part he
had never for twenty years satisfied, himself either in point
of eating, or drinking, or sleeping;—that he always
weighed out the small quantity of bread he eat;—that he

ways drank his water by measure; and instead of lying down, leaned always against a wall, when he stole, as it were, the little sleep which he could not absolutely dispense with.

But if he was so perfectly mortified in his eating, drinking and sleeping, we may truly say he was as much, or more so with respect, not only to his passions, but his whole interior, and that he himself practised diligently the excellent lessons he had so often taught his disciples. He used frequently to say, that he only was a *true monk*, who overcame himself in all things: that the way to escape the death of the soul by sin, was to receive and embrace *contempt* like *praise*, *poverty* like *riches*, and *hunger* and *want*, like *plenty* and *feasting*. A young man having once addressed himself to our Saint, desiring to learn of him the practice of religious perfection, he sent him to a place where there were a great many dead bodies, and bid him treat them with reviling, scornful language, and such other like affronts and injuries, and even to pelt them with stones to try if he could provoke them to passion. Having done as he was ordered, when he returned back, the Saint asked him how the dead had received all those outrages, and what they had said? He answered that they had said nothing. On the day following he sent him again, and bid him treat them with honour, with fine speeches and commendations, and then see how they would behave; and as they still remained equally insensible both to his good and mal-treatment, the Saint told him, that if he would be a perfect religious man, he must follow their example, and neither suffer himself to be provoked to anger or resentment by ill treatment, nor to be puffed up with the esteem or praises of men, but always to have his eye on Jesus Christ, and seek to please him him only.

St. Macarius had now arrived at the age of seventy-six, when a violent persecution was raised against all the religious by Lucius the Arian, who, after the death of

11

St. Athanasius, had usurped the see of Alexandria, by the favour of the emperor Valens. This unhappy man, finding the monks in general averse to his wicked tenets, and the people very much influenced by their example, to adhere to the catholic faith, led out a multitude of soldiers into the deserts, in order to oblige these servants of God, by all manner of cruelties, to renounce the ancient faith. A great number of the solitaries of mount Nitria were martyred on this occasion, and a vast multitude of other religious, together with many bishops, priests, and deacons, were sent into banishment. Amongst these were Macarius, and his name-sake, the other St. Macarius, of Alexandria, St. Isidore, of Scete, and St. Pambo, the holy abbot of Nitria; who, by the orders of Lucius, were taken out of their cells privately in the night, and carried away into a certain island in Egypt, which was inhabited only by pagans, to the end that they might have no opportunity of exercising their priestly functions, nor meet with any comfort or support from any one. There was in this island an ancient temple of the devils, for which the inhabitants had so great a veneration, that it was this that kept them in their idolatry. But behold the wonders of God! as soon as the boat that brought the saints thither drew near the land, the devils who inhabited the temple were all in an uproar, and one of them presently entered into the daughter of the priest of the temple, whom the people venerated almost as much as their god, and caused in her strange and violent agitations and contortions, accompanied with such loud shrieks and cries as reached the very heavens, and drew all the people about her. In this condition she ran about amongst the people, falling down sometimes and rolling herself on the ground, foaming and gnashing with her teeth, till all of a sudden she was lifted up into the air, and carried to the place where the saints by this time were set on shore, the people all following to see what would become of her. Here she fell down at the feet of Macarius and his companions, and cried out (the devil speaking by her mouth, as he did heretofore by the girl at Philippi, Acts xvi.) "Ah! ye servants of Jesus Christ, how terrible is your power! ye servants of the great God, why do you come to drive us away from a place of which we have so long kept possession! Here have we hidden ourselves, after we were expelled from the rest of the land; for you have banished us from the towns and villages, from the mountains and hills, and even from the places where none before you durst inhabit. We expected to be quiet at least in this little island, in the midst of bogs and marshes, and now you come to deprive us of our last refuge," &c. Whilst the devil was uttering these and other similar words, by the mouth of the girl, the Saints, on their part, made use of the power their Lord had conferred on them, and commanded the devil, by the sacred and awful name of Jesus Christ, the Son of God, to depart out from her; whilst he, unable to resist, was immediately constrained to obey, and left the girl stretched out on the ground as if dead. The Saints prayed for her, and lifting her up from the ground, presented her to her father in perfect health, both of mind and body. Then taking occasion from what had passed, they began to preach Jesus Christ to the people, already disposed, by the miracle they had seen, to hearken to their words; and so great was the blessing God gave to their preaching, that instantly both the priest himself, with his daughter, and all his kindred, cast themselves down at the feet of these new apostles, desiring to learn of them what they must do to be saved. All the people of the island, by their example, were immediately converted to Jesus Christ, and embraced the faith with so much fervour, that they presently demolished their temple which they had before so much revered—built up a church in its place, and after proper instructions received baptism. Thus the expulsion of these servants of God contributed to the propagation and illustration of the faith for which they were banished, and to the confusion of their enemies and persecutors, who, upon receiving the news of what had passed, gave orders to have them removed again out of the island, and privately conveyed back to their former solitudes.

St. Macarius outlived this persecution many years; and after having attained the age of ninety, sixty of which he spent in the wilderness, he passed to the enjoyment of his God about the year 390 or 391. His name is recorded among the Saints in the Roman Martyrology on the 15th of January.

There are extant in the *Bibliotheca SS. Patrum*, fifty homilies, or discourses of piety, which St. Macarius made to his religious on several occasions, truly worthy of his spirit and sanctity.

ST. MACARIUS OF ALEXANDRIA.

From Palladius, Bishop of Helenopolis, some time disciple of the Saint, Historia Lausiaca, chap. 19, Rufinus and others.

St. Macarius, commonly called the Alexandrian, to distinguish him from the other St. Macarius, of whom we have been just treating, was born at Alexandria about the beginning of the fourth century. In his younger days he endeavoured to obtain an honest livelihood by selling fruit, sweetmeats, and such like wares, till being called by God to greater perfection, he forsook all things to follow Christ in an anchoretical life, and put himself under the direction of St. Antony, in order to learn from so great a master the true science of the saints. The progress he made in this school of grace, was so extraordinary, that he became qualified to instruct many others in the way of perfection, as St. Antony himself saw and acknowledged, when one day Macarius being with him, and asking him for some beautiful palm-branches, which he kept for his work, he told him it was written : *Thou shalt not covet thy neighbour's goods* : at which words the palm-branches in an instant actually withered away, and grew quite as dry as if they had been touched by the fire, which St. Antony, seeing told Macarius that he perceived the Spirit of God had taken up his abode in his soul ; and that from this time forward he should look upon him as the heir and successor of all those graces and gifts which the divine bounty had bestowed upon himself.

Shortly after the devil seeing him in his wilderness exceedingly fatigued with travelling, and quite exhausted for want of food, suggested to him, since you have received the grace of Antony, why do not you make use of his power, and ask the necessary supply of food and strength from God, that you may be enabled to pursue your journey ? The Saint replied : The Lord is my strength—the Lord is my glory ;—but as for thee, Satan, be gone, and don't presume to tempt one that is determined to be the servant of his divine Majesty." The devil upon this assumed the shape of a camel that appeared to be wandering about the desert, laden with all kinds of necessaries for life, and coming up he stood near to the Saint, who suspecting it to be a diabolical illusion, prayed to God, and presently the phantom sunk into the earth, and disappeared.

From the desert of Thebais, where St. Antony resided, Macarius passed to that of Scete, and partly there or on mount Nitria, or in the neighbouring wilderness called Cellia, or the place of the cells, he spent the greatest part of his mortal life. In this last place he was, on account of his eminent sanctity, ordained priest, and in that quality had the charge of the church, and the superiority and direction of all the saintly souls that lived dispersed in separate cells throughout that holy solitude. Here

11*

his virtues shined forth with such extraordinary lustre and miracles, as to make him be looked upon, both then and ever since, as one of the brightest lights of the Church of God in his time, and on that account he had also a great share in the persecution which fell in a particular manner upon the religious of these quarters, under Valens the Arian emperor; when he was also, as we have seen above, sent into banishment with some other servants of God, who had miraculously converted the inhabitants of the island to which they were banished from idolatry to the faith of Christ.

As to the employment of his time in these wildernesses, we find he distributed it in such manner, as to spend the best part of it in prayer, in which he exercised himself a hundred times in the space of every twenty-four hours; another part he dedicated to manual labour, in order to obtain his livelihood; and the remainder he gave to those that came to consult him about the affairs of their souls, and to receive his instructions. In the mean time, the austerities of the penitential life to which he condemned himself were so great, that we may truly say, they were more to be admired than imitated. His fasts were long and rigorous:—for seven years he never eat and thing but raw herbs or pulse, moistened with cold water, without bread, or any thing whatever that had come near the fire.—For three years more he lived only upon four or five ounces of bread in the day, with water in proportion. Once, for the space of twenty days, he laboured to live without any sleep whatever; and to this purpose, during all that time, he never entered under any cover, but exposed himself the whole day to the parching heat of the sun, and all the night abroad to the cold air, till unable to hold out any longer, he was at length constrained to yield to nature. At another time, to punish himself for a small fault, or as others say, no fault, but to extinguish a temptation of the flesh, he condemned himself to pass six whole months in the marshes of Scete, in the remote parts of the desert, infested by a number of large gnats with stings like wasps; by which, during his course of penance, he was so roughly treated, and stung in so terrible a manner, that at his return home his whole body appeared like that of a leper, and he could only be known by his voice.

The reputation of the extraordinary austerities, and the excellent lives of the religious of Tabenna, under their holy founder St. Pachomius, inspired Macarius with a desire of going thither and joining their holy company, yet so as not to be known who or what he was. In order thereto, having changed his habit for the dress of a common labourer, he travelled fifteen days' journey through the deserts till at length he arrived at the monastery of Tabenna. Here calling for the Abbot St. Pachomius, he begged to be admitted amongst his monks. The abbot told him, that at his time of life he could not be able to conform himself to the austerities which were practised in his monastery, and therefore refused to admit him. Macarius however did not desist, but continued seven days at the gate, begging for admission, and fasting the whole time, till his perseverance prevailed with the abbot and community to receive him. And now the penitential time of Lent arrived, in which the religious assigned to themselves the particular exercises of devotion and penance in which they designed to pass that holy time: some of them resolving to eat but once in two days,—others only twice in a week,—others again, after spending the whole day in manual labour, proposing to watch and pass the night in prayer without ever lying down to take their rest. Macarius for his part said nothing; but gathering together a large provision of the leaves of the palm-trees for making mats, passed the whole time standing at work in a corner by himself, with his heart raised to God in silent prayer, without once sitting down or leaning against any thing whatever. He eat only on the Lord's day, and then nothing but some raw leaves of cabbage, without bread or any thing else, or even drinking any liquid whatsoever. The rest of the religious observing him to practice these extraordinary austerities, began to murmur against their abbot for having admitted amongst them, for their condemnation, a man that seemed not to be made of flesh and blood; whereupon St. Pachomius, who was frequently favoured with divine revelations, applying himself to God in prayer, with a desire to know who this person was that had passed the Lent in so extraordinary a manner, learnt from God that it was the Abbot Macarius, of whose sanctity he had heard so much. Whereupon taking him by the hand, and leading him into the chapel before the altar of the monastery, he said: " Is it then you, venerable Father ? Are you the celebrated Macarius, and would not let me know it ! As it is a long time since I have had a desire to see you, now I must return you thanks for the stay you have made amongst us, by which you have humbled my children, and taught them not to think much of their own austerities. You have sufficiently edified us by your presence, I beg of you, therefore, to return home and pray for us." And thus dismissed the Saint, requesting him to go back to his former habitation.

But if these rigorous penances and extraordinary austerities of St. Macarius may seem to be beyond the reach of our imitation, we cannot say as much with respect to the following instance of the spirit, as well of mortification as of charity, which both himself and his brethren shewed upon a less occasion, as recorded in the history of his life. Some one having sent him a fine bunch of grapes at a time when he had a longing desire after that kind of fruit, in order to exercise himself at once both in abstinence and charity, he sent them to another solitary, who being sick and infirm stood more in need of them. The good sick man, after thankfully receiving the present, which, had he followed his own his own inclinations, he would gladly have eaten, through the same spirit of mortification and charity, refrained from eating them, and sent them to a third who lived at some distance in the wilderness, the third again in like manner to a fourth; and so on till they had passed from one to another of most of the inhabitants of the cells dispersed through the desert, without any one ever tasting them. At length he who received them last, not knowing from whom they first came, and thinking they might be agreeable to their holy father, sent them to St. Macarius. The Saint perceiving the grapes to be the very same, and learning also upon enquiry through how many hands, they had passed, gave God thanks for that spirit of abstinence and self-denial which his brethren had showed on this occasion; and for his own part was animated thereby to a greater fervour in all the exercises of a spiritual life, but nevertheless could not be induced to eat of the grapes himself.

As to the miracles of our Saint, church history assures us, that the two Saints Macarius were equally illustrious, not only for the works of faith, but also for the miraculous graces, and other supernatural gifts wherewith God favoured them ;—that they equally excelled in the knowledge of the secrets of God,—in the power they had to make themselves terrible to the devils,—to cure diseases, and work all kinds of wonders. It is particularly recorded of our Saint, that he had an extraordinary grace in casting out unclean spirits, and delivering numbers that were either possessed or assaulted by them. The tempter one day took occasion from thence to suggest to him thoughts of vain-glory, which tended to withdraw him from his solitude, under the specious pretext of doing good to many, and to carry him to Rome, that he might exercise his talents in casting out devils, and curing all diseases in the capital of the universe. Macarius saw through the deceit, and strongly resisted the suggestion : and as the temptation did not cease, but rather acquired additional strength, he laid himself prostrate on the threshold of his cell, and cried out to the demon of vain-glory, by whom he was tempted, that he would remain there till the evening; and that if he would remove him from thence, it should be by main force, for that with his good will he would never go, how violently soever he he might tempt him.   After sun-set finding the temptation returning again with more violence than ever, he took a large basket that held two bushels, and filling it with sand, laid it on his shoulders, and being loaded in this manner, walked up and down in the desert.   Theosebius, surnamed Cosmetor, a native of Antioch, having met him whilst he was at this exercise, said; "What is the meaning of this, holy father?   Why do you thus torment yourself?   Let me ease you of your burthen." Macarius replied: "I am plaguing one that is plaguing me: and who seeing that I am lazy at home, will needs have me go and travel abroad:" and thus he continued carrying about his load of sand, till being quite wearied and spent, and all bruised with his burthen, he returned to his cell.

As to the particulars of the many miracles wrought by St. Macarius, we shall not pretend to recount them here: we shall only take notice of one recorded by Palladius, of which he was an eye-witness. This prelate relates, that being at that time himself a disciple of the Saint, he came one day to his cell, and found there lying before the door, a priest of a country parish, in the most wretched condition that can be imagined; his head being eaten in such a manner by a cancer, that a great part of his skull was seen quite bare. He came hither to seek his cure from the Saint, who would take no notice of him whatsoever. Upon which Palladius going in, began to intercede for him. The Saint answered, that he was unworthy to be delivered from this evil, which God had sent him for a punishment. "But," said he, "if you desire he should be cured, prevail on him to resolve never more to presume to approach the altar to celebrate the sacred mysteries. For this punishment has been sent him on account of being guilty of acts of impurity, and saying mass in that sinful condition." Palladius told the poor man what the Saint had said; when upon his promising with an oath never more to exercise any of the priestly functions, the Saint received him into his cell, and after he had confessed his sins, with a sincere resolution of never more returning to them, he laid his hands upon him, and in a few days sent him home perfectly cured and glorifying God.

As to the other extraordinary gifts and graces of St. Macarius, it is recorded of him that he frequently saw in spirit, not only the state of the souls of his religious at the time of their communion, but also their inward thoughts and dispositions in the time of prayer. One night the devil knocked at his cell, crying out; "Arise, abbot Macarius, that we may accompany the brethren to midnight prayers." The Saint knowing, by the light of God, that it was the enemy, replied: "And what hast thou to do, O lying spirit, thou enemy of all truth, with the assembly of the Saints, or their night prayers?" "Assure thyself, Macarius," replied the devil, "that the religious never meet to pray without us: Come along, and thou shalt see." The Saint having previously prayed to God that he might know whether what the devil vaunted of was true or not, went to the place where the brethren were assembled for the night office; and at the time they were reciting the psalms, saw a number of these wicked spirits in the shape of filthy blackamoors, running about the church, and playing a variety of tricks, with a view either to distract the religious, or overcome them with sleep; and when, after the twelve psalms were ended, they prostrated themselves in silent prayer, he perceived how busy they were about them, representing to one the figure of a woman, —to another a building or a journey,—and to others a prodigious variety of such like phantoms and images.

Now there were some of the brethren who seemed to drive them away by a superior force, and to fling them down upon their backs with so much violence that they durst not approach them any more ; whilst others, more indolent and negligent, suffered them to ride upon their heads and shoulders, and to make a mockery of them at pleasure. The Saint being much moved with this spectacle, addressed himself to God, with many tears, in behalf of his religious, begging he would deliver them from all the snares and deceits of these spirits of darkness : using these words of the royal prophet, Ps. lxvii. *Let God arise, and his enemies be scattered : and let them that hate him flee from before his face.* After the prayers were ended, calling to him the brethren, he found upon enquiring of each one in particular that had been so distracted with those vain or wicked imaginations which the Saint had seen represented to them by those blacks; hence they came to understand that those distracting thoughts, which so often interrupt the attention and devotion of the soul at the divine office or other prayers, are illusions of the wicked spirit : and that the best way to repel them and keep them at a distance, is to watch over ourselves, and to keep our souls closely united to God by a fervent application of all its powers and faculties.

It is also recorded of St. Macarius, that being one day in company with the other Saint of the same name, and obliged to pass over the Nile in a barge that served for that purpose, it happened that two tribunes or colonels were ferried over at the same time, each having a pompous equipage and great retinue to attend him. These officers beholding the two Saints in their mean garb at one end of the barge, with all that serenity, recollection, and interior peace of mind, which seemed apparent in their faces, together with a sovereign contempt of all that this world admires, could not help extolling to each other the happiness of such a kind of life as that which these servants of God led. Accordingly one of them addressing himself to the Saints, said : " You are both happy, who are thus above the world, and tread it under your feet. You speak as if it were by a prophetic light," replied our Saint, " in calling us *happy*, for the name of both of us is *Macarius*, which in the Greek signifies *happy*. But if you have great reason to say, that they who have renounced all things else to consecrate themselves entirely to the service of God are happy, inasmuch as they tread the world under their feet, we have also great reason to compassionate your unhappiness, in being slaves to the world, and suffering yourselves to be mocked by it." These words of the Saint made so deep an impression upon him, that on his return home he resigned his commission,—distributed his substance to the poor, —and quitting the world, embraced a solitary and religious life.

We shall conclude our account of the life of St. Macarius with a remarkable history, recorded by St. Jerome, of a certain solitary of Nitria, who by the price of his work, which was making linen-cloth, had saved so much money, that when he died there was found by him the sum of one hundred crowns. The religious assembled on this extraordinary occasion to deliberate what should be done with the money; which some thought should be given to the poor or to the church, and others to the kindred of the deceased. But Macarius, our Saint, Pambo, Isidore, and others who were called the fathers, being inspired by the Holy Ghost, ordained that they should cast the money into the grave together with the corpse, repeating those words of St. Peter to Simon Magus, *Keep thy money to thyself, to perish with thee.* And this wholesome severity spread such a terror amongst all the religious of Egypt, that they looked upon it as a crime for any one of them to leave so much as one crown behind them after death.

St. Macarius, after having served God for sixty years
12

in a religious life, departed to our Lord about the year 395. His name is registered in the Roman Martyrology on the second of January.

SS. ISIDORE AND PAMBO.

WE join these two together, and give them a place immediately after St. Macarius, with whom, as we have seen above, they are joined by St. Jerome, as having been inspired by the Holy Ghost, and the most eminent in their days amongst the fathers of the deserts; with whom also, as well as with the other St. Macarius, they are celebrated by all our church historians, for the brave stand they made against the Arian heresy, under Valens the emperor;—the persecutions they suffered on this occasion,—the eminence of their sanctity;—and finally, on account of the great signs and wonders which God wrought by them. They were each of them, for some time, disciples of St. Antony, and afterwards on account of their extraordinary virtues and merits, advanced to the priestly dignity, and made chief superiors; *Isidore* of the religious of the desert of *Scete*, and Pambo of those of mount *Nitria*.

It is recorded of St. Isidore, that he received so singular a grace from God, and had so great a power and authority over evil spirits, that whenever any possessed persons were brought to him, they never failed to be delivered, even before they reached the door of his cell. The brethren having asked him one day, what could be the reason why the devils were so much afraid of him; he alleged no other, than that from the time of his entering into religion he had made it his constant endeavour not to suffer the passion of anger to rise up so high as to reach his tongue. As a proof of his zeal for suppressing in himself the least emotion to this passion, we are informed by an ancient writer, that having one day carried some little baskets to market for sale, upon meeting there with some provocation, which began to excite in his heart emotions of anger and wrath, he immediately flung down his baskets, and ran back as fast as he could to the wilderness. By this diligence in watching against, and suppressing all the irregular motions and suggestions of his passions, and by the aid of incessant prayer, he attained so great a mastery over himself as to acknowledge one day, to the greater glory of God, that for the space of forty years, though he had often experienced the motions and suggestions of sin, he was not conscious to himself that he had ever given his voluntary consent, either to any irregular desire or the least emotion of wrath.

From his first entering into religion, instead of setting himself a task, as many did, of reciting daily a certain number of psalms or prayers, he chose rather to pray, without ceasing, night and day; and yet he was always so great a lover of manual labour, that after he was grown very old he could not be prevailed upon to give over working even at night; and when the brethren, upon these occasions, would sometimes beg that he would afford himself a little more rest, he replied, that all he could do or suffer was nothing in comparison of what the Son of God had done and suffered for him, and he therefore thought he could never do nor suffer enough for the love of his Saviour. He one day addressed himself thus to the assembly of the Solitaries of Scete: "Have we not retired hither, my brethren, in order to suffer many labours and pains in the body, by the means of which we may merit everlasting rest for our souls in heaven; and yet how little do we suffer here at present? For my part I think of taking my sheep-skin, and seeking some other place, where I may find something more to suffer." This he said, because at this time the number of those that resorted to this desert gave occasion to the introducing of certain conveniences of life, and some better accommodations than they had been accustomed to in the beginning, when they were in a manner quite destitute of every thing.

" It is also recorded as a maxim of St. Isidore, " That the whole science of the Saints consists in knowing and following the will of God; because then only can a man be perfect indeed, when raising himself above all other things he subjects himself to the eternal Truth and Justice. For since man was made after the image and likeness of God, who is that same eternal Truth and Justice, he cannot expect to meet with either perfection or happiness, only in a conformity with his divine original. On the other hand, he said, that the most dangerous of all temptations was to follow the suggestions of our own hearts and thoughts, instead of the will of God;—that the pleasure which a man pretends to find in the gratification of his own inclinations is quickly changed into bitterness, and leaves nothing behind but the regret of having been ignorant of the secret of true beatitude, and of the way of the Saints. From whence he concludes, that the true way to happiness consists in being willing to labour and take pains in the service of the Lord, and in patiently suffering the short tribulations of this life, in order to secure the eternal salvation of our souls."

This Saint had also a special talent from God of healing the spiritual maladies of the religious when any of them were diseased in their souls; insomuch that whenever it happened that the other superiors were for dismissing any of their subjects, on account of negligence, slothfulness, impatience, passion, or other defects, he desired they might be brought to him : when, by treating them with his usual charity, humility, and patience, he generally brought them to a right sense of their duty, and in time cured them effectually of all their vices and faults of what kind soever.

When Theophilus was made patriarch of Alexandria, anno 385, St. Isidore went thither to pay him a visit. On his return from thence to the wilderness, the brethren enquired of him, what news he brought from the city ? " I have seen nobody there," he replied, " but the patriarch." Being much surprised at his answer, they asked him, " What then was become of the inhabitants of that great city ? Surely," said they, " they are not all swallowed up by an earthquake." This obliged him to explain himself, by letting them know that he had kept so strict a guard over his eyes, as not to allow them to look upon any one.

St. Isidore departed to our Lord shortly after, in a good old age, though the particular year is not known, and his name stands recorded in the Roman Martyrology on the fifteenth of January.

Amongst several great men of the name of Isidore, there was another, a contemporary with our Saint, who was abbot in Thebais, over a thousand monks in great reputation for sanctity, and under such strict enclosure that none of them were ever allowed to go out, nor any from abroad permitted to enter the monastery, except he came to remain during life, never more to depart from it. They had gardens and wells within their own enclosure; and when there was a necessity of any thing from abroad, two of the ancients were deputed to provide such necessaries, all the rest attending only to their regular exercises.

But to come to St. Pambo : it is recorded of him, that being in his younger days a disciple of St. Antony, he desired his master to instruct him in the most efficacious manner of saving his soul; St. Antony told him, that in order to this, he must be careful to do true penance for his sins;—that he must never place any confidence whatsoever in his own righteousness;—that he must always endeavour to act in such manner, as to never after have any occasion to repent of what he had done ;—and

12*

that in particular he must labour to put a restraint as well upon his tongue as upon his appetite.

In those days he also applied himself to another of the religious to be instructed in some of the psalms. This brother began with the thirty-eighth psalm : *I said I will take heed to my ways, that I sin not with my tongue ;* which words Pambo had no sooner heard, but without waiting for the second verse, he retired to his cell, saying, it was enough for one lesson, and that he would go and endeavour to learn it in practice. Six months afterwards the brother, finding that he did not apply to him for any more lessons, asked him the reason why he staid away so long from him. O brother, said he, I have not yet perfectly learnt to practise the first verse which you taught me. Many years after this, one of his friends asked, if he had not now at least learnt his lesson? To whom he replied, that it was with much difficulty he could yet reduce it to practice, notwithstanding his nineteen years application. However, by his perpetual attention not to offend in his words, he arrived at length at so great perfection in this particular, that he is thought in this to have equalled if not excelled St. Antony himself. When any one consulted him, either upon any passage of the scripture, or any other spiritual matter, he never would answer upon the spot, but desired time to consider of it. Sometimes he employed whole months on these occasions in examining before God what answer he should give ; but then, the answers he returned carried with them so much weight, and were so holy, that they were received by all like oracles dictated by heaven.

St. Pambo did not continue always with St. Antony ; but leaving Thebais, he took up his abode, either in the desert of Scete, as some say, or in that of Nitria, where he had a monastery on the mountain. He was also for some time in the wilderness of the Cells, where, Rufinus says, he went to receive his benediction, anno.

374. As to his exterior practices, St. Pemen used to relate, that he had remarked three things in St. Pambo, which he judged to be very extraordinary, viz. his fasting on all days till the evening,—his continual silence,—and his great diligence in manual labours. He also related that St. Antony had given testimony in favour of St. Pambo, that the fear of God which possessed his soul, had induced the Spirit of God to take up his resting place within him. The eminent grace of his interior is said to have broke forth and discovered itself in his exterior, by a certain brilliant majesty in his countenance, like what we read of Moses, so that a person could not look stedfastly on his face. He often earnestly begged of God, during the space of three years, that he would cease to glorify him in this manner upon earth ; but his divine Majesty, instead of attending to his prayers in this particular, chose rather to establish so profound a humility in his soul, as not to be altered or any ways prejudiced by this glory.

St. Athanasius once desired St. Pambo to come from his desert to Alexandria, in order that by the testimony of so holy a man to the divinity of Jesus Christ he might confound the Arians : upon which occasion it is recorded of him, that seeing an actress in that city dressed up in an extraordinary manner for the stage, he wept bitterly ; and being asked the the reason of his tears, he answered that he wept partly for the wretched condition of the soul of that unhappy woman, and partly to think that on his part he did not take so much pains to please God as she took to make herself agreeable to sinful man.

Palladius relates, in the tenth chapter of his *Historia Lausiaca*, that Melania the elder, a noble Roman lady, on coming into Egypt, and hearing of the sanctity of St. Pambo, went to visit him in his monastery on mount Nitria, taking with her three hundred pounds weight of silver, which she presented to him, desiring he would accept of some part of the store with which God had blessed her. The holy man was sitting at his work making matts when she came in, accompanied with Isidore, the administrator of the hospital of Alexandria ; and without interrupting his work, or looking at either her or her present, he contented himself with telling her, God would reward her charity. Then turning to his disciple, he said : Take this, and distribute it amongst the brethren that are in Lybia and in the islands, whose monasteries are the most poor of all ; but give no part of it to the monasteries of Egypt, because this country is more rich, and abounds more in all things." The lady stood still, expecting that he would give her his benediction, or express at least his esteem for so considerable a present, by word or other sign ; but seeing that he went on with his work, without once casting so much as an eye towards the chest of money which she had given him, she said to him : " Father, I do not know whether you are aware that here is three hundred pounds weight of silver ?" " Daughter," said he, without once taking off his eye from his work, " he, to whom you make this offering, knows very well how much it weighs, without your telling him. If indeed you had given it to me, you might have had some reason to inform me of its weight ; but if you designed it as an offering to God, who did not disdain, but even preferred the poor widow's two mites before the large offerings of the rich, do not say any more about it." This passage Melania herself related to Palladius.

When Theophilus was made patriarch of Alexandria, he went to visit the religious of mount Nitria, who were all assembled on this occasion to do honour to the patriarch. They desired St. Pambo, as their superior, to make some discourse to this prelate, with which he might be edified : the holy abbot, agreeably to his maxims and practice, replied, " If he is not edified by my silence, I shall never edify him by my words." The Saint did not long survive this visit : Melania was present at his death, to whom he bequeathed, by way of legacy, a basket which he had at that time just finished. When he was near his end, he blessed God, that from the time of his first coming into the wilderness of Nitria, and built himself a cell, he had never been burthensome to any one, having always earned his bread with the labour of his own hands; and that he could not recollect a word he had spoken of which he had afterwards cause to repent: nevertheless, said he I am now going to the Lord as one that hath not yet begun to serve him. He expired without any sickness, pain, or the least fever or agony. Melania took charge of his burial, and carried away the basket he had given her, which she kept till her death.

There was also another abbot Pambo, or rather Pammon, whose monastery was in the neighbourhood of Antinoe, greatly esteemed by St. Athanasius, who, together with St. Theodore, the disciple and successor of St. Pachomius in the monastery of Tabenna, accompanied this Saint when he fled from the persecution of Julian and who, together with the same St. Theodore, assured him on this occasion, by prophetic light, that his persecutor was now actually slain in Persia, and had for his successor in the empire one that was a good Christian, but whose reign should be short: all which proved to be actually true. This holy man departed not long after to our Lord, full of years and good works; and St. Athanasius, in a discourse he made in the great church of Alexandria, in the presence of his own clergy, and of many bishops, has given the most ample testimony of his extraordinary sanctity, declaring that he was indeed a great man of God, and worthy to be compared with St. Antony himself.

ST. JULIAN SABBAS.

From Theodoret, in his Philotheus, or Religious History, chap. 2.

St. Julian, surnamed *Sabbas*, or *the venerable father*, was a native of Mesopotamia, who, following the divine call, withdrew himself in his youth from the world, and took up his habitation in a den or cavern, in a vast wilderness on the borders of Osrhoena, a place, on many accounts, inconvenient to dwell in, but preferred by him on account of its solitude, before the most commodious palace in the world. Here he undertook a life of perpetual penance and incessant prayer, eating but once a week, and then only some coarse bread made of millet, with a little salt, and drinking so small a quantity of water at his meal, as was insufficient to the quenching of his thirst,—continually nourishing his soul with the singing of psalms, in which he took great delight, and with an interior conversation with God in prayer; by means of which the divine love took such possession of his heart, that he had no relish for any worldly thing, passing the night and day always thinking of his Beloved, insomuch, that even in his sleep he could dream of nothing else.

The great reputation of his sanctity attracted by degrees many disciples to join him in the desert, who were desirous to learn the science of salvation. These he received into his cavern, and trained up to an imitation of the exercises which he himself followed ; teaching them to discard all care and solicitude for this perishable carcase, and be content to lodge and eat like himself. However, as their number increased, and as the dampness of the cavern spoiled the little provisions of pickled herbs which they provided for the sick, he consented that a hut should be built for their better preservation. Having

gone out at this time, as he frequently did for greater solitude and recollection in prayer, to a distant part of the
wilderness, employing several days by himself in spiritual exercises, and at his returning home, finding they had
erected a larger building than he had ordered, he told
them : " I fear brethren, that whilst we are enlarging our
earthly dwelling, which we can occupy but for a short
time, we shall suffer detriment with respect to our heavenly mansions which are eternal."

The method of prayer and of performing the divine
office which this saint taught his disciples, was as follows :
before day they all sung hymns, psalms, and canticles to
the praise of God together within the cave; then early in
the morning they went out into the wilderness, two by
two, and observed the same manner of worship; with this
difference, that one of them sung fifteen psalms, standing
upright, whilst the other lay prostrate on the ground in
silent prayer and adoration, till the fifteen psalms being
ended, he that had sung them prostrated himself in his
turn on the ground, and adored, whilst his companion,
rising up, sung other fifteen psalms : and thus alternately
singing and adoring, they passed a considerable part of
the day. Before sunset, they betook themselves to a
little rest, and afterwards meeting all together in the
cave, they sung their evening hymns to the praises of
their Creator.

As to the Saint himself, he made, as we have already
said, frequent excursions to a great distance from his cave,
and spent eight or ten days together in the remoter parts
of the wilderness in his spiritual exercises. On these
occasions he often took one of the brethren with him,
particularly a holy man named James, a native of Persia,
but never without desiring his companion to keep himself
at a distance, that he might be no occasion of distraction
to him in his devotions. One time, whilst James was following him in the wilderness, he found a monstrous serpent lying dead in the way, which the Saint had killed

by the sign of the cross, as he acknowledged upon his disciple's putting it home to him, but with a strict injunction to keep the matter a secret during his life. Another time, when Asterius, a young religious, endued with more courage than strength, had by his importunity obtained leave to accompany him in one of those excursions in the heat of the summer, which in those deserts is very violent, after two or three days the young man was so parched with thirst by the sun continually beating upon him, and no water being to be found in those sands, he was just upon the point of perishing, had not the Saint by his prayers and tears obtained of the Father of mercies, that a fountain of water should spring up to save the young man's life, in the very spot which he had sprinkled with his tears ; which fountain, says Theodoret, continues to flow to this day. The same Asterius was afterwards one of the most illustrious amongst the disciples of St. Julian, and propagated the holy discipline he had learnt of his master, by founding a famous monastery near Gindare, in the territory of Antioch, where he trained up many souls to religious perfection.

But these were not the only miracles wrought by the prayers of St. Julian, for he frequently cast out devils, and healed divers diseases. To avoid the concourse of people which the fame of his sanctity and miracles brought to see him, as well as the honours they shewed him, which were troublesome to his humility, he withdrew himself from his Mesopotamian cavern, and taking with him some of his disciples, with necessary provisions for a long journey, he travelled as far as mount Sinai in Arabia, taking care to avoid any town or village that lay in his way. Here he took up his habitation, being charmed with the tranquillity he enjoyed in this holy solitude; but after having built a church, or oratory, and sanctified for some time his new residence with the holy exercises of prayer and penance, it was the will of God he should return again to his disciples whom he had left behind him in his former habitation.

Here he was informed of the threats of Julian the Apostate, who was then engaged in his expedition against the Persians, and of his impious designs against the church of Christ, if he should return with victory. Wherupon, to divert this impending storm, he employed ten whole days in most fervent prayer, to implore the divine mercy and protection for the church. At the end of which time he learnt, by divine revelation, the unhappy death of that prince, and declared the same to his disciples.

Valens, an Arian, who succeeded not long after to the empire, was a great persecutor of the church and an earnest promoter of such as were addicted to his heresy. In his time the Arians made a great havoc in the church of Antioch, where also they had the impudence to publish that St. Julian was of their sentiments. Upon this occasion the Saint, at the request of the Catholics, leaving his desert, took a journey to Antioch, to bear testimony to the faith, and to repress the insolence of the heretics. In his way thither he miraculously preserved the life of the child of a good woman who had entertained him at her house, that by accident had fallen into a deep well, and was given over for lost, but was afterwards found sitting and playing upon the water. Upon being drawn out, he declared he had seen the Saint all the while holding him up, and keeping him from sinking to the bottom. When he arrived at Antioch, great multitudes from all parts flocked about him; some to behold a man so much renowned for his sanctity, others to seek by his prayers a deliverance from the evils wherewith they were afflicted. Here it pleased God that he himself should be seized by a violent fever. But as the Catholics were apprehensive that the people would be shocked on the occasion, at their desire, he prayed to God, that if his recovery might be of any service to the church, he would be pleased to restore him to health. His prayer being immediately followed by a sweat, his fever abated, and he presently recovered. Many others were healed upon the

13

spot by his prayers. After which he went to the place, out of town, where the faithful assembled to their devotions. In his way thither he passed by the gate of the emperor's palace, where a poor cripple, who had been deprived of the use of his legs, was instantly cured by the touch of his garment, so as to be able to rise up immediately and leap or run. The report of this miracle being noised abroad, brought an immense crowd about the Saint, to the great confusion of the Arians, whose impostures were not only clearly discovered, but confuted by the public testimony the Saint gave to the catholic truth, and by his confirming it by evident miracles which they could not contradict, as the governor of the eastern district (who being grievously ill, had sent for the Saint), was one of the number of those who were miraculously cured by him.

On his return home from Antioch, he passed through Cyrus, a city of which Theodoret was afterwards bishop. Here the faithful represented to him the danger they were in from one Asterius, an Arian, who had been intruded upon them for a bishop, and was perparing a sermon against the faith of the Trinity, to impose upon them by his eloquent sophistry. The Saint exhorted them to fasting and prayer; and joining with them in these spiritual exercises, by the efficacy of his prayers in their favour, Asterius was suddenly seized upon with a mortal illness, which within twenty-four hours hurried him before the judgment seat of Christ, on the very eve of the festival which he designed to have preached his impious doctrine in the cathedral of that city.

The Saint after this returned to his solitude, and there continued his accustomed exercises, till having attained to a good old age, he exchanged his mortal pilgrimage for a happy immortality. He is spoken of with the greatest eulogium by St. Jerome, Epist. 13. and by St. John Chrysostom, writing upon the epistle to the Ephesians. His name is recorded in the Roman Martyrology, January 14.

ST. ABRAHAM.

From his Life by St. Ephrem.

St. Abraham was born in Mesopotamia, abou t th year 300, of wealthy parents, by whom he was tenderly beloved, and who provided him with a worldly spouse, to whom they from his childhood had promised him in marriage, designing to procure him an advantageous settlement, and desiring nothing so much as to see him advanced to some post of honour or dignity in the world: but God, who had other designs upon him, inspired him with the love of purity, and an early affection to the practices of piety and devotion. He was remarkably diligent in frequenting the church,—in attending to the holy scriptures, —and in carrying home the divine lessons he there heard, in order to make them the subjects of his meditation both day and night. When he had come to man's estate, his parents pressed him so closely to marry the girl to whom they had before contracted him, and after having resisted their solicitations for some time, he was at length constrained to acquiesce. But after celebrating the marriage feast, when night came on, a ray of divine light having penetrated his heart, accompanied by so strong a call to quit all for the love of God, that he immediately arose, and left both his spouse untouched and his father's house, and going to some distance off, hid himself in an empty cell which he found fit for his purpose, and there with great joy began to sing hymns of praise to his divine Deliverer.

His parents and friends not knowing what became of him, after a diligent search of seventeen days discovered him in his cell at his prayers. But as they found him fixed in his resolution to remain there, in order, as he said, to bewail his sins, and dedicate the remainder of his life to prayer and penance, they left him to follow the call of God, and returned home. At parting he desired that they would not come any more under pretence of visiting him, to interrupt his spiritual exercises ; and that he might have as little communication as possible with the world, he walled up the door of his cell, leaving only a little window through which he received, form time to time, the slender provisions which maintained his life. Here, free from the cares and distractions of the world, he lived in the greatest austerity, abstaining even from bread,— in watchings, penitential tears, and a continual practice of the most profound humility, wonderful charity and meekness, which he shewed, without respect of persons, to every one. In this solitary state he continued for the space of many years, without ever remitting or being wearied out by his long penance, but rather finding an unspeakable sweetness therein, with which he was never satisfied. He considered every day as if it were the day of his death, and suffered not so much as one day to pass without weeping, but was never seen to laugh. Yet with all this austerity and continual mortification, he always preserved a fresh countenance, an agreeable air, and a strength and vigour of body, which must have proceeded from grace, and not from the slender nourishment he allowed himself. Nay, his very habit, which must be considered as a kind of a miracle, was not worn out during the fifty years that he remained in this penitential course of life.

The reputation of his sanctity brought many of all conditions to him, to whom he gave admirable lessons for their spiritual profit ; for our Lord had rewarded his early piety with the gifts of wisdom and understanding in so eminent a degree, that his light shone forth to all that approached him for their instruction and edification. In the mean time his parents dying, when he had been about ten years in this solitude, left him their worldly substance, which was very considerable, which he desired a friend of his to charge himself with, and to dispose of the whole in alms and other pious uses, in order that himself might not be distracted or interrupted in his spiritual exercises by any temporal concerns.

There was in the neighbourhood of the Saint's cell, not far distant from the city of Edessa, a large country town, inhabited by pagans, who were not only obstinately addicted to their idolatrous worship, and heathenish superstitions, but also excessively barbarous and cruel towards all such as sought to reclaim them from their idolatry, by preaching to them the faith of Christ, insomuch that several of the clergy and religious in those parts, who had from time to time attempted to convert them to Christianity, instead of succeeding in their undertaking, meeting with nothing but insults and outrages, were forced by their barbarity to abandon their enterprise. The bishop hearing of the heroic virtues of Abraham, cast his eyes upon him as one whose charity, zeal, meekness, and patience, seemed most likely to prevail over the blindness and obstinacy of these infidels; wherefore assembling his clergy, he proposed to them the advancing of the man of God to the priestly dignity, to the end that he might go and convert them. Having unanimously applauded his proposition, they went in a body, with the prelate at their head, to the cell of the holy man. The bishop told him upon what occasion they were come, and how great and charitable a work it would be in him to go and endeavour to procure the salvation of so many poor deluded souls. Abraham, at the hearing of this proposal, being struck with surprise, begged that the prelate would never think of sending such a miserable wretch as he was upon so important and arduous an enterprise, but rather suffer him to remain in his cell to lament and to do penance for his manifold sins. The bishop encouraged him, assuring him that God would assist him in this great work; that his having forsaken all things for his love, was not suf-

13*

ficient to make his sacrifice complete, unless he were also ready to renounce his own will by the virtue of obedience, which is the true way to find out the will of God; that whilst he stayed in his cell, he was labouring only for his own salvation; but by going where he was about to send him, and labouring in the conversion of those infidels, the grace of God co-operating with him, he would become the instrument of saving the souls of many, and be entitled to a much greater reward in eternal bliss. The man of God, on hearing this, could resist no longer; but cried out with tears: "The Lord's will be done! I am ready to go to whatsoever place you shall be pleased to send me." Thus the bishop, having brought him out of his cell, ordained him priest, and sent him to preach to that pagan people.

He began his mission by pouring out prayers and tears before God in behalf of these poor souls, in whom he found no manner of disposition to profit by his words. Then sending to his friend, whom he had charged with the disposal of the worldly substances left him by his parents, he procured from him a sum of money with which he in a short time built a church, and adorned it for divine service. In the mean time the people, for whose conversion he ceased not continually to sigh and pray, made no opposition, although their curiosity brought them daily to behold the building. But when he had finished the church, and dedicated it to the living God, with a most fervent prayer, accompanied with many tears for the conversion of the idolaters, his zeal carried him from the church to the temple of the idols, where he overthrew their altars, and broke their statues in pieces. Hereupon their rage knew no bounds, but falling upon him with merciless fury, after having discharged innumerable blows and stripes upon him, they drove him out of the town.

The next morning when they came to the church (as they daily did, not out of devotion, but from a certain curiosity and pleasure they took in seeing its decorations) they were surprised beyond measure to find him at his prayers before the altar. But upon his beginning to preach to them, and to conjure them to turn from their idols to the living God, they again fell upon him, and having beat him worse than before, they fastened a rope about his feet, and dragged him like a dead dog out of the town, where they pelted him with stones till they thought they had made an end of him. About midnight he, whom they had left for dead, came to himself, and after fervently praying, with abundance of tears to the Father of mercies, for the conversion and salvation of his persecutors, got up, and returned again into the town, and early in the morning was again found in the church singing psalms. The pagans, although astonished at the sight of him, yet were no way mollified, but rather more enraged, so that they repeated the treatment they had given him the preceeding day, and dragged him again by the feet with ropes out of their town. He returned nevertheless the next day, and thus for the space of three whole years, he still persevered constant in his labours and fervent prayers for their conversion, under a perpetual succession of grievous sufferings, pains, mockeries, and outrages, without ever shewing the least anger or impatience, or returning them a single angry word, or even entertaining in his soul any hatred or aversion towards them whatever, but, on the contrary, the more cruelly they treated him, the more tenderly did he love them, and the more affectionately invite them to come to Christ, *the way, the truth, and the life.*

After three years had elapsed in this manner, the patience and prayers of the Saint at length prevailed over the resistance he had hitherto met with from this obstinate people. Upon a certain occasion, when they were all assembled together, they began to declare to each other their great admiration at the unwearied patience and charity of the servant of God, and from thence to

argue that the God whom he preached must needs be
the true God, and the religion which taught him so
much patience and charity the true religion. Continuing to reason after this manner with one another, they
further observed how he, being but one man, had cast
down and broken in pieces all their gods, without their
being able to resist him, or to revenge themselves on
him. These reflections, being matured by the grace of
God, opening their eyes and softening their hearts, produced a general resolution upon the spot of their all going in a body to the church, to yield themselves up to
the man of God, and to embrace the faith he preached,
which resolution they instantly put in execution. The
Saint received them with inexpressible joy, and having
first instructed them in the necessary articles of the christian doctrine, he afterwards baptized them, to the number of about one thousand persons, men, women, and
children. After which he continued for the space of
one year, watering these young plants, till he saw them
not only deeply rooted in the christian faith, but also
diligent in bringing forth the fruit of every christian
virtue, some thirty, some sixty, and others an hundred
fold.

Having thus accomplished the great work for which he
was sent, and finding the affection of the people towards
him to be so great, that they would never willingly suffer
him to return to his solitude, he, when they least suspected
it, withdrew himself from them privately by night : having first recommended them in the most earnest manner
he could, to the divine goodness, and making three times
the sign of the cross over their town. The afflicton which
these good people suffered, when on coming to church
the next morning they could not find their pastor, and
the diligence wherewith both they and the bishop, who
was sensibly affected with their grief, made search after
him, was inexpressible, but all in vain, for he concealed
himself with so much secrecy, that they could learn no

tidings of him ; so that the good prelate, to console and assist them, went amongst them himself, and after having greatly edified them by his instructions, &c. he ordained priests, deacons, and subdeacons, amongst them, for the preaching the word of God, and administering the divine sacraments in their infant church. When Abraham was informed how matters stood, he gave thanks to God, and then ventured to return to his ancient cell, where he was frequently visited by his flock, in order to nourish their souls with the food of the words of life, which issued in copious streams from his sacred lips.

We pass over several other particulars of the virtues of this man of God, and the frequent assaults he underwent from the malice of the common enemy, who had oftentimes visibly appeared to him, but was always so effectually vanquished by his humility, and the confidence he placed in our Lord, as not to be able to inspire him with the least fear. But there remains a remarkable passage of the life of this servant of God which must not be omitted, as it relates to the fall, the conversion, and penance of his niece.

After the Saint had gone back to his cell, it happened that his brother, dying in the world, left an only daughter, named Mary, an orphan of seven years of age. This child was brought to her uncle in his wilderness, who undertook to train her up to a religious life, and placed her, for this purpose, in a cell adjoining to his own, with a little window between both, through which he instructed her. Here she made such good use of the lessons she daily received from him, as to become a perfect model of piety and penance, in which happy state she persevered for twenty years, till a false religious, or rather a wolf in sheep's clothing, under pretence of coming to be edified by the conversation of her uncle, found means to tempt her to sin, and ceased not till she was so unhappy as to quit her cell, and yield to the temptation. The horror and remorse that followed her crime was so

excessive, that it threw her into despair; so that instead
of rising after her fall, and returning to her uncle to
confess and do penance for her sin, she was resolved to
fly from him, and accordingly went to a distant town,
where she abandoned herself to a sinful course of life.

The Saint having taken notice that for the space of
two days he had not heard her sing psalms, according
to her custom, called out to her to know the cause of
her silence, and as no answer was returned, it presently
occurred to his recollection that she was the dove he had
seen in a vision swallowed up by a dragon. His grief
for the loss of his dear child became inexpressible : he
wept and prayed for her without ceasing, till at the end
of two years, having heard where she was, and the
wicked course of life to which she had abandoned herself, he took the resolution of seeking after the lost
sheep, in order to bring her back to Christ's fold. In
order thereto, he procured, through the means of a friend,
a horse, together with a soldier's habit, and a large cap
or hat, which covered a great part of his face, and taking some money with him, went to the inn in which she
lived, where having ordered a splendid supper to be prepared, he told the host that he had heard much of the
beauty of a young woman in his house, whose name
was Mary, and desired she might sup with him. Supper
being ended, and the waiters having retired, he took off
his cap, and mingling tears with his words : " My
daughter," said he (for so he used to call her), " dont
you know me ?—My child did not I bring you up ?—
What has befallen you ?—Who is the murderer that has
killed your soul ?   Where is that angelical habit that
you formerly wore ?—Where that admirable purity ?—
Where are those tears which you poured out in the presence of God ?—Where, those watchings employed in
singing the divine praises ?—Where that holy austerity
that made you take pleasure in lying on the bare ground ?
—Why did you not, after your first fall, come presently

to acquaint me with it, since I should certainly have done penance for you, with my friend Ephrem (*the writer of this life*), who has been ever since under an unspeakable affliction on your account ?—Why had you so little confidence in me ?—Alas! who is there without sin but God alone ?" On hearing these words she stood like one struck dumb and motionless with confusion and horror, and it was not without extreme difficulty, after many affecting speeches,—lively representations of the tender mercies of God to repenting sinners,—and even promises to take all her sins upon himself, that she at length put on the resolution of returning to her cell. Then prostrating herself at his feet, she spent the remainder of the night in prayers and tears. At break of day he bid her get upon his horse, and thus conducted her back to his cell, ordering her to leave what money and goods she was possessed of behind her, as inheriting them of the devil, whom she had been serving. After her return, she gave herself up with so much ardour to the exercises of a penitential life, and bewailed her sins day and night with so deep a sense of sorrow and contrition for them, joined with so lively a confidence in the divine mercy, that God was pleased, within three years, to give her, as a token of his acceptance of her penitence, the grace of even working miracles, by restoring health to the diseased by her prayers. However, she continued her penitential course with incredible austerity during the fifteen years that she lived after her conversion, never ceasing to lament her sins, till at length God was pleased to take her to himself. At the hour of her death a certain extraordinary brightness was observed on her countenance, which gave all that were present occasion to glorify God.

As to St. Abraham, he passed to a better life five years before her, after having, as we have already seen, spent fifty years in serving God in the most consummate sanctity. No sooner was the news of his death spread

abroad, than the whole city, in a manner, crowded
about his cell, and as many as could procure the least scrap
of his clothes, carried them home with them, as so many
precious relics which would bring a blessing along with
them to their houses; and we are assured by St. Ephrem,
that the very touch of them cured all diseases upon the spot.
St. Abraham is commemorated in the Roman Martyrology, on the 16th of March, but the Greeks celebrate
his festival, jointly with St. Mary, his neice, on the 29th
of October.

Theodoret, in his Philotheus, gives us the life f another
St. Abraham, a native of the city of Cyrus, who from
an anchoretical life was called forth by divine inspiration to the conversion of the inhabitants of a certain
town on mount Libanus; which having happily effected,
by his zeal and charity, after three years abode amongst
them, he returned to his solitude. · The extraordinary
sanctity of his life, and the general esteem wherein his
eminent virtues and great talents for the gaining of souls
to God were held, determined his superiors to send him
with the episcopal character to the city of Carræ (or
Haran) in Mesopotamia, which as yet had not received
the faith of Christ, but was given up to the worship of
devils.   Here God gave such a blessing to his labours
and preaching, continual prayer, wonderful sanctity and
austerity of life, that this idolatrous people, by his means
was soon brought over to Christ.   He flourished in the
fourth century.

ST. JOHN OF EGYPT.

From Rufinus's Lives of the Fathers, chap. 1.   Palladius, Historia
Lausiaca chap. 43. and Cassian, l. 4.   Institut. chap. 23, 24, 25.

AMONGST all the saints of the Egyptian deserts, there is
perhaps none, St. Antony excepted, whose name is so
illustrious in church history, and the writings of the holy
fathers, as that of St. John of Lycopolis (so called from
the place near which he dwelt in the hither Thebais.) He
was not only greatly renowned for his extraordinary sanctity and miracles, but also consulted as an oracle from all
parts, on account of his eminent spirit of prophecy, not
only by persons of an inferior rank, but even by the emperor Theodosius the Great himself, to whom, amongst
other things, he foretold his glorious victories over the
mighty armies of the two usurpers, Maximus and Eugenius.
This Saint was born about the year 305, and brought up
at first to the trade of a carpenter, but when grown up
to manhood he withdrew himself under an ancient religious man, whom he served with so much diligence and
humility, that the good old father was quite wrapt in
admiration at his virtue.   However, to put it to the trial,
whether his virtue was built upon a solid foundation or
not, he often enjoined him to do many things seemingly
absurd, or extremely difficult, or altogether impossible,
which the humble disciple immediately took in hand,
and endeavoured to accomplish with a wonderful faith,
simplicity, and perseverance, without so much as once
allowing himself to reflect on the unreasonableness or
impossibility of the injunction: but believing all things
possible to obedience, and looking upon the ordinance of
his superior as the commandment of God himself, an instance of which is recorded by Cassian.   The old father

14

one day fixing a *dry stick* of wood in the ground, bid his disciple water *that tree* twice a day, which task, with his usual punctuality in matters of obedience, he constantly performed for the space of a whole year, whether sick or well, or whatever other occupation required his attention, though he was obliged to walk the distance of two miles each time to fetch the water, till at the expiration of the year, the old father asked him, whether the tree had as yet taken root or not, and he simply answering that he did not know, the father pulled the stick out of the ground, and bid him water it no longer.

After the death of his master, having spent about five years in different monasteries in the exercises of a religious life, being then about forty years of age, he retired alone to a steep mountain, about two miles distance from the city of Lycopolis, and there chose a hollow rock of difficult access for his place of abode, which he divided into three rooms or apartments: one of which served him for an oratory, another for a work-room, and the the third for his ordinary uses. The entrance of this cavern he closed up so effectually, that for the space of fifty years he neither went out himself nor admitted any one to enter his enclosure, conversing only on certain days through a window with such as either came to be edified by his heavenly discourses, or to seek counsel, consolation, or a remedy for their diseases; but for the accommodation of such as came from a remote distance, he permitted a dwelling to be erected near to his grotto, where some servants of God, who had placed themselves under his direction, took care to provide them with food and lodging. But as for women, none were suffered to approach him upon any account whatsoever. He employed the whole week in conversation with God, except the Saturdays and Sundays, when he let himself be seen through his window by such as came to visit him; and after having prayed for and with them, and entertained them with excellent lessons out of the word of God, according to their exigencies, he resolved their doubts, comforted them in their spiritual afflictions, and encouraged them to fervour and perseverance in the love and service of God. His words were seasoned with that heavenly wisdom which he acquired by a continual conversation with God; for the more he withdrew himself from earthly things the nearer the Spirit of God approached to him, with such heavenly light as not only to endow him with a clear understanding of things present, but also with so perfect a knowledge and foresight of things to come, that few or none of the saints since the Apostles have been found to excel, or even to equal him in the spirit of prophecy. He not only often declared the most secret thoughts of their hearts to those that came to visit him, and reproved them in private for sins of which he could have no knowledge but by revelation, but also foretold public calamities, and cautioned the people against the sins by which they were about to draw down the severe judgment of God upon their heads; and on many other occasions relating to the public welfare, he not only gave directions to those in power how to act, but punctually foretold the success. He became also illustrious for innumerable miracles; though to avoid ostentation he would never undertake to cure the diseased in his cell, but rather chose to send them some oil he had previously blessed, which never failed to heal them of all their disorders.

Palladius relates how himself had undertaken a journey of eighteen days from mount Nitria to the neighbourhood of Lycopolis, on purpose to visit this saint; and that as soon as he saw him, he told him his name, and mentioned the monastery from whence he came; and that shortly after the governor of the province coming in, and the Saint having entertained him for some time in private upon the affairs of his soul, when the governor was gone he let Palladius know what had passed in the mean time in his thoughts. He told him also the temptations he lay under of quitting his solitude, and of returning to his native country, under the specious pretext of comforting his aged father, and of inducing his brother and his sister to embrace a religious life, assuring him that such an undertaking was needless, for that they had both of them already renounced the world, and that his father would live seven years longer; and moreover, that he should hereafter be a bishop, and afterwards suffer great troubles and afflictions; all which came to pass, for when Palladius, some time after, going into Palestine for a change of air, and from thence into Bithynia, he was there made a Bishop of Helonopolis, and became a partaker in the persecution raised against St. John Chrysostome, being himself also expelled from his see on the same occasion.

Rufinus also with six others, his companions, went in like manner from Jerusalem to visit the great Saint not long before his happy death. At their first coming, when according to custom they were about to join with him in prayer, and then to receive his benediction; he asked if there was not one amongst them in holy orders? They answered, no. But he looked on them one by one, and then pointing to the youngest of the company, he said, *this man is a deacon;* which was actually the case, though he desired to conceal it, and as only one of the company knew it, he therefore continued to deny it; upon which the saint taking hold of his hand, and kissing it, said: "My son, take care not to disown the grace you have received from God, lest that which is good should be an occasion of your falling into evil, by telling a lie under the pretext of humility. An untruth must never be told, not even under the pretence of good, nor upon any account whatever; for a lie can never proceed from God, but always from evil, as our Saviour himself teaches." The deacon received this charitable correction with respectful silence. After which, having all united in prayer, as soon as they had finished, one of the company, who was grievously tormented with a tertian ague, humbly entreated the Saint to cure him. He told him, that he desired to be delivered from what was sent him for his good, for that sicknesses, and such like chastisements, contributed to purify the soul. He however gave him some blessed oil, by the application of which he was suddenly and perfectly healed. The man of God gave orders, says Rufinus, for our entertainment, according to the strictest rules of hospitality, taking much care of us, whilst he was altogether regardless of himself; for he never eat till after vespers, and then but a very small quantity of what had never been near the fire. This was his manner of fasting, in which he still persevered, though he was now ninety years of age.

After refreshing their bodies by the entertainment the saint had ordered for them, they returned again to receive from him the food of their souls. Having asked them, from what place they came, and what was the motive of their journey? They answered, that they came from Jerusalem, with a desire to be edified by seeing what they had heard so much of. Upon which he told them, with a cheerful serenity of countenance, which, proceeded from the inward joy and peace of his soul, that he wondered how they should take so much pains, and suffer the fatigues of so long a journey, merely to see a poor frail imperfect mortal, in whom there was nothing worthy of any one's seeking after or admiring; for even supposing they had conceived an opinion that they might be edified by what they should see in him, or hear from his mouth, yet how inconsiderable would all this be in comparison of what they might learn at any time without going abroad, from the prophets and apostles, or rather from the spirit of God in the holy Scriptures. However, seeing they came so far with a desire to hear something from him, he made them a most divine exhortation, set down at large by Rufinus; in which, after cautioning them against the danger of being puffed up by vanity;

14*

on account of their journey, or any thing they should see, or hear from the servants of God, either by harbouring a better opinion of themselves, or seeking to raise themselves in the esteem of others, he proceeds to expatiate on the pernicious effects of pride and vain-glory, which not only rob us of the fruit and reward of all our good works, but is capable of even casting the soul, that seems to herself to have already ascended to the top of the hill of religious perfection, headlong down the precipice that leads to the bottomless pit, as was the case with Satan and his angels. Of this he told them a dreadful example, which had lately happened in that very desert, of a solitary, who dwelt in a cavern by himself, and led an austere life, labouring with his own hands for his subsistence, and passing both day and night in prayer ; after having attained to an eminent degree of virtue, suffering himself to be puffed up with pride and a conceit of his own strength, he fell an easy prey to the enemy ; who assuming the shape of a woman in distress, and being admitted by him into his cave, excited in his heart impure thoughts and criminal desires ; to which, when he had consented, and was seeking to put them into execution, the phantom vanished away with a most hideous noise, whilst a multitude of devils was heard in the place, with a loud laughter mocking and insulting him. The wretch was so much cast down and confounded at his shameful fall, that abandoning all thoughts of endeavouring to rise again, and repair, by penance and humility, the fault into which his pride had betrayed him, he fell, into the deep gulph of despair, and returning into the world, he gave himself up to all manner of impurities, industriously avoiding the meeting or conversing with any holy person, who by their wholesome admonitions might seek to reclaim and convert him.

In the sequel of his discourse the Saint also inculcates the necessity of keeping a strict guard upon our hearts and thoughts, in order to prevent any passion, or disorderly affection of the will, or the vain desire of any thing which is not according to God, from taking root in the heart; for from these roots a thousand distractions presently shoot up, to the great prejudice of our attention and devotion in prayer, as well as to the purity of the soul; " so that it is not enough," says he, " to have renounced the world, and all the works of Satan, the prince of the world, nor even to have left our goods, our lands, and all we possessed in the world, we must also renounce our imperfections, and all vain pleasures, and *unprofitable and hurtful desires*, which, as the apostle tells us, 1 Tim. vi. 9, *drown men in destruction and perdition.*——For without renouncing these things, we never effectually renounce the devil and all his works; since it is by their means the devil enters and takes possession of our heart. These disorderly affections hold a correspondence with our enemy; nay, as they proceed from him, and open to him the door of the soul, it is no wonder such souls should never enjoy rest, but rather be always agitated by troubles and commotion, since they are always encompassed by so wretched a guest to whom they have given admittance by their passions and vices. On the other hand, he that has indeed renounced the world, that is to say, retrenched all his vices and passions, and banished all disorderly affections to sin far from his soul, so as to leave no gate open by which the devil may enter;——he who represses his anger, resists and overcomes all irregular motions to evil,——avoids all lying,——abhors envy,——who not only speaks well of every one, but even denies himself the liberty of thinking evil of any one, and who always considers the good and evil of his neighbour as his own, and behaves accordingly on every occasion, such a one as this opens the gate of his soul to the Holy Spirit, who enters in and fills it with his light, and with those admirable fruits of *charity, joy, peace, patience,* &c. which are produced in the soul by this heavenly Comforter." Wherefore the

Saint proceeds to recommend in a particular manner to all who are desirous of being truly religious to labour to acquire such perfect purity, both of conscience and of heart, as may enable them to offer up to our Lord such a perfect and pure prayer as may introduce them to a certain familiarity with his divine Majesty and his holy angels, and to such a happy union of love, as to be enabled to say with St. Paul, Rom. viii. 38, 39. *That neither death, nor life, nor angels, nor principalities, nor powers, nor things present, nor things to come—nor any other creature shall be able to separate me from the love of God which is in Christ Jesus our Lord.* He further adds, that the best means to attain this perfect purity, so pleasing to God, is to retrench by the virtue of mortification, vanities, inordinate affections, and sensual delights of every kind, even in small things, and to walk resolutely in the narrow way of self-denial and penance ; with which, if we join the love of solitude, silence, and recollection of spirit, we shall easily arrive at perfection, and even begin to enjoy a kind of heaven upon earth.

With these and such like heavenly discourses the Saint entertained his guests, and after three days dismissed them, giving them his blessing, and telling them at parting, that on that very day the news was brought to Alexandria of the victory which the emperor Theodosius had obtained over the tyrant Eugenius, but, said he, that good emperor shall not long survive this happy event, but shall die a natural death. All which they soon after found to be true. The man of God himself did not survive that year. During the space of three days before his death, he let no man see him ; and on the fourth day, being on his knees in prayer, he breathed out his pure soul into the hands of his Creator, whom he went to enjoy for a happy eternity.

Palladius relates, as having learnt it from the Saint himself, that during the many years he had lived in his cavern he had never seen any woman, nor one piece of money, nor ever beheld any man eating, nor had any man ever seen him either eat or drink.

But we must not here omit a very remarkable history relating to this Saint, which we find not only attested by Rufinus and Palladius, but also by St. Augustine, L. *de Cura pro Mortuis,* c. 17. which he had learnt from those who had been informed thereof by the very parties themselves to whom it happened. A certain tribune or colonel came to the Saint and begged he would allow his wife to see him, as she had undertaken a long and dangerous journey out of an extreme desire she had of visiting him. The man of God answered, that he never saw, nor admitted of visits from any woman. But as the colonel still pressed him, affirming that it would cost his wife her life, through the greatness of her affliction, if she were not admitted to see him, the Saint bid him go, and assure his wife she should see him without giving herself the trouble of either coming to him, or so much as going out of her own bed chamber. Accordingly that very night the man of God appeared to her in a vision in her sleep, said to her: " O woman, great is thy faith, which has obliged me to come hither to satisfy thy request. However I must warn thee against desiring in future to see the mortal and earthly visage of the servants of God, but rather to contemplate with the eye of the spirit their lives and other actions: *for the flesh profiteth nothing, but it is the spirit that giveth life.* Know this also, that I, not in the quality of a Saint, or of a prophet, as thou imaginest, but only in consideration of thy faith, have prayed to our Lord for thee, and he has been pleased to grant to thee the cure of all the corporal diseases under which thou labourest ; and henceforward both thou and thy husband shall enjoy good health, and all thy house shall be blessed. But take care that thou never forget the benefits of God ; live always in the fear of the Lord, and desire no more for thy worldly subsistence than the appointment due to thy post. Content thyself then with having seen me in thy sleep, and desire no more." When the woman awaked, she related the whole vision to her husband, describing the habit of the Saint, and all the lineaments of his face, which to his great astonishment all perfectly agreed. Upon which he went the next day to return thanks to the man of God; who as soon as he saw him, said : " behold I have fulfilled my promise, depart then in peace, and may the blessing of God go along with you both."

St. John of Egypt is celebrated in the Roman Martyrology on the seventeenth of March.

ST. ARSENIUS.

From the third and fifth book of the Remarkable Actions and Sayings of the Ancient Fathers, published by Rosweidus.

ST. ARSENIUS was a nobleman in great favour with the emperor Theodosius, who committed to him the care of the education of his two sons, Arcadius and Honorius, in quality both of their godfather and of their governor. In this eminent station he lived at court the life of a courtier, in the midst of honours, riches, and pleasures, till he was about forty years of age, when God was pleased to call him from a worldly life into the wilderness, there to seek, by flight, silence, and repose, the salvation of his soul. For, whilst he was one day at his prayers, earnestly begging of our Lord to teach him what he should do to secure his eternal salvation, he heard a voice that answered him, saying, Arsenius, flee the company of men, and thou shalt be saved." Wherefore, in compliance with this heavenly call, he instantly abandoned his secular glory for the love of Christ : and quitting all his wordly possessions, retired into the desert of Scete, in order to

dedicate the remainder of his days to the love and service
of his Maker, in solitude, prayer, labour, and penance.
Whilst he repeated the same prayer, he heard again the
same voice, saying, " Arsenius, flee, be silent, and quiet,
(*fuge, tace, quiesce*) these are the principles of salvation,
or the first things to be done in order to salvation. *Hæc
sunt principia salutis.*"

To fulfil this repeated injunction of fleeing from the
company of men, he chose a cell at a great distance from
the other solitaries, and very rarely admitted of any visits
from them. Even when he went to church, which was
thirteen leagues distant from his habitation, he used to
place himself behind one of the pillars, in order to conceal himself as much as possible, so as neither to see nor
be seen by others. When Theophilus, the patriarch of
Alexandria, went one day to visit him with some others
in his company, and desired he would make some discourse to the company for their spiritual edification ; the
Saint asked them whether they were all disposed to observe and put in practice what he should say to them ?
Yes, replied they, very willingly. Why then, said he, I
beg of you, that in what place soever you may hereafter
hear Arsenius to dwell, be pleased to let him be alone,
and never to come near him. Another time the same
patriarch being desirous to see him, sent to know if he
would admit of his visit. Arsenius answered, that if he
came alone he should open the door to him, but if he
brought any others in his company he would seek out another place, and remain there no longer ; so that Theophilus, for fear of driving him away, refrained afterwards
from visiting him. The abbot Mark having asked him
one day, why he kept at such a distance from men, and
shunned the conversation of all the other solitaries ? He
answered : "God knows how dearly I love them all ;
but I cannot be at the same time with his divine Majesty and with them. For whereas the angels, though their
number be almost infinite, yet have all but one will ; it

is quite otherwise with men, whose dispositions and wills are different ; therefore I cannot think of leaving God to converse with men."

As to the manner in which he spent his time in this solitude, it was divided between working and prayer, or rather his whole life in the wilderness was one continual prayer ; for even whilst he was sitting at work and making baskets, which was his daily employment, his soul was ever attentive to God in prayer, and for ever bewailing his sins ; insomuch that he was obliged to have always a handkerchief in his bosom, to wipe off the flood of penitential tears which continually flowed from his eyes. As for the nights, he generally spent them, as we learn from his disciple Daniel, in watching and prayer ; only towards the morning, when nature could hold out no longer, he used to suffer sleep, which he called his *naughty servant*, to close his eyes ; but after a very short repose, which he took sitting, he rose up again to his accustomed exercises. The same disciple relates, that on Saturday evenings the setting sun usually left him at his prayers, with his hands extended towards heaven, and that he continued praying in this same posture till the sun beams, rising the next morning, came beating upon his eyes. In order to renew his fervour in his spiritual exercises, he would frequently say to himself: *Arsenius, Arsenius, to what end didst thou leave the world and come hither?* He used also often to say that whenever he had been talking, he had always found matter whereof to repent, but had never regretted his having kept silence. He was also a great lover of holy poverty. The other solitaries said of him, that as no one was more richly clad than Arsenius whilst he lived at court, so none of the inhabitants of the desert wore a more mean or poor habit than he, after retiring from the world. His poverty was so great, that having occasion for a trifle of money to procure some little necessaries for him in sickness, he was obliged to receive it in alms, upon which he cried out : I give thee thanks, O my God, that thou hast made me worthy to be thus reduced to the necessity of asking an alms in thy name." After he had lived for many years in the wilderness, a kinsman of his, a senator, dying, left him by his last will a considerable estate. When this will was brought to the Saint, by a proper officer, in his solitude, it displeased him so much that he would have torn it in pieces, had not the officer flung himself at his feet, declaring that it would cost him his life if the will were destroyed. Upon this Arsenius returned him back the will, saying, "How is it possible this man should by his will make me his heir, since he, as it appears, died but a little while ago, whilst I have been dead so many years."

As to his method of fasting, and other austerities of this kind, it is hard to describe them in particular, on account of his keeping himself so much to himself. His disciple Daniel only informed us, that during the whole time he knew him, they laid him in but a very slender provision for his whole year's sustenance ; and yet that he managed it so well, as not only to make it suffice for himself, but also to impart some of it to his disciples whenever they came to see him. The same disciple also took notice, that whilst he was sitting at his work, making baskets, according to his custom, of the leaves of palm-trees, when the water in which he was obliged to moisten and soften them began to corrupt, he would never change it, or fling it away, but if there were any need of fresh water, he would pour it in upon that which was already corrupted, that so it might always continue to yield a disagreeable smell. The brethren asked him one day, why he would not suffer that corrupt water to be flung away, since it infected his whole cell with its stench ? "Because," replied he, "I was used when I lived in the world to gratify myself with the most agreeable perfumes, and therefore it is no more than just that I should now, during the time that remains of my life, in punishment of my former

15

sensuality, support this stench, in hopes that at the last day God will deliver me from the insupportable stench of hell, and not condemn my soul with that of the rich man who had passed his days in feasting and delights."

But nothing was more remarkable in this Saint than his extraordinary humility, which made him so industrious in keeping himself out of sight, and in concealing every thing that might procure him the applause or esteem of men. Although he was so learned in the human sciences before he quitted the world, as to be perfect master both of the Greek and Latin, and had, after his retiring into the wilderness, received such extraordinary lights from God for understanding spiritual matters, that no one had a more perfect knowledge, or could better explain the most difficult passages of the holy scriptures than himself, yet he would never speak of these matters by his own choice, nor shew at any time his knowledge of them, but rather chose to consult and hearken to the most illiterate of the brethren, provided he were truly humble. Being asked one day why he, being so learned a man, sought instruction and counsel from a certain solitary, who was quite destitute of all human literature, he replied : " It is true, whilst I was in the world I acquired some knowledge in the sciences of the world, and in the Greek and Latin tongues, but since I have left the world, I have not yet been able to learn even the A, B, C, of the true science of the Saints, of which this ignorant rustic is master." Such were his humble sentiments of himself.

After he had spent forty years in the desert of Scete, the Mazices, a barbarous people of Lybia, made an irruption on that side, where they massacred St. Moses and other solitaries, and forced all the rest from their cells. Upon this occasion Arsenius was obliged to change his earthly residence, but not the true dwelling place where his heart was fixed. He went therefore to a place called Trohe, not far from the ancient Babylon of Egypt (now Cairo), and there he continued his usual course of life for ten years, till fresh irruptions of the barbarians forced him thence. From Trohe he went to Canopus in the lower Egypt, which is not far distant from Alexandria, where, being too much disturbed with the importunity of visits from that great metropolis, he remained no longer than three years, and then returned again to Trohe, where he spent the two last years of his mortal pilgrimage. When his end approached, he told his disciples that he desired they would bury him privately, no matter how, only taking care that he should be remembered in the offering of the holy sacrifice. They that were present at his death, seeing him, said to him : "Father, why do you weep ? Are you, like the rest, afraid to die ?" " Yes," said he, " very much ; and this is no new fear, but a fear that has stuck close to me ever since I first came into the desert." He departed to our Lord in a good old age, being ninety-five years old, of which he had spent fifty-five in the desert in the exercises of a religious life. St. Pemen seeing him expire, cried out : " O happy Arsenius, for having wept and mourned for yourself so much in this world ! since they who do not mourn in this life, shall mourn for all eternity in the next." It is also recorded of the patriarch Theophilus, that when he was at the point of death, he said ; " O how happy wast thou, O Arsenius, who hadst this last hour continually before thine eyes !"

The name of St. Arsenius is recorded in the Roman Martyrology on the nineteenth of July.

ST. NILAMMON.

From Sozomen, an ancient Church Historian, lib. 8. c. 19.

NILAMMON was a holy anchoret, who had made himself a little cell near Geres, a small city of Egypt, in the neighbourhood of Pelusium, where he dwelt for many years in admirable sanctity. When the bishop of that city died, the clergy and people, who had conceived a high opinion of the eminent virtues of this servant of God, desired to have him for his successor. But whatsoever advances they made, Nilammon's humility repelled, by refusing to submit his shoulders to a charge which even an angel might have reason to dread; but being apprehensive that they would use violence, he closed up the door of his cell, and fenced it with stones, that they might not be able to come at him.

In the mean time it happened that Theophilus, the patriarch of Alexandria, coming by sea from Constantinople, where he had been too much engaged, in the unjust deposition of St. John Chrysostom, was driven by a storm upon the coast of Geres. The people therefore took this opportunity of the presence of the patriarch to entreat him to oblige Nilammon to accept of the bishopric. Whereupon Theophilus going to his cell, used his utmost endeavours to prevail upon him to accept of episcopal consecration, and continued to press him so closely, that Nilammon finding the patriarch would not hear any thing that he could alledge to excuse himself, desired at least one day's respite to set his affairs in order, telling him, that on the following day he might do with him as he pleased.

The patriarch failed not to return on the following day, accompanied by all the people, and then challenging the

Saint to fulfil his promise, he desired him to open the door, that they might proceed to his consecration. Nilammon proposed that some time should be allowed him for prayer before his consecration. Theophilus applauded the proposition, and betook himself also to prayer; but the fervour of Nilammon's prayers was so excessive, that he breathed out his soul into the hands of his Creator. In the mean time, the patriarch and people who remained without, after having allowed him, as they thought, competent time for his devotion, began to be impatient, and to call aloud on him to open his door; but finding that a great part of the day passed in this manner, and that he returned no answer, they forced their way into his cell, where, to their great surprise, they found him dead. Having buried him with great honour, they erected a church over his monument, where they celebrated his festival amongst the Saints.

He died anno 403, and his name is recorded in the Roman Martyrology on the sixth day of January.

ST. SIMON STYLITES.

From Theodoret in his Philotheus, chap 26, and Antonius, Disciple of the Saint, in his Life.

ALTHOUGH there were, during the life-time of St. Simon Stylites, almost as many eye-witnesses of his extraordinary course of life, and of the innumerable prodigies which God wrought by him, as there were men in all the eastern regions, not to say in the then known world, yet the great Theodoret, who undertook, whilst the Saint was yet living, to transmit, by writing, to posterity a faithful account of this wonder of the world, was afraid lest he should seem to succeeding ages to have delivered to

15*

them a fabulous rather than a true history. But the divine providence which raised up this Saint in so extraordinary a manner, in order to shew forth the power of his grace to the whole world, and to rouse up by so great an example the drooping spirits of lukewarm Christians, as well as to enlighten the eyes and touch the hearts of thousands of infidels and sinners, was pleased that the wonderful life of Simon should not only be perfectly well known at the time he lived through the whole extent of the Roman empire, and all the eastern nations bordering thereon, but that for the edification of posterity it should also be written by cotemporary authors, and in so public a manner, that we may safely aver, there is no fact in history better authenticated.

Our Saint was born towards the latter end of the fourth century, at a place called Sisan, upon the confines of Syria and Cilicia.   In his tender years he was employed by his parents in feeding their sheep in the country, so that he seems to have had but little opportunity of frequenting the church or hearing the word of God.   But a great snow happening to fall one day, obliged him to leave the sheep under shelter at home, which afforded him leisure to go to church.   No sooner had he entered the church than he became so extremely affected, and penetrated with the fear of God, as to give the utmost attention to the divine lessons that were read out of the Epistles of St. Paul and the gospel ; and after deeply reflecting on those words of the sermon upon the mount, *blessed are they that mourn :* and *wo be to you that laugh :* and *blessed are the clean of heart,* &c. he addressed himself to an old man, who was one of the congregation, desiring to be further informed what he should do, and what course of life he should follow, that he might live up to these heavenly lessons and save his soul ?   The good old man recommended a retired and solitary life as the most proper to establish solid virtue in his soul ; and spoke to him in so moving and affecting a manner, that the holy seed im-

mediately sunk so deep into his heart as to already begin
to produce its fruit. The first thing he afterwards did,
was to retire to a solitary place, where there was a church
of the martyrs, and there, prostrate upon the ground with
the utmost fervour of soul, he besought him who desires
that all men should be saved, to vouchsafe to direct him
in the way of perfect piety, in order to secure his eternal
salvation. Having continued a long time in prayer, he
fell into a profound sleep, in which he had the following
vision. He seemed to himself, as he related to Theodoret, to be digging the ground, in order to lay the foundation of a building, and that he heard a voice which bid
him *dig still deeper.* He did so, and then would have
rested himself, but the voice a second time bid him *go
deeper still.* And the same thing having been repeated
four times, one after another, at length it was said to him
that is deep enough, and that he had now nothing more
to do but to build.

Arising from the ground, he went directly to a neighbouring monastery, which was governed by a holy abbot
named Timothy. Here he prostrated himself before the
gate, employing three whole days and nights in fasting
and prayer, without ever being taken notice of. At
length the abbot coming out, he cast himself at his feet,
and besought him with many tears to take pity on a poor
soul in danger of perishing, who was desirous to learn
how to serve God. The abbot taking him by the hand,
encouraged him, led him into the monastery, and recommended to the brethren to teach him the rule of the house,
which he, being then only thirteen years old, quickly
learnt, and practised with such perfection as to surpass
all the rest in humility, as well as in the exercises of fasting and penance. Here also, in four months, he learnt
the whole psalter by heart, and took great delight in meditating on, and feeding his soul with these heavenly hymns.
In this monastery he remained two years, exhibiting a
perfect pattern of a consummate virtue and piety in so

tender an age. In the mean time his parents sought after him, and bewailed him as lost, whilst he, with greater reason, rejoiced at having now happily found both himself and his God.

For his greater improvement in the silence of the saints, he went from this religious house to another monastery, founded at a place called Teleda, near Antioch, by the disciples of the Saints Ammian and Eusebius, and governed at this time by the abbot Heliodòrus, where he remained for about nine or ten years. There were in this monastery about eighty monks, but Simon excelled them all in the exercises of a religious life; for, whereas all the rest were accustomed to eat once a day, or at least once in two days, he fasted the whole week with such rigour as to eat nothing, except only one meal on the Lord's day. Here, having procured a rope or cord, made of the leaves of palm-trees, so hard and rough that it could scarcely be even handled, he privately girt himself with it beneath his habit, next to his skin, so tightly, that it forced its way into the flesh, till it was almost covered, and the flesh itself became perfectly corrupted with it. He concealed what he suffered on this occasion with as much care as possible, till the religious at length found out how the case stood with him, and the abbot insisted upon his parting with the cord, which was with much difficulty, and, not without putting him to great tortures, disengaged from the flesh.

After the wound occasioned by the cord was cured, the abbot dismissed him from the monastery, fearing lest any of the other religious might suffer prejudice, by aiming at an imitation of his extraordinary austerities. Simon, on this occasion, retiring into a more remote and lonesome part of the mountain, found there a dry well, into which he went down and there sung the praises of God. Here he remained for several days without either eating or drinking, till Heliodorus, repenting that he sent the Saint away in that manner, desired two of the brethren to seek after him, and bring him back again. These by the direction of some shepherds, who had heard him singing, found him out in his well, and with the help of a rope brought him up, and conducted him back to the monastery, where he continued for a short time, and then betook himself to an abandoned hut near a village called Telanissus, situated at the foot of that mountain on the top of which he afterwards finished his course.

In this hut he lived shut up during three years; and here our Lord first inspired him with a desire of fasting the forty days of lent, without taking any manner of corporal nourishment during the whole time. Upon this he desired Bassus, who was the ecclesiastical superior in that district, to wall up the door of his cell for that lent, and leave him quite to himself without any thing for his food. Bassus remonstrated to him, that this would be an undertaking beyond the strength of man, and that to destroy himself, which would be the inevitable consequence of such a fast, could be no act of virtue, but, on the contrary, a grievous crime. Leave with me then, father, said the Saint, ten loaves of bread and a pitcher of water, that I may make use of them in case I find it necessary. Bassus accordingly furnished the loaves and the water, and then stopping up the door, departed, and did not return till the forty days were ended. As soon as Easter was come he hastened to visit the servant of God, carrying with him the blessed sacrament; but behold, after he had removed the stones and opened the door, he found the Saint lying extended on the floor like one dead, without speech or motion, with the ten loaves and the water quite untouched. However, as he found life still remaining in him, he dipped a sponge in the water with which he moistened his mouth, and then gave him the holy communion. With this heavenly food he was again raised up, and further enabled to recover his strength, by taking in a little nourishment from the juice of herbs and pulse. This fast of forty days during lent, without either eating or drinking any thing whatever, from this time foward, he constantly observed every year throughout the remainder of his life, which time and custom had at length made easy to him. For at the beginning, after passing the first part of lent, standing and praising God, he was obliged, as he grew weaker, to sit down, and in this posture to perform the divine office, till towards the latter end his weakness forced him to lie down stretched out at full length, as one half dead, and on this account, during the first years of his living and standing upon the pillar, he was obliged, for the latter part of his forty days fast, to support himself by the help of a post fastened to his pillar for this purpose, to which he caused himself to be tied as he became weaker. But for many years before his death God had strengthened him so far as not to stand in need of any help, but pass the whole time of lent with all the cheerfulness imaginable, without any nourishment or human support whatsoever.

From his hut near Telanissus, the Saint went up to the top of the neighhouring mountain, and there made for himself an inclosure of stones, without any covering, in which he remained for some years, taking no other nourishment but boiled lentiles and water, and by the means of a chain, one end of which he fastened to his right leg, and the other to a great stone, he confined himself to such narrow limits as not to be able to go beyond the length of his chain. But if he was chained in body, his soul remained at liberty, and was continually flying up towards God, by mental prayer and contemplation. This chain, upon the remonstrances of Melecius, a Chorepiscopus under the patriarch of Antioch, he suffered to be taken away. At which time, as Theodoret learnt from Melecius himself, after the smith had filed off the iron, when they came to take away the leather which the Saint had put next to his skin, to hinder the chain from entering into his flesh, as the cord had done before, they found in it about twenty large puneezes, or bugs, which this prelate thought worthy of particular notice, to shew the wonderful patience of the Saint, who had quietly suffered for so long a time the troublesome bites of these insects, when he might with so much ease have rid himself of them at once by destroying them.

And now the reputation of Simon's sanctity being spread far and near, great multitudes began to resort to him on account of the many miraculous graces of every kind that were obtained through the efficacy of his prayers and benedictions, struggling with each other who should first come near him and touch his garments, believing that those coarse skins wherewith he was clad, would impart to them a blessing. This became so troublesome and insupportable to the Saint, as to first suggest to him the thought of living upon a pillar, in order to be out of the reach of the crowd ; to which he was no doubt instigated by a particular inspiration from God, who designed, by the means of this extraordinary manner of living, to draw great numbers of infidels to the faith, and of Christians to a virtuous and penitential life.

He began this new way of life, which was never before attempted by any other, about the year of Christ 423, and continued it till his death, which happened about seven and thirty years afterwards. The pillar which he caused to be made at first was but six cubits, that is three yards high, which he afterwards exchanged for one of twelve cubits, and again, for one of twenty-two cubits ; but that on which he finished his course was thirty-six cubits, that is eighteen yards in height. Its diameter, as we learn from Evagrius, was at the most but two cubits, or one yard ; so that he could not, if he would, lie down upon it at his length. In the mean time he had no covering or shelter to defend himself either from the rigour of the winter, the heats of the summer, the violence of the rain or wind, or from other injuries of the air. His ordinary posture was standing night and day, without any other support but the strength of faith and divine grace.

In his prayer he very frequently bowed himself down to adore God, and that in so profound a manner as to bring his forehead almost to his toes.   His rigorous fasts, for he never eat but once a week, and then next to nothing, reduced his body to so low a condition as to make it easy to him.   These adorations he repeated so frequently, that we learn from Theodoret, that whilst this holy prelate was himself present, one of his attendants counted them to the number of 1244.   He often remained for a considerable space of time in prayer, bowed down in this manner with his forehead upon the pillar and this, it is probable, might also be the posture in which he slept; for certain it is, that he sometimes slept, though fame had published that he lived without either sleeping or eating.   Be this as it may, he certainly slept but very little; for, as he generally passed the greatest part of the night in prayer, so he did the best part of the day, even till the ninth hour, viz. three in the afternoon, when he made his exhortations to the people.   But on the eves, or vigils of the festivals, he not only passed the whole night in prayer, but stood all the time on his feet, with his hands stretched forth and extended towards heaven.

The other holy inhabitants of the oriental deserts hearing of the new and extraordinary manner of life which the Saint had undertaken, having consulted together, sent a deputation to him, as we learn from the historian Evagrius, lib. 1. chap. 13, to ask him the reason of his leading so unheard of a course of life, or of leaving the common road which had been beaten by all the Saints and the holy fathers who were gone before him; and to order him to come down immediately from his pillar: giving, nevertheless, instructions to their deputy, that if Simon should shew himself ready to obey, he should suffer him to remain thereon, and encourage him to proceed in his undertaking, as shewing by his ready obedience that what he did was not from caprice, but by divine inspiration; but that if he refused to obey, he should oblige him to come down by force. The deputy had no sooner delivered his commission, than the Saint, without making the least reply or demur, presently disposed himself to obey, and to come down. Whereupon the deputy told him to continue where he was, for his undertaking was from God.

This the Almighty himself sufficiently manifested by the many miraculous gifts and graces he bestowed upon him, of which there were in his life-time millions of witnesses, as there was an incredible multitude from all parts of the world continually assembled to behold this wonder of the world, to hear his divine instructions, and seek remedies through him for all their evils. " For you shall not only see there," says Theodoret, " the inhabitants of our province, Syria, but also the Ishmaelites, Saracens of Arabia, Persians, Armenians, Iberians, Ethiopians, and other nations which are still more remote. There came also people to him from the farthest part of the west, viz. from Spain, Britain, Gaul, and other neighboring provinces ; and as to Italy, it is needless to say any thing, since we are assured that his name is so illustrious in Rome, that they even set up little pictures of him in their shops and porches for a protection and defence." So far Theodoret writing, whilst the Saint was yet living, the things of which he himself had been witness. He also gives several instances of the spirit of prophesy which he had experienced in this Saint, and of great and evident miracles wrought before his own eyes, and adds, that great numbers of infidels, by occasion of this Saint, were daily brought over to the faith of Christ. " One," says he, " may see the Iberians, Armenians, and Persians coming to receive baptism. And as to the Saracens, they come to him in large companies of two or three hundreds, or even of a thousand at a time, abjuring, with a loud voice, their false religion. treading their idols under their feet, in the presence of this bright light of Christianity, embracing the divine mysteries of our holy faith, and re-

16

ceiving from the sacred mouth of this man of God the
rules of life which they were to follow for the time to
come. "I myself," says Theodoret, "have been witness
of all this."

As to the rest, the same learned and holy prelate gives
an ample testimony to the unparalleled modesty and humility of this great servant of God, and of his wonderful
meekness and affability to persons of all conditions, how
poor or mean soever they were according to the world.
But nothing was so admirable in him as that invincible
patience, constancy, courage, and alacrity wherewith he
underwent, for so long a series of years, the voluntary
austerities of so severe and rigid a course of penance,
which for a greater part of the time was rendered still
more difficult and insupportable by a dreadful ulcer in
his left foot, which he had contracted by his continual
standing, and which sent forth corrupted blood and ver-
min. Nevertheless, with all his fasting, watching, prayer,
and other austerities, he ceased not to labour daily for
the salvation of the souls of his neighbours, by delivering to them from his pillar twice a day excellent exhortations to take off their hearts from this wretched earth
—to set always before their eyes that everlasting kingdom which we hope for hereafter—to tremble at the
threats of eternal torments—to despise all that passes with
time, and ever to aspire after the good things of the Lord,
in the land of the living. He was also ever ready to
give ghostly counsel to all who came; to hearken to their
demands, cure their diseases, accommodate their differ-
ences, &c.; and not only to attend to the private necessities of particulars, but much more to every occasion by
which he might promote the common good of the church;
dictating sometimes letters, to this end, to prelates, to
governors, and even to the emperor himself. Thus he
usually employed his time from the third hour after mid-
day till the sunset, and then he gave his benediction to
the people, which they received with great reverence,

and thus bid adieu to men to converse with his God alone.

At length the time being come in which God had decreed to crown the patience and labours of his servant with eternal glory, upon a Friday, anno Christi, 400, having bowed down, according to his custom in prayer, he gave up his happy soul into the hands of him whom he had so constantly and so faithfully served. His body, after his death, remained in the same posture from Friday till Sunday in the afternoon, no one in the mean time knowing that he was dead; because it was no unusual thing for the Saint to pass whole days in prayer, so as to omit his ordinary times of speaking to the people. But on Sunday in the afternoon, his disciple Antonius going up the pillar by a ladder, found that he was dead, and immediately gave private notice of it to the patriarch of Antioch, and to the governor of the province, in order to prevent any tumult that might be raised by the people contending about his body. The patriarch Martyrius, accompanied with six other bishops, and escorted by the governor with 6000 soldiers, came without delay, and taking the body of the Saint down from the pillar, carried it away with great solemnity to Antioch, where it was interred. God was pleased to work many great miracles by his intercession, as well at his monument in that city, as at his pillar where he lived and died. His name is recorded in the Roman Martyrology on the fifth of January.

There were diver other saints of the name of Simon, who are also celebrated in church history. Amongst the rest *St. Simon the ancient,* whose life is also given by Theodoret in his Philotheus, of whom he relates that he had the very lions of the desert at his beck. *St. Simon Stylites the younger*, who also passed his life upon a pillar, and is recorded in the Roman Martyrology, September the third; St. Simon, surnamed Salus, whose name is registered in the same Martyrology, July the first, with the following eulogium: " *At Emesa, St. Simon, confessor, surnamed Salus, who became a fool for Christ; but his profound wisdom God declared by great miracles.*"

ST. EUTHYMIUS.

From his Life, by Cyrillus, a faithful cotemporary writer.

EUTHYMIUS, surnamed *the great* was born at Melitene in the lesser Armenia, of noble and virtuous parents, anno 377. He was a child of prayer, his parents having obtained him of God after a long barrenness, by the intercession of St. Polyceutus, the martyr; and having dedicated him to God from his mother's womb, at the age of three years he was put in the hands of the holy bishop Otteus, and from that time was brought up like another Samuel, in the temple of God, in the exercises of an early piety, and in the study of the holy scriptures, on which he constantly meditated, even in those leisure hours which others of his age spend in their diversions. He was ordained lector when yet a boy, and gradually promoted to the higher orders, giving great edification through them all, till he was thought worthy of the priestly function, and then had the conduct, by commission, from the bishop, of all the monasteries of the diocese of Melitene. In the mean time it was his custom to retire as often as he could, from all other business to attend to God and himself in solitude and silence, to which he had a great inclination from his childhood, to spend a great part of his time in prayer in the churches of the martyrs, and to make an annual retreat alone by himself during the whole time of lent, in a desert mountain, at some distance from the city. His love for solitude and retirement still increasing upon him, at length determined him to withdraw himself entirely from his own country, his friends, and acquaintance, and to go into the Holy Land; where, after visiting and reverencing the places consecrated by the mysteries of our redemption, he chose for his abode a solitary place, about six miles from Jerusalem, called Pharan, in the neighborhood of a *Laura*, or residence of divers religious men, living in separate cells at some distance from each other, but meeting for their devotions in the same church, as the hermits of Camalduli do at present.

This solitude was quite congenial with his inclinations to retirement and silence, and therefore he made himself a cell here, employing his hands in making mats, or in other manual labours, that he might live without being burthensome to any one, and be enabled to relieve such as were in want, having his heart entirely fixed on God, and making it his whole study to please him. Here divine providence brought him acquainted with a holy solitary, named Theoctistus, who had his cell not far off, and who followed the same manner of life; and the likeness of their dispositions united them so closely together in the bands of a most perfect friendship and charity, that they seemed to be animated with one and the same heart and soul. Amongst other exercises of piety, these two servants of God never failed to make every year a spiritual retreat, which they began after the Epiphany, and continued till Palm-Sunday. At this time they quitted their cells and retired into the wilderness of Cutila, where being wholly separated from all conversation with mortals, they spent their whole time with God in prayer and contemplation till Palm-Sunday, when they returned home again, laden with the spiritual riches which they had acquired in their retreat, to offer them up to our Lord Jesus Christ, at the festival of his passion and resurrection.

Euthymius had practised this for some years, when he and Theoctistus, going according to their custom into the wilderness, were conducted by providence to the

16*

banks of a rapid torrent, where they discovered a large cavern of very difficult access, which they embraced as a place assigned by heaven for their happiness. Here they lived for some time, quite secluded from all human society, having no other food whereon to subsist but the wild herbs of the dersert. But as the Almighty designed to bring about the salvation of many souls by the means of these his servants, he did not suffer the place of their abode to remain long a secret. They were at first discovered by certain shepherds, who published to the neighbouring village their place of residence and manner of life. This discovery brought about visits from the inhabitants, who cheerfully furnished them with necessaries for their temporal life, and in return received from them wholesome instructions and exhortations, in order to their eternal life.

Shortly after the monks of Pharan also came to visit them, when the sanctity of their discourse and manner of life moved two of them, Marinus and Lucas, who were afterwards great Saints, and by degrees many others from other places, to put themselves under their direction, so that after some time they built a monastery in the same place, and converted their cavern into a church. Euthymius committed the direction and superintendency of this monastery to Theoctistus, whilst he himself enjoyed the sweets of his beloved silence and repose, seated with Mary at the feet of our Lord, yet so as often to interrupt his contemplation, by labouring to purify the souls of his brethren from their stains, and, like a skilful physician, to apply proper remedies for the cure of all their evils ; for they came daily to discover their most secret thoughts to him, and to receive the rules and lessons of a spiritual life from his mouth, while Theoctistus for his part did nothing without his advice and concurrence.

He spoke to them all with the affection of a father, and constantly inculcated to them, " That they who by their religious profession had renounced the world, and

the things of the world, should make it their principal
study to exercise themselves in humility and obedience,
and divest themselves of their own will; they should have
always the hour of their death before their eyes—tremble at the apprehension of a miserable eternity, and continually aspire, with the most ardent desires, after the
kingdom of heaven ;—that they should also incessantly
employ themselves in manual labours, more especially
when of an age in which the passions of youth stand in
need of being kept under, for in that case the body must
be brought down by labour, that it may be obliged to
submit to the spirit; and that they should ever remember
both the example and the doctrine of St. Paul, who says,
1 Thess. iii. 10. *If any man will not work, neither let
him eat,* &c. He also strenuously recommended silence,
particularly in church and at meals, and could never endure to see any of the young religious, by a motion of their
own will, affect to appear more austere than the rest in
fasting, being desirous that, according to the precept of
the Gospel, they should rather hide their good works than
make them known. He preferred that kind of abstinence,
as the most commendable, which at every meal, and
upon every occasion, restrains the appetite from taking
its fill, and always retrenches, without ostentation, some
part of what it craves. He added; that they should always be upon their guard to resist every irregular desire ;
—that they should carry their arms always about with
them to defend themselves against their invisible enemies,
and meditate day and night upon the law of God.

Whilst Euthymius was in this monastery, Aspebet, governor of a canton of Saracens, brought his son Terebon,
who had quite lost the use of one half of his body by a dead
palsy, to be cured by the Saint. The religious seeing a
multitude of these barbarians coming towards their monastery were all in a fright; but Theoctistus, as Euthymius was then employed in his spiritual exercises, encouraged them; and going forth to meet the band, he asked

them what they wanted? Aspebet answered, we want to see Euthymius. He is in his retirement, said Theoctistus, and will neither see nor speak to any one till Saturday. Then Aspebet showed him his son, whose whole right side was withered in such a manner as to appear quite dead, and made a sign to the youth to tell him his case. " The boy said he had been struck with this disorder in Persia, where his father then resided in the service of king Isdegerdes; that in order to his cure they had not only employed all the natural remedies of physic, but also the secrets of magic, to no effect; and that since he came with his father into Arabia, they had again tried new experiments upon him, but all to no purpose. Wherefore finding that there was no succour to be had from man, he had turned his thoughts towards the great God that made man, and prayed to him one night with great fervour, to restore him to health, promising in that case, that he would dedicate himself to his service, and become a Christian. That after this prayer he had fallen asleep and seen, in a dream, a venerable monk, who said his name was Euthymius; that he lived upon the bank of the torrent in the wilderness, near the road that leads to Jericho, at about ten miles distance from Jerusalem: and that if he desired to be cured, and was disposed to fulfil his promise, he should come to him, and that God would restore him again to his health.

Theoctistus having heard this, went in and related the whole to Euthymius, and both of them concluding that the visions must certainly have come from God, the Saint interrupted his retreat upon this occasion, and going out prayed over the young man, and made the sign of the cross upon him, at which he was in an instant perfectly cured, to the great astonishment of the multitude of barbarians present, who were all converted upon the spot, and after proper instructions received baptism. Aspebet took the name of Peter, and made such progress in christian piety, as to be afterwards ordained bishop of the

Saracens, and Maris his brother-in-law, quitted the world entirely to become a disciple of St. Euthymius.

The fame of this great miracle being spread throughout the country, brought such numbers from all parts to visit the Saint, and seek the cure of their maladies, which they usually obtained by his prayers, that partly to avoid the danger of vain-glory, and partly to enjoy his beloved solitude with more freedom, taking with him a holy man whose name was Domitian, he withdrew himself privately from his monastery into the desert of Ruban, that lies more to the south, near the lake of Sodom. Here for some time he fixed his abode in a high mountain, on the top which he discovered a well, and some ancient ruins, with which he built a chapel and an altar, living the whole time on the wild herbs he found there. From hence he went to the desert of Ziph, where David formerly had concealed himself when the was persecuted by Saul, the recollection of which pleased him much; but it was rot long before the inhabitants of a neighbouring town, called Auistobulias, found him out, by means of a young man possessed by an evil spirit, who had frequently the name of Euthymius in his mouth, and was wonderfully delivered as soon as he was brought within sight of the Saint. This miracle brought him many disciples, for whom the people of the neighbourhood built a monastery, which the Saint for some time directed in the ways of religious perfection. But his love of solitude induced him to quit this monastery also, where he found himself much importuned and distracted by visitors from all parts, and to seek out with his companion Domitian a place more agreeable to his inclination for retirement, which he at length met with in a cavern not far distant from his former monastery. Theoctistus, whom he had left superior there, with all the rest of the brethren, besought him to return to them again: but the most they could obtain of him was, that he would visit them every Sunday, and be present at their assemblies.

Aspebet, now named Peter, hearing where the Saint was, introduced a great number of the Saracens to him who were desirous of becoming christians, whom Euthymius instructed and baptized. These new converts being desirous of remaining under his direction, he appointed them a place at a small distance for the building themselves a church and other dwellings, where he often visited them to instruct them in the way of eternal life, till finding them sufficiently grounded in christian piety, he procured them a priest and some deacons for the care of their church, and the administration of the sacraments. But as by the daily arival of many more, the number of his converts became very considerable, he proposed to Juvenal, the patriarch of Jerusalem, to give them also a bishop, who might take charge of all the Saracens of Palestine. The patriarch readly complied with the Saint's proposition, and ordained Aspebet, or Peter, to this function, by whose means God daily added others to his church.

Hitherto Euthymius, through his love of solitude, had recommended all such as resorted to him in order to embrace a religious life to the monastery of Theoctistus, till he was admonished in a vision to build a *laura* and church for the recepttion of such desired to put themselves under his direction, which was soon filled with a multitude of religious souls. The number of the monks, joined to the barrenness of the place, made it difficult to procure sufficient provisions in that wilderness; but the providence of God never forsook his servants whose whole care was to please him. It happened one day, that four hundred Armenians, in returning from Jerusalem toward the Jordan, missed their way, and came down to the laura of Euthymius. The Saint seeing them, immediately gave orders that they should be hospitably entertained. Domitian represented to him, that the community was reduced to so great straits that they had not bread enough for the brethren, not even for one meal. The Saint full of confidence in God, bid him go to the bakehouse, and see what he should find there. He obeyed, and found the room covered with bread and other provisions in such abundance that he could hardly thrust the door open.

God also favoured his servant with the gifts of prophesy, of which our author mentions several remarkable instances. As to the manner of life which he here followed, he assures us, from the testimony of those that were the best acquainted with him, that he was never seen to eat but on Saturdays or Sundays—that he never wilfully broke silence nor opened his lips but when necessity obliged him to speak,—that he never laid himself down to repose, but slept sitting ; and adds, that he was a close imitator of the great St. Arsenius, and was highly delighted with hearing from the religious who came from Egypt the particulars of his life and conversation. He had always these words of Arsenius present in his mind ; *Arsenius, Arsenius, on what account didst thou leave the world?* and strive to copy out in his own practice all the great examples that Saint had given of humility—recollection—poverty of spirit—love of silence and solitude —perpetual compunction of heart—profusion of tears in the sight of God—and continual watching, fasting and prayer.

There happened in those days so great a drought in Palestine, that it seemed, according to the expression of the scripture, as if the heavens were of brass, and the earth of iron. The cisterns and receptacles which they had made for water were filled with nothing but dust, and the whole country was reduced to the utmost extremity for want of rain. As the evil increased daily, an infinite multitude of the people of the towns and villages round about, carrying crosses in their hands, and singing *Kyrie eleison*, to implore the divine mercy, came to the Saint on the very day when he was going out, according to his custom, to make his retreat in the wilderness, as a preparation for Easter. The sight of their distress moved him to compassion, and he spoke to them as follows.

" My children, as for my part, I am but a wretched sinner, and stand more in need than any other of the mercy of God, especially at this time in which we see his wrath thus enkindled against sinners, and therefore I am not so bold as to dare to lift up my eyes to him, as I know that he sends these afflictions when he pleases ; and that, as no one can shut when he is pleased to open, so no one can open when he is pleased to shut. Our sins have separated us from him——we have disfigured his image——we have defiled his temple——we have suffered ourselves to be carried away by our passions ;——envy and avarice reign amongst us, and our hatred against each other renders us hateful to him : but as he is the fountain of all goodness, and as his mercy knows no bounds, let us all prostrate ourselves before his face, and pray to him from the very bottom of our hearts, and I make no doubt but that he will forgive us, and give us a proof of his fatherly love by the seasonable aid he will send us ; for as David says, *The Lord is near to all them that call upon him.*" After he had thus spoken to the people, all cried out, begging that he would pray for them ; whereupon, after exhorting them to join in prayer to the Lord with the greatest fervour of which they were capable, he retired with his religious into there oratory, and lying prostrate on the ground with many tears implored the divine mercy; when behold a sudden wind arose, the heavens were obscured by thick clouds, and immediately such an abundance of rain came pouring down as quite soaked the whole earth which was followed by the most fruitful year that had ever been known in Palestine in the memory of man.

The Saint had such an extraordinary zeal for the maintenance of the purity of the catholic faith, that he, who was otherwise the meekest of men, could not endure the obstinate abettors of condemned errors. In his days a wicked heresy was broached by Eutyches, a monk of Constantinople, who denied the distinction of the divine and human nature in Christ. Though his impious doctrine was condemned by the Council of Chalcedon, still there were not wanting many children of iniquity, who instead of submitting to this great authority, spread abroad such infamous slanders against that council, and misrepresentations of the Catholic doctrine, as alienated the minds of many from the faith; the principal of whom was Theodosius, a monk of Palestine, who under a religious habit covered a diabolical spirit, and by his wicked insinuations and downright calumnies, prejudiced the mind of the empress Eudocia, who was at that time in Palestine, against the council, and by the means of her interest, and the great liberalities she exercised towards the religious, gained the greatest part of them over to the Eutychian faction, the disciples of St. Euthymius excepted. Not content with this, having intruded himself into the partriarchal see of Jerusalem, he declared open war against all such as opposed themselves to his impiety, banished the orthodox bishops from their sees, and even imbrued his hands in the blood of some of them. In the mean time Euthymius opposed himself as a wall for the house of Israel, and constantly refused to have any manner of communication with this false patriarch; but as he was continually plying him with messages, in order to bring him over to his side, by reason of the neighbourhood of the laura of the Saint to the city of Jerusalem, he assembled his disciples, and having powerfully exhorted them to constancy in the catholic faith, he withdrew into the desert of Ruban, where he remained till the usurper was obliged to quit Jerusalem, and the patriarch Juvenal was restored to his see.

In the mean time he brought back to the Church an excellent anchoret, whose name was Gerasimus, who had been also imposed upon, with many others, and drawn in to be an abbettor of the impious Theodosius, till hearing of the eminent sanctity of Euthymius, he went to confer with him in the wilderness of Ruban, and by his heavenly discourses was fully reclaimed from his error,

17

and conceived a deep and bitter regret at having suffered himself to be deceived, for which he did severe penance. His exanple was followed by four other anchorets, who, in like manner, renounced the communion of Theodosius. Gerasimus afterwards built a laura and a monastery near the Jordan, where he trained up many souls in great perfection, and closed a life of extraordinary sanctity by so happy a death as to have his name enrolled amongst the saints. See the Roman Martyrology, March the fifth.

The empress Eudocia, after, having for a long time resisted the solicitations of her nearest relations, began at length to open her eyes to the bright rays of the catholic truth, and in order to her instruction therein she sent to St. Simon Stylites, as one to whom God imparted extraordinary lights to direct souls in the way of salvation, and opened to him, by her messenger, the bishop Anastasius, the whole state of her interior. The Saint exhorted her to disengage herself effectually from the nets of Satan in which her soul had been entangled by the means of the impious Theodosius, and for this purpose desired she would address herself to St. Euthymius, and to receive from his mouth the pure words of life. Having complied with the advice of the Saint, and being reconciled to the Catholic Church, her example was followed by great numbers both of the religious and laity. This princess, after having built a great many churches, monasteries, and hospitals, conceived a design of extending her beneficence also to the *laura* of St. Euthymius, which the Saint had founded in great poverty; but before she had declared her mind to any one living, Euthymius, who by a divine light often discovered the secrets of hearts, told her, "Daughter, your departure out of this world is near at hand; wherefore, instead of busying yourself with all these cares, attend to your own interior, and think of preparing yourself for your journey hence, rather than of settling revenues upon us; we want nothing else of you, but that you would remember us in your prayers." The empress followed his advice, and some months after made a happy end.

Amongst other favours which our Lord did to his servant Euthymius, our author relates, from the testimony of the anchoret Cyriacus, who learnt it from two eye-witnesses, that one day whilst the Saint was saying mass, a bright fire was seen to come down upon his head, which encompassed both him and his disciple Domitian, and remained from the *Sanctus* till after the communion. He was also often favoured with the vision of angels at the time of his offering the holy sacrifice; and when he distributed the holy communion, he saw in spirit the different dispositions of the communicants; perceiving how the sacred host cast rays of light upon some, and darkness upon others, who, by being unworthy, received it to their own condemnation. The Saint was so affected with this vision, as to be ever after perpetually inculcating to his religious, the necessity of keeping their conscience always pure, that they may worthily approach to the divine mysteries: that *holy things were for holy persons:* and therefore when any of them found their conscience charged with the guilt, either of hatred, or the desire of revenge, upon receiving an injury; or of envy, or of wrath, or of pride, or of speaking evil of their neighbour, or of entertaining loose thoughts or criminal desires, or of any other vice, they should by no means present themselves at the divine table, till they had in a proper manner, expiated their sins by penance.

And now the man of God, after having passed about sixty-seven years in the deserts of Palestine, which by this time he had peopled with a multitude of Saints, was given to understand, by divine revelation, that the time of laying down his earthly tabernacle was near at hand. It was his custom, after the Epiphany, to begin his annual retreat, and to withdraw himself into the remoter parts of the wilderness, where he continued his spiritual exercises till Holy Week. Wherefore, his disciples Elias and Martyrius (both of them afterwards, according to his prediction, patriarchs of Jerusalem), who were used to accompany him on this occasion, came on the octave of that festival to ask him, if they were not to set out with him on the day following? The Saint replied, that he would spend that week with them at home in the *laura*, but that on Saturday at midnight he would leave them. He passed the vigil of the feast of St. Antony, Jan. 17, with them in prayer, and after the morning lauds, told them this was the last vigil he should keep with them. Then having ordered all his religious to be assembled, delivered to them an excellent discourse, telling them that his hour was now at hand, and conjuring them, if they had any regard or affection for him, to show it, by faithfully and constantly practising the lessons he had taught them. In particular he recommended to them *charity* and *humility* as the two principal ingredients of christian perfection, telling them, that if all Christians were bound to exercise themselves in these virtues, much more they who by their religious profession had in a particular manner consecrated themselves to Jesus Christ, to the end, that being freed from all secular cares and affections, they might have no other solicitude but to please him. "Labour then," said he, "my brethren, with all your might to keep both your bodies and minds ever chaste;—continue all of you together to praise and glorify God;—practise with all possible diligence the rule he has given us,—do all in your power to comfort the afflicted, and to fortify by your exhortations and instructions such amongst the brethren as labour under temptations, that they may not fall a pray to the enemy. Let your gate be always open to hospitality;—divide the little you have with the poor and indigent, and the divine bounty will not fail to furnish you with all that shall be needful for yourselves."

After having spoken to this effect, he asked them whom they desired to have for their superior after his death? They all, with one voice, desired it might be Domitian.

" That cannot be," said the Saint, " for he shall not survive me above seven days." Whereupon they made choice of Elias, to whom the Saint earnestly recommended the care of his flock. After this they retired, and Domitian alone remained with the Saint, who, after three days, departed to our Lord at the precise time he had foretold, and his happy soul was seen at that very time by St. Gerasimus carried up by angels towards her heavenly country. His individual companion Domitian, within seven days, took the same happy road, being invited on the eve of his death in a vision in his sleep, by St. Euthymius, to come with him to the regions of light and life everlasting, where they should live together for ever in the kingdom of their Father. St. Euthymius has a place in the Roman Martyrolgy on the twentieth of January.

ST. THEODSIUS THE CENOBIARCH.

From a cotemporary Writer, published by Bollandus.

THEODOSIUS, surnamed the Cenobiarch, from the multitude of religious whom he trained up in a conventual life, was born near Cesarea in Cappadocia, anno 423. Being educated by his parents in the fear of God, he from his tender years gave such proofs of virtue and piety as to be ordained a lector to read the holy scriptures to the faithful in the church. What he read to others penetrated and made a deep impression on his own heart. The words of God to Abraham, Gen. xii. *Go forth out of thy country, and from thy kindred, and out of thy father's house*, &c. affected him as much as if they had been addressed to himself; as also that promise of our Lord in the Gospel of conferring everlasting life on those who should quit all things for love of him. By frequently

17*

meditating on these and such like passages of holy writ, he was at length determined to follow the call of God, and forsake every thing in this world, that he might more securely find the kingdom of heaven.

In consequence of this resolution he set out to go and visit the holy places at Jerusalem, taking Antioch in his way, in the neighbourhood of which St. Simon Stylites was then living upon his pillar. Theodosius went to see the Saint, being desirous to reccommend himself to his prayers, and receive his benediction. No sooner had he come near the pillar, than Simon cried out, *Welcome Theodosius, servant of God*, and presently desired he would ascend to him by a ladder. After mutual embraces, he foretold to him all that should afterwards befal him, and in particular that he should have the direction of a numerous flock, and should rescue by the aid of divine grace, many souls from the jaws of the infernal wolf. Theodosius being confirmed in his good resolution by his conference with so great a Saint, proceeded in his journey to Jerusalem, where, after reverencing the holy places, he went and placed himself under the direction of Longinus, an eminent servant of God, who dwelt by himself in a small lodge in the tower of David, where partly under him, partly under Marinus and Lucas, disciples of St. Euthymius, he learnt the true science of the saints to such perfection, as to become himself a most excellent master and teacher, both by word and example, of this heavenly discipline.

Some time after he was moved, by divine inspiration, to seek a more retired solitude, where he might lead an anchoretical life. For this purpose, withdrawing himself into the wilderness, he made choice of a cavern, which he found on the side of a mountain, for the place of his habitation during the remainder of the days of his mortality. Here he lived for the space of thirty years in a mortal body, as if he had been an immortal spirit, in the constant exercise of watching, fasting, and prayer, together with such a continual recollection of thought, fervor of spirit, humility of heart, and abundance of tears, as could not fail to draw down the graces and gifts of the spirit of God, in the most abundant manner upon his soul. His only food during this long period of time, was dates or pulse, moistened in cold water, or wild herbs, without any bread whatsoever. He embraced labours with as much ardor as others do their pleasures, and avoided pleasures as much as others do labours. Although he desired nothing so much as to live concealed from the eyes of men, yet it was impossible for him to keep himself so secretly in his cavern, but that the bright light of his extraordinary sanctity should break out and cast its rays both far and near, and invite many to him, who were desirous to place themselves under his conduct, and learn the secrets of religious perfection. It was with difficulty he at first received any one into his company; but his charitable solicitude for the salvation of the souls of his neighbours, prevailed over his love of solitude, and the great success which attended his conduct and direction of souls, proved that it was the holy will of God he should be thus employed.

Although the number of his disciples did not at the beginning exceed six or seven, who all lived with him in his cavern, yet they gradually increased; and as they all made it their business to seek in the first place the kingdom of God with all their power, divine Providence never failed to add over and above the necessaries of this present life. One Easter-eve, when the Saint had now twelve disciples with him in his cavern, it happened that they had nothing whatever to eat: but what gave them most concern was, that they had not even bread for the divine sacrifice. This they represented to their holy superior, who being full of confidence in God, bid them nevertheless prepare the altar for the celebrating mass on Easter-day; when behold, about sun-set Providence sent a man to their cavern with two mules laden with bread and other provisions in such quantity as abundantly sufficed them until Whitsuntide. At another time, when they were reduced to the same extremity, Providence sent them a supply in a manner still more remarkable, which happened thus. As a man was leading his horse with a load of provisions to some other place, when he came into the neighbourhood of the cavern where the servants of God dwelt, he could not, with all his might, force his horse to go forward ;. so that conceiving there must be something supernatural in the case, he gave him liberty of the bridle to go which way he pleased. The horse being then left to himself, immediately, as if he were guided by an invisible hand, went straight up to the cavern, where the master perceiving the distress of this holy community, relieved them very plentifully, and glorified God for having thus wonderfully made him the instrument of his divine goodness, in supplying his servants with food.

But the number of the disciples of the Saint, amongst whom were persons considerable for their worldly birth and fortune, daily increasing, and his cavern being too small to contain them, they with difficulty prevailed upon him to consent to the building a spacious monastery and a church, close by, in the very place appointed to him by heaven, by the remarkable circumstance of the coals in his censor catching fire of themselves. Here he received all that came to him ; and as their number became very considerable, he was afterwards obliged to add several other buildings, as well for the relief of the spiritual as the corporal necessities of the multitude that resorted to him. In no place was hospitality exercised with greater affection, or with more cheerfulness and joy than in this monastery ; for amongst all the virtues of the Saint, his tender compassion and charity for his neighbours, and diligence in relieving all their necessities, seemed to claim the first place. So great was his solicitude for the sick and distressed, that he even built several hospitals and infirmaries about his monastery for their accommodation; of which extensive charity of his servant, God was pleased to testify his approbation more than once in a miraculous manner. At the time of a great famine, when an incredible multitude of people flocked to the monastery upon a Palm-Sunday, and the religious not having wherewith to feed so great a crowd, would have kept the gates shut, the Saint, trusting in God, bid them open the gates and give them all to eat. And though the number was so great as to fill every part of the house, yet by a miracle not unlike that wrought by our Lord in feeding the five thousand in the desert, they all eat and were filled; and there still remained more bread than they had at first. The like miracle happened also another time, upon the feast of the Annunciation of the Blessed Virgin.

As to the disciples of our Saint, the number who put themselves under his conduct was so great, that, according to our author, during the time of his superiority, he buried with his own hands no less than six hundred and ninety-three religious men, whom he had trained up in the way of sanctity; and that his successor, St. Sophronius, did as much for four hundred more, who both in life and death followed the same happy course. He also adds, that many illustrious bishops and abbots were taken out of this monastery; that many others who had been here brought up under our Saint, betook themselves afterwards to an anchoretical life, in which they became eminent for holiness;—that several who had followed the profession of arms quitted the service of Cæsar to enrol themselves amongst the soldiers of Jesus Christ, and to learn his heavenly discipline of Theodosius; that many who enjoyed posts of honour in the world, as well as several who were renowned for their learning, came also to our Saint, to take up, under his direction, the sweet yoke of christian simplicity and humility, and become his scholars in the study of the science of the saints. His conduct towards all who were under his care was ever regulated by so consummate a prudence as to accommodate his directions and prescriptions to the different exigences and dispositions, as well as to the strength of his disciples. Whenever any of them were guilty of a fault, instead of penances, he only used words of admonition, correction, and exhortation, which were animated with such unction as made them penetrate into the very midst of their souls. In these corrections he had the art of associating meekness and affability with a just severity, in so engaging a manner as to make himself at once be both feared and loved. The lessons of all virtues which he gave to others, were enforced by his own practice. His conversation was always extremely edifying and instructive, and his spirit ever attentive to God. Whether alone or in company, or in whatsoever manner he was employed, his temper was ever calm and even, always the same. His chief delight consisted in reading the holy Scriptures, which he made the subject of his perpetual meditation both day and night, even to the day of his death. Although our Saint had not been educated to any degree in secular learning, nor ever studied the rules of human eloquence, yet in the discourses which he delivered to his disciples, he far excelled the greatest orators in the arts of moving and exciting the affections, and inflaming the heart; because his words did not proceed from human wisdom, but from divine grace and the spirit of God. He was always so great an admirer and imitator of St. Basil, that in his words and with his spirit he would often address himself to his monks to the following effect : " I beseech you, my children, by the charity of our Lord Jesus Christ, who delivered himself up to death for our sins, let us, once for all be quite in earnest, as seriously to set about the business of saving our souls. Let us conceive a lively sorrow for having passed our time hitherto so unprofitably; let us now at least begin to fight manfully in the service of God and of his Son Jesus Christ, that we may be made partakers one day in their glory.

Let us shake off this sluggishness and lassitude, which makes us still love to put off from day to day the labouring in good earnest to advance in virtue; for if by suffering ourselves to be deceived by the enemy, we be found void of good works here, we can have no pretension hereafter to the joys of heaven, but shall hereafter lament in vain for having let slip the time and means of working out our salvation, when it shall not be in our power to recover them. The nature of this life, and of that which is to come, are quite opposite; the one is a time of penance, and the other of reward;—the one a time of labour, the other of repose;—the one a time of suffering, and the other of consolation. At present God is infinitely good to those who turn from their evil ways, and are converted to him; but then he shall be a just and inexorable judge, who will call us to a strict account for all our thoughts, words, and actions. Now he is patient, but then he shall be terrible. How long then shall we remain deaf to the voice of Jesus Christ, who invites us to the possession of an eternal inheritance? Shall we never awake out of this long and profound sleep? Shall we not, now at least, renounce our ill-spent life, to embrace evangelical perfection? Ah! why do we not tremble at the thoughts of that dreadful day of the Lord, when he shall receive those whose good works shall entitle them to a place at his right hand, into his kingdom; and shall condemn those who, being void of good works, shall be placed at his left, to eternal fire? We say indeed that we desire to go to heaven; but do we labour in earnest; do we pursue the means of acquiring and securing to ourselves that eternal kingdom? If we neglect to put in practice what our Lord has commanded, it is in vain that we flatter ourselves with the expectation of receiving from him that glorious recompence wherewith he will reward those only who shall persevere to the end in fighting courageously against sin."

So far the Saint in the words of St. Bazil.

St. Theodosius was also inflamed with an extraordinary zeal for maintaining the catholic faith against all condemned heresies; of which he gave signal proofs during the reign of the emperor Anastasius, who was a great abettor of the Eutychian heresy, condemned by the general council of Chalcedon. This prince, in hopes of drawing our Saint over to favour his impious tenets, sent him a very considerable sum of money by the way of an alms, as he pretended, for the relief of the poor, and the comfort of his religious in their sicknesses. The Saint thought it not prudent to offend the emperor, by refusing his charity, though he suspected that an ill design lay concealed under this specious pretence. Not long after Anastasius sent to desire of him a confession of his faith, agreeable to the Eutychian heresy. Theodosius, instead of coming into his measures, declared himself ready to suffer a thousand deaths, rather than betray his conscience, or consent to heresy. The emperor, though chagrined and disappointed, dissembled his resentment, and proceeded at that time no farther: but not long after, he furiously attacked the catholic faith, and raised a violent persecution against its professors. In this distressed state of the church, when the orthodox pastors were either banished from their churches, or intimidated into a criminal silence, which is always advantageous to error, —when the heretics triumphed, and a great part of the people either joined with them, or were in doubt which side to take, the Saint seeing the dreadful danger to which the sheep of Christ lay exposed in the midst of these wolves, fearless of the rage of the emperor, or of the violence of his officers and ministers, went boldly into the great church of Jerusalem, at the time of the divine service, and going up to the tribune from whence the holy Scriptures used to be read to the people, pronounced a loud anathema against all who did not receive and revere, like the four Gospels, the four general councils of Nice, Constantinople, Ephesus, and Chalcedon, in which the and the Incarnation of the Son of God, had been defined and declared against the Arians, Macedonians, Nestorians, and Eutychians. This courageous profession of his faith in so public and solemn a manner, made a wonderful impression on the minds of the people in favour of the catholic religon, and struck all who heard him with such astonishment, that none of his adversaries, as he passed through the crowd to go out of the church, durst so much as open their mouths to speak one word to him, much less presume to stop him. After this he was seized with a long and painful illness, which he bore with extraordinary patience and fortitude; until it pleased his Divine Master to call him to the enjoyment of that reward which he has prepared for all who labor and suffer for his sake.

Theodoret, in his Philotheus, has given us the acts of another saint, named also Theodosius, a native of Antioch, who led a life of wonderful austerity and sanctity in a mountain of Cilicia, ever praying and singing psalms, without ceasing to labor with his hands, and training up many disciples in the same exercises. In order to accommodate the monastery he had built for them, he miraculously caused a never-failing stream of water to flow from the hard rock on which it was erected. So great and general was the esteem in which he was held, even amongst the barbarians and infidels, on account of his sanctity and miracles, that such as were in danger at sea, though at ever so great a distance off from his place of residence, who called upon the God of Theodosius, saw the tempest immediately cease by the invocation of his name. He flourished in the fourth century.

18

ST. SABAS.

From his Life by Cyrillus, a faithful contemporary Writer.

SABAS, or Sabbas, was born at Mutalascus, a small town in the district of Cesarea, in Cappadocia, anno 437. His father, who was an officer in the army, being obliged to go to Alexandria, in Egypt, left his son, who was then but five years old, together with his estate, in the care of an uncle, whose name was Hermias. But the evil treatment Sabas met with from his aunt, the wife of Hermias, obliged him to leave them, and go to another uncle, named Gregory. This produced a violent contest between the two brothers which should have the care of his person and of his estate, which inspired in the nephew, young as he then was, so great a disgust for the world, that resolving to quit it, he retired to a monastery called Flavian, at about three miles distance from Mutalascus, where the abbot received him, though as yet but a child, amongst his religious, and took care to have him well instructed in the knowledge of the holy Scriptures, and of all things necessary to acquit himself worthily of so holy a profession. Here, as he was working in the garden one day, he observed an apple tree laden with fruit, which appeared so very fair and tempting, that he plucked off one of them with a design to eat it; but immediately suspecting it to be a snare of old serpent, who had heretofore driven our first parents out of paradise, by tempting them to eat of the forbidden fruit, and that he throws out no baits so efficacious to ensnare youth as that of pleasure; after reproaching himself with the fault he had committed, he flung down the apple, trod it under foot, and made a resolution never to eat of that kind of fruit as long as he lived. From that day forward he led

a life of the most extraordinary abstinence with respect
to eating and drinking. As to sleep, he slept no longer
than the necessity of nature absolutely required; and excepting the time whilst his hands were lifted up to God
in prayer, they were perpetually employed in some manual labour, for he dreaded nothing more than idleness, on
account of the opportunity it affords the enemy to creep
insensibly into the soul. By this continual application of
all his faculties to attain to perfection, he made such a
progress in the way of virtue, that not one of the religious,
who were to the number of seventy in this community,
equalled him in obedience and humility, or in any of the
exercises of an evangelical life.

His uncles, being at length reconciled together, both
joined in soliciting him to come out of the monastery, and
to settle himself in the world in a married life. But he
resisted all their solicitations, and with the leave of his
superior, being now eighteen years old, went away to
Jerusalem, in order to reverence the holy places, and then
to visit the Saints that inhabited the neighbouring deserts,
that he might acquire still greater proficiency in the true
science of the saints. Here after a short stay in the monastery of St. Pasarion, he went and flung himself at the
feet of the great St. Euthymius, desiring to serve God
under his holy discipline. Euthymius told him he was as
yet too young for the solitary life of the laura, but sent
him to the neighbouring monastery of his friend Theoctistus, with a particular recommendation of him to the abbot,
as of one who was likely to become a most illustrious
saint. In this monastery the young Sabas consecrated
himself entirely to divine love. He spent the day in manual labours, and the night in fervent prayer, and was ever
ready, young and strong as he was, to comfort and assist
the brethren in their respective offices. He brought in
water and wood for the use of the community:—regardless of his own health, he took particular care of the sick,
and was ever the first and last at the divine office, which

he always recited with a most edifying devotion:—in a
word, the religious were so charmed with his obedience
and humility, that they could not, without admiration, behold so great perfection in one of such tender years.

It happened about this time that one of the monks obtained leave of the abbot to go to Alexandria, in order to
dispose of an inheritance that fell to him by the death of
his parents. Sabas, being ordered to accompany him in
this journey, unexpectedly met with his own father and
mother, who lived at Alexandria. Having rejoiced excessively to see him, they endeavoured, by the most pressing
solicitation, to prevail on him to stay with them ; but Sabas, having set his hand to the plough, absolutely refused
to look back, remembering what our Lord had said, that
such as love father or mother more than him, are not
worthy of him. "If they, said he, who, after enrolling
themselves in the service of an earthly king run away
from their colours, are severely punished for their deser-
tion, what punishment then should not I deserve, if after
having engaged myself in the service of the King of
heaven, I should abandon so holy a warfare? Wherefore cease, I beseech you, to persuade me to quit this way
of life, which I find so advantageous to my soul, or else
you will oblige me to consider you no longer as my
parents and friends, but as strangers and enemies."—
They told him that if he would not stay with them, he
would at least accept of a considerable sum of money,
which they would have given him. But this he also
refused, and it was with much difficulty that they prevailed upon him to receive three pieces of silver ; which
as soon as he returned to the monastery he immediately
gave to the abbot, fearing nothing more than the demon
of the love of money.

After the death of the holy abbot Theoctistus, with
the approbation of St. Euthymius, he betook himself to
a cavern belonging to the monastery, where he passed
five days of the week in perfect solitude ; fasting, work-

ing, and praying the whole time. On the Saturday and Sunday he performed his devotions in the monastery, and then returning to his cavern, he carried with him the materials of which he made every week to the number of fifty baskets. And now St. Euthymius, who used to call him *the young old man*, by reason of his extraordinary wisdom, desired to have him nearer himself, and therefore took him along with him, when he entered upon his yearly retreat, on the 14th January, into the desert of Ruban, where he was accustomed to pass the holy time of lent. After they had walked for a long time together over the barren sands of this vast wilderness, where nothing green could grow, nor any water be found, Sabas was so much exhausted with weariness and thirst, that he could hold out no longer, but was obliged to lay himself upon the ground like one half dead. Euthymius pitying his distress, prostrated himself in the presence of God, and cried out from the bottom of his heart: " Thou seest, O my God, the extremity to which this thy young soldier, who fights under thy standard, is now reduced, be pleased therefore to relieve and assist him, by causing water to issue forth out of this dry and thirsty land." Having finished this prayer, and thrust his staff three times into the ground, behold there presently issued forth a spring of clear and excellent water, from the drinking whereof Sabas not only quenched his thirst, but found in himself such vigour, strength, and comfort, as enabled him cheerfully to support all that he had afterwards to suffer in the desert.

After the death of St. Euthymius, Sabas retired into the same wilderness near the river Jordan, which St. Gerasimus at that time illustrated with the rays of his sanctity. Here, according to custom, passing the night on a solitary mountain in prayer, he was directed by a heavenly vision to go and take up his abode in a cavern to the east of the torrent of Siloe, with a promise that God, who takes care of the meanest of his creatures,

18*

would not fail to provide for him. Having immediately
obeyed this ordinance of heaven, he went down from
the mountain, and was led, as it were, by the hand to
the cavern, which lay on the side of a steep hill, of very
difficult access. Here he lived for some time, without
any other food for his subsistence but the herbs that grew
wild about his cave, and being obliged to go six or seven miles for water, which, with the utmost difficulty he
carried up to his lodging by means of a rope, which he
made to hang down for that purpose from his cavern to
the foot of the hill. But divine providence at length
conducted some of the country people to the place, who
ascending by the help of the rope to the cavern, and admiring the sanctity of the servant of God, from that time
forward furnished him with the little provisions he stood
in need of.

After he had dwelt about five years in this solitary
cavern, God inspired him with a desire of exercising his
charity towards his neighbours, by receiving, instructing,
and directing as many as desired to quit the world, and
to put themselves under his guidance in the ways of God
and religious perfection. To these he gave excellent lessons of a spiritual life, and appointed them separated spots of ground for building their cells after the
manner of a laura, which, in process of time, became the
most considerable of any in all Palestine. He built them
also a chapel, wherein, as often as any priest came into
the wilderness, he procured that the divine mysteries
should be celebrated; for as to his own part, his humility made him decline the priestly dignity, of which he
deemed himself altogether unworthy. The first disciples
of the Saint were men of the most eminent virtue, so full
of the Spirit of God, that they lived in the wilderness
like angels in human bodies, continually employed in
singing the praises of their Maker. Their number was
about three score and ten, amongst whom were several
who afterwards became founders and superiors of other

religious communities. Having at the beginning laboured under great inconveniences, especially for want of
water, which they were forced to fetch, as was observed
before, from a spring that was seven miles distant, the
Saint one night in his devotions, earnestly besought the
Lord to remedy this evil, by affording his servants a
source of water nearer home; when behold at the conclusion of his prayer he heard a noise, and looking towards the place, he perceived by the moonlight a wild
ass making a hole in the ground with his foot, and then
bowing down his head, as if it were to drink. The
man of God conceiving by this signal that his prayer was
heard, went to the place, and opening the hole a little
wider, a stream of living water issued forth, which from
that time never ceased to flow through the midst of the
laura, in such a manner, as neither to be swelled in winter nor to be diminished in summer, though almost all
the people of the country resorted thither for water.

And now the number of those who came to place
themselves under his direction increased exceedingly;—
but, alas! they were not all led by the same spirit as their
predecessor; on the contrary, some of them formed a
faction against the holy abbot, and went to Salustius,
who upon the death of Martyrius was lately made patriarch of Jerusalem, to desire he would give them another
superior: for as Sabas was clowhish and simple, they
wanted one who was a priest. The new patriarch, who
was no stranger to the merit of the Saint, instead of regarding his accusers, sent for him and ordained him priest
in their presence, and confirmed him in his charge of abbot and superior; and going with him to the laura consecrated for him a church, and erected an altar in a spacious subterraneous den, which had been shewn to the
man of God by a pillar of fire which reached from heaven to earth. Many others after this resorted to the
Saint to put themselves under his discipline, amongst
whom were several excellent men of the Armenian na-

tion, to whom the man of God made over his own first habitation with the neighboring oratory, in which he directed them to sing the praises of God in their native language. About this time also the father of the Saint having died at Alexandria, his mother Sophia came to visit him, and having by his counsel entirely renounced the world, passed the short time that remained of her life in preparing her soul, by spiritual exercises, for a better, and made a most happy end under his directions. The Saint consecrated a considerable sum of money which she bequeathed him, to the service of God, by building two hospitals ; the one for the entertainment of passengers, the other for the religious of other communities who came to visit his laura.

Our Saint was united in a most holy bond of friendship with the great St. Theodosius, and always joined him in promoting the cause of their common Lord, as well in defending the purity of the catholic faith against all the attacks of heresy, as in propagating religious discipline. Their union was so remarkable, that the people of Jerusalem called them the two apostles; and the patriarch Salustius, at the desire of the religious of his district, put under their care all the monasteries around Jerusalem, in such a manner that Theodosius had the charge of all that lived in convents, from whence he was named the Cenobiarch, and Sabas the charge of all the anchorets and solitaries. But Euthymius was the Saint whose life St. Sabas particularly chose for the model of his own ; after his example he withdrew himself every year into the most remote part of the wilderness, and there passed the whole time of Lent, till Palm-Sunday, in perfect solitude, fasting, and prayer. In one of these excursions he was conducted by divine providence to a steep mountain, on the top of which he found a cavern, and in this cavern a holy anchoret who had lived there for eight and thirty years upon nothing but wild herbs, without either seeing or being seen during all that time by any one. The edi fication he received by the heavenly conversation of this man of God brought Sabas thither again another year to receive his benediction, but he found him dead in the posture of one at his prayers, and interred him in his cavern.

In another of these excursions he came to a hill called Castel, lying at a great distance from all communication with men. This place he pitched upon to erect a monastery, and after the Easter holidays he led thither a colony of his disciples, who found in the neighborhood an old desolate building, which they converted into a church, and afterwards built themselves cells around it. As the first inhabitants of this holy solitude were men of eminent virtue, wholly disengaged from all earthly cares and affections, our Lord was pleased in the beginning to provide for their subsistence in a wonderful manner, by charging Marcian, the superior of the monasteries of Bethlehem, in a vision, to furnish them with all necessaries, which he carefully executed.

In the meantime the malecontents of whom we spoke before were gathering strength, by seducing several others over to their faction, so that no less than forty of the religious entered into a conspiracy against the holy abbot, resolving to use all means in their power to get rid of him. The Saint being apprised of their design chose to withdraw himself quietly from them, rather than proceed to any measures against them which might be inconsistent with that meekness, patience, and humility, which constitute the character of a disciple of Jesus Christ. Wherefore retiring into a desert, not far from the city of Scythopolis, he took up his abode in a cavern near the river of Gadar. Although this cavern happened to be a lion's den, yet the beast finding the Saint there, not only refrained from offering him any violence, but quietly yielded up to him the possession of his dwelling-place. Here the reputation of his sanctity, which could no where lie long concealed, brought many to visit him from the neighboring cities of Scythopolis and Gadara;

amongst whom was a young gentleman named Basil, who by an inspiration of heaven had entirely renounced the world and came to dwell with Sabas in his cavern. Some thieves who had imagined Basil to be rich, and that he had carried off his money with him, came one night in hopes of booty to visit the cavern; but finding nothing, not even the necessaries of life, they were struck with astonishment, and retired, not without deep remorse for the evil they had proposed to commit, and a dread of meeting with some rigorous punishment from the justice of God. This apprehension was greatly increased, when a little after they had left the cavern they saw some lions approaching, whose terrible looks seemed to threaten them with immediate death and destruction. In this extremity they bethought themselves of the sanctity of Sabas, and commanded the lions in the name, and by virtue of the prayers of that venerable servant of God, to be gone; when behold they had no sooner pronounced the name of Sabas, but these furious beasts turned their backs upon them and ran away. This miracle not only wrought the total conversion of the thieves, but being rumored abroad brought such multitudes to visit the Saint as determined him, after having recommended his disciples to God and leaving to them the cell he had lately built, to seek some other solitude, where he might attend to his God with less distraction.

After some time he returned again to his laura, where to his excessive grief he found no amendment in the disposition of the malecontents, since whatsoever he could either say or do to bring them to a right sense of their duty made them rather worse than better. Upon this he retired towards Nicopolis, and fixed his abode for some time under a tree in an open field, till the master of the field, admiring his sanctity, built him a cell, which in a short time was converted into a monastery. In the meantime the malecontents applied to Elias the patriarch of Jerusalem for another superior, pretending that Sabas was devoured by a lion. The patriarch gave no credit to the fable; and not long after Sabas himself coming to Jerusalem to celebrate the feast of the dedication of the Church, he obliged him to return to his laura, with an order to the rebels either to submit to him or depart. They chose the latter, and retired towards the torrent of Theon, and repaired some old cells which they found there, and called this place the *new laura*. But as they were destitute of all things, and no one was willing to assist them, the Saint in his great charity, not only labored to procure them all necessary provisions, but went himself in person to carry them to them; nor did he cease to ply them with benefits, both for their temporal and spiritual well-being, till overcoming evil with good, he at length brought them over to dispositions more suitable to the sanctity of their profession, and established them in regular discipline under a holy superior whom he appointed for them.

It would be endless to descend to all the particulars of the great things which St. Sabas did, during the many years that remained of his life, for the glory of God,—for the sanctification of souls,—and the propagation of the kingdom of Christ,—the spirit of prophesy which he manifested on many occasions,—the great miracles God wrought by him,—his labors for the public good of the Church, and maintaining the purity of faith, as well during the reign of Anastasius, the Eutychian, as during that of his successors Justin and Justinian, since these would suffice to fill a volume, they are therefore omitted as exceeding the bounds of our intended brevity. Wherefore we shall only add, that as he always lived the life of a Saint, so he died the death of a Saint, on the fifth of December, (on which day he is honored by the church) anno 531, at the age of 94; and that after his death many miracles were wrought through his intercession.

ST. JOHN THE SILENT.

From his disciple Cyrillus, the same who wrote the Lives of SS. Euthymius and Sabas.

JOHN, surnamed *Silentiarius*, or the *Silent*, from his great affection to silence, was born in the lesser Armenia, of illustrious and wealthy parents, anno, 453, who being themselves good Christians, gave him a christian education. At the age of eighteen he abandoned the world, and employed that part of the estate which fell to him by the death of his father and mother, in building a church in honor of the blessed Virgin, together with a monastery into which he retired with ten other persons, who like himself were desirous to think of nothing else but the salvation of their souls. Here he led a life of the most perfect purity of soul and body, joined with a most profound humility. The heavenly prudence with which he conducted the religious committed to his charge recommended him first to the priestly character, and shortly after, upon the death of the bishop of Colonia, determined the metropolitan, the archbishop of Sebaste, to consecrate no other than him to fill up this vacancy. In order thereto he sent for John, as if it were upon some other business, and when he came, in spite of all his remonstrances to the contrary, he ordained him bishop. Being then about thirty-eight years of age, he for ten years discharged himself in a most edifying manner, of all the duties of the episcopal ministry, continuing to practise the same religious exercises as he had been accustomed to in his monastery.

Towards the latter end of this time, finding his church and his clergy grievously oppressed by his brother-in-law, the governor of the province, and that all his remonstrances only served to make him still worse, he took a journey to Constantinople, to seek a remedy for these evils. Here having, with the assistance of the patriarch Euphemius, settled the affairs of his diocese in the best manner he could, and following a divine inspiration, having resolved totally to withdraw himself from the world, without acquainting any one with his design, he privately got on board a ship, and went to Jerusalem, where he took up his lodgings in an hospital, to which was annexed a chapel of St. George the Martyr; and during the time he remained there, continued to pray with many tears, that God would direct him to a proper place where he might attend to nothing else but the working out his own salvation. Whilst he was praying one night to this effect, having lifted up his eyes to heaven, he perceived a light in form of a cross coming towards him, and heard a voice that said to him: " If thou desirest to save thy soul, follow this light." He immediately obeyed, and following this heavenly light, he was conducted to the great laura of St. Sabas, where he found one hundred and fifty solitaries, living in extreme want of all temporal things, but rich in the treasures of divine grace.

The holy abbot having received this new comer without knowing who he was, recommended him to the procurator of the community, who employed him for some time in various offices for the service of the other religious, such as fetching them water,—preparing their victuals,—carrying stones for the building which they had at that time in hand,—dressing and carrying the workmen their dinners, at the distance of about a mile from his lodgings,—entertaining such strangers as came,—and, in a word, doing all that any of the monks desired, with such humility, readiness, and cheerfulness as made him both admired and loved by them all. After this St. Sabas appointed him a little cell, in which for the space fo three years, he lived in silence, taking no manner of nourishment during five days of the week, and only coming out to the church on Saturdays and Sundays, where

19

he was always the first and the last, and there sung the psalms of the divine office with such respectful awe, modest gravity, and fervent piety, as edified all who saw him ; and assisted also at the unbloody sacrifice and sacrament of the altar, with such deep compunction and devotion, that he could not refrain from shedding floods of tears during the time of the celebrating those divine mysteries.

After these three years of silence, St. Sabas appointed him to the office of procurator of the laura, to the great advantage of the whole community, God giving his blessing to his servant, and assisting him in all things. The time of exercising this office be ng expired, and the holy abbot seeing him so accomplished in all virtue, took him to Jerusalem, and desired the patriarch St. Elias, the successor of Salustius, and formerly disciple of St. Euthymius, to impose his hands upon him, and to ordain him priest. The servant of God, on this occasion, desired he might be first allowed to speak to the patriarch in private ; and having obtained of him a promise of secrecy, told him, that he had been a bishop, but that the multitude of his sins had determined him to quit his see, and to fly into the desert in order to bewail his offences and obtain the divine mercy ; and in the mean time, as long as he was strong and robust to labour, all he could to assist and comfort those good religious to whom God had associated him. The patriarch was astonished at the hearing of this, and calling for St. Sabas, said to him : " This monk has discovered to me in private some particulars, which will not allow me to ordain him priest. Take him therefore back with you, and let him live in silence, and suffer no one to disturb him." St. Sabas being thus not only disappointed, but also very much concerned, through the apprehension lest some great evil might have been discovered by the patriarch which had prevented him from admitting his disciple to holy orders, betook himself to his prayers, and ceased not to importune our Lord to let him know whether John was indeed, as he had thought, a vessel of sanctification, and worthy of the priestly function or not. At length an angel, after he had spent the whole night in prayer appearing to him, told him, that John was indeed *a vessel of election*, but being already a bishop could not be ordained priest. St. Sabas, who was often favoured with such visions, went immediately to St. John's cell, and embracing him, said, " I find, father, that you have hidden from me the grace you have received from God, but he has been pleased to reveal it to me." " You mortify me exceedingly, said John, by speaking to me thus. I was in hopes this secret would not have been known to any one, but now I perceive I must quit this country.", Sabas desired him to be at rest, and made him a solemn promise that he would keep his episcopal character a secret. Upon which he was content to continue with him ; yet so as to remain close in his cell, where he spent four years more in perfect solitude and silence. When the insolence of the monks drove St. Sabas away from the laura, John would remain there no longer, nor hold any communication with the rebels, but retired to the desert of Ruban, where he found a cavern in which he passed nine years, conversing with God alone, and living upon what wild herbs or roots he could find in the wilderness.

Whilst he dwelt in this solitude one of the religious came to visit him, and staid a short time with him ; but being quickly wearied with so austere a kind of life, and such close retirement, he proposed that they should return together to the laura, in order to celebrate the approaching feast of Easter with the brethren, and not to starve in that barren desert.——The Saint, who could not think of returning to the laura as long as Sabas was absent from thence, exhorted the brother to a confidence in divine providence, which, as it had heretofore fed six hundred thousand men for the space of forty years in the wilderness, could with as much ease abundantly provide for them both. But this exhortation having made no impression on the mind of his companion, he presently took his leave of him and departed. He was scarcely gone when an unknown person came to the cavern of the Saint, driving an ass laden with all sorts of provisions, which he bestowed upon the servant of God; whose faith his divine Majesty was pleased to reward in this wonderful manner: whilst the other, instead of going back to the laura, lost his way in the wilderness; but after wandering about for the space of three days, being now quite exhausted and famished, returned to the Saint, and seeing all the good things that God had sent him, acknowledged his own error, and asked pardon for it.

Whilst St. John dwelt in this desert, the Saracens made an inroad upon the borders of the empire on the side of Palestine, and committed great outrages. On this occasion the Saint was pressed by the monks of the laura to come and take shelter amongst them, where he would be more remote from the danger of the enemy's parties, and protected by the Roman soldiers; but he, who had found by experience how sweet it was to converse alone with his God, chose rather to remain where he was putting his whole trust in him, who has given his angels charge over his servants to guard them in all their ways; and his divine goodness was pleased to shew his approbation of this entire confidence which his servant placed in him, by sending him as our author learnt from the Saint's own mouth, a great lion to be his visible guardian. At the first sight of the beast, the man of God was struck with some fear, but he quickly recovered himself, and found that the creature, instead of meaning him harm, carefully attended him by day and night, and suffered no enemy to approach near his cavern.

At the expiration of the nine years, St. Sabas visited him, and brought him back to the laura, where he lived for many years shut up in his cell, no one, except the holy abbot, knowing all the while of his being a bishop, till God was pleased it should be made known to the whole community, by the means of Atherius, an Asiatic prelate, who having made a pilgrimage of devotion to Jerusalem, was directed from heaven to go and visit our Saint in the laura of St. Sabas, and there acquainted the religious with the treasure they possessed, as well as with all the particulars of this former course of life. When John was now seventy years of age, it pleased God to take St. Sabas to himself. Our Saint was sensibly touched with the loss of his holy father, and the more because, being shut up in his cell, he had not been present at his death. But behold St. Sabas appeared to him in a dream, desiring that he would not be afflicted as his death; for that though they were now separated in body, they were still united in spirit. John desired he would pray to God for him, that he would be pleased to take him also out of this miserable world; but Sabas told him that could not be as yet, because his longer stay in the world was necessary to support the brethren under the grievous conflicts and temptations to which they were like to be exposed from the enemies of the faith.

Twenty years afterwards, when the saint was now fourscore and ten years old, my author, who had been received whilst a child by St. Sabas into the number of his disciples, was directed by his pious mother to St. John, in order to be guided in all things by his counsels for the welfare of his soul. The Saint told him, if he desired to save his soul, he would advise him to enter into the monastery of St. Euthymius. But being then young and giddy, he neglected the advice, and chose rather to go towards the Jordan, to dwell in some of the religious houses in that part of the country. Having fixed on the laura called the Reedfield, he was there taken violently ill, being unaccustomed to the yoke of religious discipline, and suffered at the same time a great anguish of mind, as well as bodily pain, when behold the Saint appeared to

19*

him in a dream, saying : " Behold, how thou art now
chastised, because thou wouldst not be advised by me.
But rise up, and go to Jericho, and there thou shalt find in
the hospital of the abbot Euthymius, a very ancient religious man, follow him into the monastery into which he
shall conduct thee, and there thou shalt find the salvation
of, thy soul." Upon this he awoke, and found himself
instantly cured ; and presently after getting up, receiving
the blessed sacrament, and taking some nourishment, he
walked the same day to Jericho. From hence he went
to the monastery of St. Euthymius, and from that time
always applied to our Saint for his spiritual direction.

This afforded him an opportunity of being an eye-
witness of the wonders which God wrought by our Saint.
As when in his presence one, whose name was George,
brought his son who was grievously tormented by an evil
spirit, and left him before the window of his cell, (as no
one ever came within the door) who was immediately
delivered, upon the Saint's praying for him, and anointing him with the oil of the cross. But the miracles
wrought by him for the cure of souls were the most remarkable. The abbot Eustatius applied one day to the
Saint upon occasion of a most violent and obstinate temptation of blasphemous thoughts, desiring him to pray
for him. The servant of God did so ; and then turning
to him he said : " God be praised, my son, you will never more be troubled with the like thoughts," as was actually the case: this our author learnt from Eustatius
himself.

A lady, named Basilissa, who was deaconness of the
great church of Constantinople, having taken a journey
to the Holy Land, in the company of a kinsman, who
though otherwise virtuous and religious, was nevertheless infected with the errors of Eutyches, hearing of the
wonderful graces bestowed upon our Saint, conceived a
great desire to see and speak to him. But being informed that no woman was allowed to come within the en-

closure of the laura, she sent to Theodore his disciple, and begged of him to take her cousin along with him to the Saint, in hopes that by his blessing and prayers he might be converted and reclaimed from his errors. Theodore took the young man with him, and knocked at the Saint's window, according to custom, which when he had opened, they both knelt down and craved his blessing. The man of God told his disciple, that as for his part he gave him his benediction, but that he could not do as much for his companion, because by schism and heresy he was an alien from the Catholic Church. The young man, astonished to hear him describe in this manner the state of his soul, which he could not know but by divine revelation, was by an evident miracle of divine grace, perfectly converted upon the spot, and renouncing his heresy, after a competent preparation, was admitted by the Saint to the holy communion. The lady, overjoyed at his conversion, conceived a still greater desire of seeing the Saint, and of treating with him about the state of her soul, insomuch that she had formed a design of putting on man's clothes, that so she might have access to him; but the Saint, knowing by revelation her design, sent to her to lay aside so useless a scheme, for that he would not be seen by her in that manner; but if she would stay where she was, she should see him in her sleep and then might put what questions she pleased to him. The following night, or shortly after, the Saint appeared to her in a dream, and said to her: " God hath sent me to you, you may now propose to me all that you want to know." She then declared to him all that she had in her mind, and received from him full satisfaction in every particular, for which she returned great thanks to God. All this, says our author, I can aver for truth, having heard it from her own mouth.

And here our author concludes his account of our Saint, who was, at the time of his writing, actually living, doubting not, as he says, but that others would deliver in a more ample manner to prosterity the great things that God had wrought by him, as well as his many labours and sufferings in defence of the faith of the church. The Saint was at that time one hundred and four years old, and though weak in body, yet perfect in all the faculties of his soul, and by a cheerful countenance ever shewed forth the joy of his heart, and the purity of his conscience. How long he lived a terwards, or in what year he depart d to our Lord, we have not found; but his name stands recorded among the Saints in the Roman Martyrology on the thirteenth of May.

ST. JOHN CLIMACUS.

From Daniel, Monk of Raithu, his Contemporary, and from his own Writings.

JOHN, surnamed *Climacus*, from his celebrated book entitled *Climax*, or the *scale* or *ladder* of christian and religious perfection, was born, as it is thought, in some part of Palestine, about the year 525. After an innocent education at home in the exercises of Christian piety, joined with the study of the human sciences, when he had attained to the age of sixteen, he formed the happy resolution of quitting the world and all terrestrial things, in order to discover the treasure of evangelical perfection in the field of religious discipline. The place he pitched upon for his retirement, in which he might spend the remaining days of his mortality, was mount Sinai, where the Lord heretofore gave his law to Moses, and which from the time that St. Antony and St. Hilarion began to propagate the monastic institute, had always been peopled with holy solitaries. Some of these lived as hermits in lonesome cells, others in the vast monastery on the top of the mountain, which was at this time one of the most celebrated in the church of God; but John chose a middle way, declining the multitude of the convent, as exposing him to more distractions, and yet not venturing, because he was young and unexperienced, to live quite by himself as an anchoret, he put himself under the discipline of a holy man, who dwelt in a cell on the side of the mountain, whose name was Martyrius, and lived with him for nineteen years, in the exercises of so humble and faithful an obedience, as that he seemed, from his very first entering upon this course of life, to have left his own will behind him: and notwithstanding his great wit and learning, which is so apt to puff men up, to judge of nothing by his own choice, but to regulate himself in all things, by a humble dependence on the conduct and direction of his superior, as the surest way to be conducted and directed by God himself.

After a trial of four years he made his solemn profession, by which he eternally dedicated himself to God. At which time a holy abbot, who was present, foretold that this young religious man would be one day one of the greatest lights of the Church of God. From the time of his profession, John continued still to live with the same simplicity and humility under the direction of Martyrius, making a continual progress both in virtue and the knowledge of the holy scriptures, on which he meditated day and night. Martyrius sometimes took him to visit the saints who dwelt in that neighbourhood. One day he brought him to a servant of God whose name was Anastasius, who fixing his eyes upon him, told Martyrius that his disciple would be one day abbot of mount Sinai, which situation was looked upon in those days as one of the highest promotions in the whole monastic order, and a dignity to which none were raised but such as were most eminent in sanctity, no others being thought proper to be the fathers and superiors of so many saints as then inhabited that holy mountain. At another time, when they went together to visit John, surnamed the Sabaite, because he had been a disciple of St. Sabas, this holy man, according to the custom of the solitaries, washed the feet of his guests, beginning with the disciple, and on being asked the reason, he said he did not know who that young man was, but he believed he saw in him an abbot of mount Sinai.

At the end of nineteen years our Lord took Martyrius to himself, and then our saint, by the counsel of George the Arsilaite, an eminent servant of God, undertook an anchoretical life in a cell by himself, at the foot of the mountain, at the distance of five miles from the church, to which nevertheless he repaired on all Saturdays and Sundays to join the rest of the religious in the divine office, to assist at the sacred mysteries, and receive the blessed sacrament. In this hermitage he continued forty years, practising in the highest degree of perfection the three principal virtues of a solitary life, which he has so much recommended in his writings, viz. a total disengagement of his thoughts and heart from temporal things, an incessant watchfulness and continual prayer, which consisted, as we learn from his own doctrine (Grad. 27.) in having God always for his object, and his divine will for his rule in all his exercises, words, thoughts, and in every motion and step that he took, and in doing nothing but in the presence of God, with an internal fervour of spirit. This gift of continual prayer was accompanied by the gift of tears, which he frequently poured forth in private before our Lord, bewailing his sins with the deepest compunction of heart. Nor did his frequent application to the reading of the scriptures and writings of the saints, interrupt his prayers or tears, but rather served as a fuel to that inward fire of divine love, which produced both the one and the other. Nor was the knowledge he here, acquired, nor the particular lights which the spirit of God imparted to him for the instruction and conduct of others, in the least prejudicial to his humility, or make him think he was left upon earth for any thing else, but to bewail his sins in solitude, and do penance for them.

Many persons, as well religious as seculars, came from time to time to consult him about the concerns of their souls, to whom, with great candour and simplicity, he communicated the lights which God gave him. A solitary, whose name was Moses, not content with only coming to consult him, prevailed on him by the intercession of the ancients of mount Sinai, to receive him in quality of his disciple. This Moses being sent one day by the Saint to fetch earth from a place at some distance for the use of their little garden, the fatigue of the work and the heat of the sun, obliged him, towards noon-day, to go and rest himself on the side of a tank, under the shadow of a rock, or great stone, that hung over his head. Here laying himself down he fell fast asleep. In the mean time the Saint, who had been praying in his cell, happened also to fall into a slumber, in which there appeared to him a venerable person, that said: " Dost thou sleep, John, without any concern? "get up, for Moses is upon the brink of danger." Having immediately awoke upon this admonition, he betook himself to his prayers, to beg deliverance for his disciple. But whilst he was praying for him, the divine goodness was pleased that Moses also should hear, as he thought, in his sleep, the voice of his master calling upon him to get up with all speed; upon which he presently started up in a fright, and ran away from the bank, and within less than a minute the great stone under which he had been sleeping fell down, so that had he remained there but one minute longer, he must have been inevitably crushed to death.

The common enemy of the good of sou's beholding with an envious eye the great advantage that many reaped from the instructions and spiritual discourses which the Saint made to those who visited him, stirred up the jealousy of certain persons who pretended to be scandalized

at his speaking too much, saying that he was a vain bab-
bler, who only loved to hear himself talk. The Saint,
who sought not to promote his own fame, but the glory
of God ; who had no vain opinion of his own talents, but
had only yielded to speak through the importunity of his
brethren, and from an impulse of fraternal charity, far
from justifying or excusing himself, or even being offended at what they said of him (believing they had only
meant to give him a charitable admonition and fraternal
correction), was resolved to comply therewith, and of
consequence condemned himself to an inviolable silence,
which he kept for a whole year, till at length those very
men, overcome with his wonderful humility and modesty,
and sensible of the detriment they had done the public,
by depriving them of his wholesome instructions and
directions, joined with all the rest of the brethren in begging of the man of God to resume his former practice.

The Saint had now led the life of an anchoret for the
space of forty years in his cell, when all the religious of
mount Sinai, with one accord, chose him for their abbot ;
and notwithstanding all his resistance, obliged him to quit
his hermitage to come and be their director and general
superior. Thus was this great light set in the candle-
stick, from thence to cast his bright rays on every side,
to enlighten the whole world. The lustre of his sanctity
reached even as far as Rome, from whence our most holy
Pontiff, St. Gregory the Great, wrote to him, testifying
the great esteem he had of his eminent virtue. It was
about this time that John, the abbot of Raithu, a famous
monastery on the confines of Egypt, obtained permission
of our Saint to commit to writing the great lights he had
received from God for directing and conducting souls to
the very top of the mountain of religious perfection. This
he has happily executed in his excellent book, entitled
Climax, or the *Ladder* of thirty steps or degrees of christian virtues, by which the soul ascends to the heavenly
paradise. It appears that the Saint, before the compos-

ing of this work, had made a visit to a famous monastery in Egypt, supposed to have been of the order or congregation of St. Pachomius, of which he makes frequent mention, bestowing the highest encomiums as well on the holy abbot, as on several of the monks by name. Here he continued a considerable time, and, with the leave of the superior, went also to see the monastery, or rather prison of the penitents, which was distant about a mile off from the abbey, and remained therein thirty days. The wonders of divine grace, which he there discovered in the whole demeanor of these happy penitents, are inserted at large in his fifth step of his Ladder, viz. *penitence:* of which, as it may serve as a stimulus to penitent sinners, we shall here give an abstract.

" Being come," says he, " into this monastery of the penitents, I beheld things which the eye of the slothful has never seen, the ear of the negligent has never heard, and which have never entered into the heart of the sluggard,—things and words capable of doing violence, if I may use the expression, to the Almighty. I saw some of these penitents standing whole nights upright, without allowing themselves any sleep or rest whatsoever ;—others, in a pitiful manner, looking up towards heaven, and calling for help from thence with groans, sighs, and prayers ;—others, who whilst at prayer, had their hands bound behind them like criminals, bowing down their pale countenances towards the ground, declaring aloud that they were unworthy to lift up their eyes to heaven, and that they durst not presume to speak to God, &c.—I saw some, (says he,) sitting on the floor covered with hair-cloth and ashes, hiding their faces between their knees, and striking their foreheads against the earth ;—others beating their breasts with inexpressible contrition of heart, some of whom watered the ground about them with their tears,—others grievously lamenting that they could not weep,—several mourning with a loud cry over their own souls, as we

20

mourn over the dead corpse of a dear friend,—others ready to roar out for grief, eagerly struggling to stifle the noise of their complaints, till being no longer able to repress them, they were forced to let them break forth with greater violence;—others appeared so astonished, that one would have supposed them to be statues of brass, so insensible of all things had the excess of their sorrow rendered them. Their heart was plunged in an abyss of humility, and their scorching grief had dried up all their tears, &c. There might you have seen the words of David fulfilled in these holy penitents, *I am become miserable, and am bowed down even to the end: I walked sorrowful all the day long. I am afflicted and humbled exceedingly.* And again, *I am smitten as grass and my heart is withered, because I forgot to eat my bread.—For I did eat ashes like bread, and mingled my drink with weeping.* No other words could be heard amongst them, but such as these: woe, woe to me, a miserable sinner; 'tis with justice, O Lord, 'tis with justice; spare us, O Lord, spare us; have mercy on us.— Some of them afflicted themselves by standing parching in the most violent heat of the sun; others, on the contrary, exposed themselves to suffer no less from extremity of the cold.—Some, in the violence of their thirst, taking a small quantity of water, contented themselves with only tasting of it, whilst others, after eating a morsel of bread, cast the rest away, saying: they were not worthy to eat the food of men, who had acted more like irrational creatures: there was no room for laughter;— none for idle talk;—none for resentment, anger or contradiction;—none for mirth, the care of the body, good cheer, or the pleasures of eating or drinking;—none for the least spark of vain-glory. No earthly cares distracted them, nor did they know what it was to judge or condemn any man but themselves. Their whole employment, day and night, was to cry to our Lord, and no voice was heard amongst them but that of prayer.

Some there were who, beating their breasts with all their might, as if they were knocking for admittance at the gate of heaven, said to the Lord: O open to us through thy mercy, the gate which we have shut against ourselves by our sins.——Another, *shew us only thy face, O Lord, and we shall be saved.*——Another said, shew thyself, O Lord, to thy poor supplicants, that sit in darkness and in the shadow of death, &c. Having always the hour of death before their eyes, they would say, O what shall our end be?——What sentence shall then be pronounced upon us?——Will God revoke the judgment we have deserved?——Has our prayer been able to force its way to the presence of the Lord?——Has it been regarded, coming from such unclean hearts and lips as ours? ——Has some part at least of our sins been blotted out? for as they are very great, they stand in need of many penitential labours and sorrows to be wholly effaced.—— Who can tell whether even our good angels are near us, to present our prayers, or whether the stench of our sins has not driven them away? &c. To these interrogations some replied, who knows, brethren, as the Ninevites said heretofore, but that our Lord may grant us pardon, and deliver us from that dreadful penance of the world to come? Let us neglect nothing that depends on us; let us continue to knock at the door of his mercy, even till the end of our lives: perhaps he will yield to our importunity and perseverance; for he is good and merciful. Let us run, brethren, let us run, for we have need to run, and to run with all our speed, that we may recover what we have lost. Let us run, and not spare this filthy flesh; let us make it suffer in time, because it has exposed us to the danger of suffering for eternity. Thus said these holy criminals, and they were as good as their words. Their knees were hardened by incessant kneeling;——their eyes appeared sunk into their sockets; ——the hair of their eye lids was fallen off by their continual weeping;——their cheeks were rivelled, and, as it

were, parched with the scalding brine of their tears ;—
their breasts bruised with blows," &c.

The Saint having added a great deal more, with regard to the sentiments and dispositions of these holy penitents, and all that he saw and heard during his stay
amongst them, concludes his narration in the following
manner :   " After I had remained thirty days in this prison, I returned to the great monastery, the holy abbot,
seeing me quite altered, like a man utterly astonished,
and comprehending the cause of my amazement, said :
Well, how fares it, father John ?   Have you seen the labours and conflicts of our penitents ?   Yes replied I ;—
father, I have both seen and admired them, and cannot
but esteem them more happy who mourn in this manner,
after falling into sin, than those who have not fallen, and
therefore bewail not themselves ; because it seems to me
that their fall has been to them an occasion of a most
happy and secure resurrection."

Our Saint, after publishing this book, did not continue
long in his station of abbot, but exchanged it for beloved solitude, returning into the desert to prepare himself
for eternity.   He departed to our Lord, in an advanced
age, about the year 605, and his name is enregistered
amongst the saints, in the Roman Martyrology on the
thirtieth of March.

ST. JOHN THE ALMONER.

From his Life written by Leontius, his Contemporary, Bishop of
Neapolis, in Cyprus.

THIS Saint, whose life has been commonly published
with those of the fathers of the desert, though it does
not appear that he ever lived in the desert, was born at
Cyprus, about the year 552, his father, Epiphanius, being at that time governor of the island. He was brought
up from his childhood in christian piety, and amongst
other virtues, he was always in a particular manner addicted to alms-deeds, and to the works of mercy and charity
to the poor ; from whence he has ever since been distinguished by the surname of *the Almoner*, or *Alms-giver*.
He was confirmed in the love and practice of this heavenly
virtue, by a vision he had in his youth, which himself afterwards related in the following manner : "When I
lived in the island of Cyprus, being then no more than
fifteen years old, I saw one night in a dream a young
virgin crowned with olive, of an incomparable beauty,
and more bright than the sun, who, standing by my bed,
struck me on the side, and awaked me. Being at length
awake, I still preceived her standing in the same spot, and
supposed her to be a woman ; wherefore, making the
sign of the cross, I asked who she was, and how she
could have the boldness to come to my bed side whilst I
was asleep ? She answered, with a sweet and smiling
countenance ; I am the eldest daughter of the great celestial King : take me for thy friend, and I will conduct
thee into his presence ; for no one has so much power
and interest with him as I have, since it was I that even
brought him down from heaven to earth, and made him
become man, in order to save man. Having said these
words, she instantly disappeared. As soon as I recovered from my surprise, I began to think that this heaven
21*

ly beauty represented alms-deeds, and mercy and compassion for the afflicted; because it was indeed the mercy, compassion, and goodness of God towards mankind, that made him come down from heaven, to clothe himself with our humanity. Having arisen, I immediately dressed myself and without awaking any of the family, went at the first dawning of the day to the church. In my way I met a poor man trembling with cold, and in order to make, as it were, an experiment of the truth of the vision, I pulled off my cloak and gave it him. Presently after, before I had reached the church door, a stranger, clothed in white, came up, and put a purse into my hands, containing a hundred pieces of money, saying: Take this, my brother, and distribute it as you think fit. The joy, together with the surprise in which I then found myself, induced me to receive the purse without demur; but when, upon reflection, I turned back to follow the person, and to return him his money, as having no want or occasion for it, he vanished out of my sight. From that day I often gave alms to my brethren the poor, saying within myself: *now I shall see whether Jesus Christ, according to his promise, will return me a hundred fold;* by which I became guilty of a great sin in tempting God, and afterwards conceived a great remorse of conscience for it, yet I still received from him, at sundry times, and in divers manners, all the satisfaction I could desire." So far the Saint, speaking of his younger days.

St. John had given the most brilliant examples of all virtues, more especially of an unbounded charity in a secular life, till about the fifty-fourth year of his age, when the great reputation of his sanctity, which now spread itself far and near, recommended him so strongly to the church of Alexandria, that upon the death of Theodore its patriarch, he was chosen his successor; the emperor Heraclius, in the mean time, using his utmost influence to overcome the repugnance the Saint had to this promotion, of which he thought himself infinitely unworthy. As soon as he arrived at Alexandria, he sent for the archdeacon and officers of the church, and said to them; "It would be unjust, O, my brethren, if we should begin with any other care or concern, before that which we owe to Jesus Christ; wherefore be pleased to go through the city, and let me have an exact list of all my masters." As they seemed not to understand his meaning, he explained himself, saying, that he considered the poor not only as his lords and masters, but his coadjutors also, who, by their prayers, were to help him to heaven. The list of the poor which they brought in was found to amount, in that great and populous city, to upwards of seven thousand five hundred; yet notwithstanding their being so numerous, the Saint gave orders that a daily allowance of necessaries should be given to every one of them out of his revenue.

After his consecration, he immediately applied himself, with all diligence and fervour, to execute every branch of his pastoral charge with the utmost perfection; and, as a true father of his people, to procure them whatever was either for their spiritual or corporal welfare. He began, by putting an effectual stop to the frauds and injustices committed in trade, particularly by false weights and measures, a practice which, said he, God, as we learn from his divine word, utterly abhors; and, as he was informed, that they who had the administration of the temporalities of his church, were often biassed by presents which were made them, so as to be partial in the discharge of their office, he sent for them, and after appointing them a larger salary, strictly forbid them to receive any presents from any person whatsoever; because, said he, a fire shall consume the houses of those that take bribes. Being also informed that many who laboured under injuries and oppressions, were intimidated by his secretaries, and other officers, from laying their complaints before him; as a remedy to so great an evil, he ordered a chair to be placed before the great church, with a bench on each side, where he attended for several hours, on every Wednesday and Saturday, to give audience, and redress the grievances of all that pleased to come for that purpose, and would charge the proper officer to see that what he ordered should be presently executed. Upon which occasion he used to say; "If we poor mortals are allowed at every hour to enter the house of God, in order to address our supplications to him, and lay all our wants before him, though his Majesty be incomprehensible, and infinitely elevated above all created beings, if we," continues he, "are so anxious that he would hear our prayers, and make haste to help us, how ready ought we to be to hear the petitions, and grant the just demands of our fellow servants, remembering that saying of our Lord Jesus, *with what measure you mete, it shall be measured to you again.*" Matt. vii. 3.

On these occasions, it was the custom of our Saint, who hated idleness, either to employ his time in reading the holy Scriptures, whilst he was waiting in order to give audience to such as should apply to him, or in spiritual conferences with some servants of God; but one day having remained there till noon, without being applied to by any one, he withdrew, with tears in his eyes, saying: that none of his people had favoured him that day, or afforded him any opportunity of offering something to Jesus Christ, in order to cancel his own innumerable sins. Sophronius, a great servant of God, who sat by him, replied, that he ought rather rejoice to find that God had made him his instrument in establishing so good a harmony and perfect a peace amongst the sheep committed to his charge, that there was not even one to be found amongst them that had any difference or misunderstanding with his neighbour; for this indeed, said he, is converting men into angels.

This Sophronius, with John his companion, men

equally eminent both for their wisdom and their sanctity, were sent by divine providence to the assistance of our Saint. He made use of them, upon all occasions, as his counsellors and directors, and obeyed them with as much submission as if they had been his fathers; and his esteem, as well as his love for them, were the more increased by the success that attended the exertion of their eminent talents in bringing back to God innumerable souls who had been unhappily seduced by the Eutychian heresy, which then greatly prevailed all over Egypt, even amongst many of the religious. By means of these holy men, the Saint had the comfort of beholding in his days, not only many private houses and families, but also several churches and monasteries, delivered out of the jaws of the infernal wolf, and again restored to the true fold of Christ, the Catholic Church. As to our Saint, he incessantly warned his flock to avoid all communion in spirituals with any who were separated by heresy from the communion of the church, and not so much as to enter into their churches or meeting-houses, much less to join with them in prayer, even though any one should be so unhappily circumstanced as to be confined during his whole life to a place where he could never see a catholic priest, or receive any of the holy sacramets; for, said he, as the laws of God and man forbid any one, who has a wife living, to cohabit with another woman, how distant or for how long a time soever his lawful wife may be separated from him, so he who has been espoused to Christ in the Catholic Church, cannot without the crime of *spiritual adultery*, upon any pretext whatsoever, engage himself in the communion of heretics.

Exclusive of the assistance that our Saint received in the discharge of his pastoral office from those two great men, he was also desirous of participating in the prayers and merits of the holy solitaries, for whose manner of life, though he had never been a solitary himself, he conceived the utmost esteem.   To this end, having assembled together a number of saint-like anchorets out of the deserts, he distributed them into two bands, and built cells for them in two chapels erected at his own charges; the one dedicated to the blessed Virgin, the other to St. John; furnishing them with all necessaries out of his own farms, in order as he told them, that whilst he, under God, took upon himself the care of providing for their corporal sustenance, they, on their part, should provide for the spiritual necessities of his soul, especially by offering up to God in his behalf their evening and midnight devotions.   These foundations of our Saint were of great edification to the faithful of Alexandria, many of whom, in different parts of the city, were excited by the example of these holy men, to pass whole nights in singing the praises of God.

It would be an endless task to relate the particulars of all the great things done by our Saint during the ten years of his episcopal administration, as well for the promoting of the glory of God, as for the sanctification and salvation of the souls committed to his charge, together with the many wonderful examples he gave of humility, —meekness,—patience,—charity for all, even his enemies,—and the rest of the evangelical virtues; but as the most distinctive traits in his character were the most tender compassion for the poor and distressed, and an unbounded liberality in point of alms-deeds, we cannot refrain from adducing the following extraordinary instances.   In his time Chosroes, king of Persia, having laid waste Syria, and other parts of the eastern empire, and carried off a great number of Christians into captivity and slavery, such as could escape his hands made the best of their way to Alexandria, and presented themselves in great multitudes to the man of God, as the known refuge of all the distressed.   The Saint received them all with open arms, and as many of them were sick and wounded, he placed in hospitals or other lodgings, where they were all entertained at his charges, and as long as they themselves chose to remain, the most tender care was taken of them; and as to the rest, who were innumerable, he ordered his almoners to give a piece of silver to every man that applied to them for charity, and two to every woman or girl, in consideration of the weakness of their sex. His almoners perceiving amongst the great numbers of those that applied for relief, some to be richly clad, made a scruple of giving them any money, and came to consult the Saint on the subject; but he being highly displeased at their not having complied to the letter, with those words' of our Lord; Luke vi. 30. *Give to every one that asketh you*, desired they would not in future be so inquisitive into the circumstances of those who came to crave alms, but rather distribute that which belonged to God with a bountiful hand, according to the will and commandment of Christ. "But if your *little faith*," said he, "makes you apprehend lest my income should not be sufficient to furnish wherewith to relieve such great numbers, I will by no means become a partaker in your *unbelief*; for since it has pleased God to make me, though most unworthy, the dispenser of his goods, if all the men in the world were to come to Alexandria to crave alms I would relieve them, under an entire confidence that they would never be able to exhaust his immense stores, nor those of the church."

Whilst this great multitude of strangers remained at Alexandria, one of them, in order to put the Saint's extreme charity and compassion for the distressed to a trial, presented himself in ragged garment one day when the man of God was going to the hospital to visit the sick, which he constantly did twice or thrice in a week, and begged he would have pity on a poor captive, and order him some relief. The Saint immediately ordered his almoner to give him *six pieces of silver*. No sooner had he received this alms but he departed, and having changed his dress, and met the Saint again in another street, he cast himself at his feet, saying, he was a poor man, in the utmost distress, and begged his assistance. The holy prelate then told his almoner to give him *six pieces of gold*, although this officer had just whispered in his ear, and told him it was the very same person whom he had relieved a little before. Again he came a third time, still imploring the charity of the man of God, and when the almoner signified that it was the same identical person, the Saint answered, give him *twelve pieces of gold ;* for possibly, said he, this may be *Jesus Christ*, my Saviour, who is come on purpose *to try me ;* alluding, in all probability, to what had happened not long before to St. Gregory the Great.

In the mean time the Persians continuing their devastations in the eastern provinces, drove still greater numbers of people to Alexandria, to shelter themselves there under the charitable wings of our Saint, who not content with relieving all that came, sent also considerable alms to Modestus, the patriarch of Jerusalem, at this time reduced to the greatest extremity with all his people by the Persians, who had taken that city and burnt the churches. With this alms he sent also a letter to the patriarch, apologizing for not sending something more worthy of the temple of God, and declaring how glad he should be, if circumstances would permit him to come himself in person, and labour with his own hands in rebuilding the holy church of the sepulchre and resurection of our Lord, requesting also that he would excuse his want of the means, and obtain for him, by his prayers, that his name might be written in the book of life.

At this time the innumerable multitude of persons that came from all parts to Alexandria, made all sorts of provisions exceedingly dear, more especially as the harvest had failed in Egypt, the Nile not having overflowed that year as usual. The Saint, who could not endure to distress laid out all the money he had or could any way procure, either by begging or borrowing of good people, till at length, all being spent, no one could be found that would lend him any more, every body apprehending, lest by the continuance of the famine, they should come themselves to want; when behold, amidst these extremities, as if God had a mind to try the fidelity of his servants, a rich citizen, who was desirous of being promoted to holy orders, but was prevented by the canons of the Church, on account of his having been twice married, made him an offer of two hundred thousand bushels of wheat which he had stored up, together with a very large some of money to be disposed of in charities, upon condition he would dispense with the irregularity he had incurred by his bigamy, and ordain him deacon. The Saint told him, that although the offering which he proposed could never come at a time in which it was more wanted, he nevertheless could not accept it, as it was defective and tainted by the condition to which it was annexed, because the law of God required that the sacrifice offered to him should be clean and without blemish: and as to the present necessities of his brethren the poor, as well as those of the Church, he was confident that the same divine goodness which had hitherto taken care of them, would still continue to feed and support them, provided, said he, we inviolably observe what he commands us. No sooner had he returned this answer, and dismissed the ambitious aspirer to a spiritual promotion, but his people brought him the gladsome tidings that the two great ships belonging to the Church, which he had sent to Sicily, were just arrived in the port laden with corn; upon which the man of God prostrated himself on the ground, and returned hearty thanks to our Lord, who had not only preserved him from sin under that trial, but had immediately sent him such a seasonable and abundant provision.

It was wonderful to relate the many other occasions

21

wherein it pleased God to furnish his servant with extraordinary supplies in order to support his boundless charities, so that, generally speaking, the more he gave away, the more he received from the divine bounty through the hands of charitable Christians, and sometimes not without an evident miracle. A citizen, who after living in opulent circumstances had been suddenly reduced to extreme poverty, applied to the Saint in the church for an alms; he recollecting him to have been not long before a wealthy man, had great compassion on him, and whispered to his almoner to give him fifteen pounds of gold; which when the almoner was going to execute, he was persuaded by the secretary and the steward to give him only five pounds. The Saint returning home from the church, was met by a rich widow, who put a promissory note in his hands, in which she obliged herself to give him five hundred pieces of gold for the poor. Having received the note, and knowing in spirit that it was sent to recompence the charity given to the above-mentioned citizen, he required and found out that his officers had only given him five pounds instead of fifteen, whereupon he told them they would be answerable to God for the other thousand pieces of gold which the good lady that had given the note for the five hundred had designed for the poor, if they had not abridged her charity by not complying with his. In order to convince them thereof, having sent for the lady, he asked her in their presence, if the sum mentioned in the note was what she originally intended to give to Jesus Christ, or whether she had proposed to give him a larger sum? She suspecting by this question that what had passed had been revealed from heaven, she was struck with fear and astonishment, and assured him in the most solemn manner, that she had actually written *fifteen hundred pieces of gold*, but that looking at the note just before she had presented it to him at church, she found to her great astonishment, the fifteen hundred changed into five hundred, but knew not by what means nor by whom, as the paper had never been in any other person's hands but her own, and therefore concluded it to be the will of God that she should give no more than five hundred.

A captain of a ship, a stranger, having suffered great losses at sea, besought our Saint, with many tears, that he would have the same compassion for him as he had on all others in distress; he ordered his almoner to give him the weight of five pounds in gold; which sum enabled him to repair his vessel and put to sea again. But scarcely had he sailed out of port, when a storm arose which obliged him to fling all his goods overboard, and it was with the utmost difficulty he saved his ship. Again he applied to the saint, begging he would have compassion on him for the sake of him who had shewn pity to the whole world. The holy prelate having told him, that this misfortune had befallen him in consequence of his having mingled the charity money which he received of the church with what remained of his own former ill-gotten wealth, and that therefore he had lost both, gave him now the weight of ten pounds in gold, bidding him take care not to mix it with any other money. Thus being enabled to repair and load his vessel with a fresh cargo, he tried his fortune a second time, but with worse success than ever, for being cast away upon the coast he lost both ship and cargo, and hardly escaped with his life. This latter misfortune drove him into so violent a fit of despair, that he was almost tempted to make away with himself, if the holy patriarch, who had learnt by revelation all that had happened, had not sent for him to comfort him, with the assurance that the like misfortune should never again befal him, and that this was permitted in consequence of his having obtained by unjust means possession of his ship. Then in order to set him up in the world again the saint appointed him captain of the large vessel belonging to the church of Alexandria and sent him out laden with twenty thousand bushels of wheat. What follows is an abstract of the account given by the captain himself, with the most solemn asseveration of its veracity :—" We sailed," said he, " during the space of twenty days and twenty nights with so violent a wind that not being able, either by the stars or the sight of any land, to know in what part of the world we were, we should have given ourselves up for lost, had not the pilot assured us that he saw the holy patriarch by his side at the helm, bidding him not to fear, for that we were in the right road. On the twentieth day we came within sight of England, where, when we put to land, we found a great famine. Upon our making it known that we were laden with corn, the principal magistrate of the place told us God had sent us to assist them in their extremity ; and having given us our choice either to receive money or the weight of our corn in British tin, we chose one half in coin, the other in tin. But behold a still greater wonder wrought by our Lord, as a recompense for the charity of our Saint : as soon as the ship returned safe back to the coast of Egypt, some of the British tin being sold by the captain to a dealer in pewter, who on melting it down, found it pure silver; upon which, when he went to reproach the captain, as if he had suspected his honesty, and meant by a stratagem to put it to a trial, the whole was carefully examined, and all found to be excellent silver.

But as our Saint had, on so many occasions, received these miraculous supplies, in order to enable him to continue his extraordinary charities, so was he also sometimes tried, like Job, with great losses, which were shortly after repaid to him with interest. Nicetas, the governor, urged on by some evil counsellors, under the pretence of the pressing necessities of the state, on account of relieving of the Persian war, demanded and carried off, in the name of the emperor, all the money that had been brought to our Saint for charitable uses, leaving him master of only one hundred crowns; but on the same day, a stranger, from the coast of Barbary, brought him large sums of money, sent by charitable christians; and the governor himself, before it was night, (upon reading a paper sent on this occasion by the man of God, in which he had written these words, " Our Lord, who has said, *I will not leave thee, neither will I forsake thee,* cannot tell a lie, because he is the truth; and therefore a wretched man, who must shortly be the food of worms, cannot tie up the hands of God, who furnishes all his creatures with both food and life,") returned all the money he had taken from him, adding thereto three hundred crowns of his own, and offering to undergo what penance the patriarch should be pleased to impose on him for his crime.

At another time the Saint sustained a very great loss, when all the vessels belonging to the church of Alexandria, to the number of thirteen, meeting with a violent storm in the Adriatic sea, were constrained to fling their whole freight, consisting of corn and other goods, overboard. On this occasion the holy patriarch said with Job, *the Lord gave and the Lord hath taken away, as it hath pleased the Lord, so it is done, blessed be the name of the Lord:* and told his friends who came to condole with him on his misfortune, that with respect to himself he rather considered it more to his advantage than his loss, imputing it entirely to his having taken too much complacency in his alms, without sufficiently guarding against the danger of being infected by vainglory;—that he was very sensible of what service afflictions and humiliations are to purify the soul from the dross of pride and vanity, being convinced as well as the psalmist, *'Tis good for me that thou humbled me, that I may learn thy justifications,* Ps. 118;—that however severely, as to his own part, he deserved to be punished on account of his having given occasion, by his vanity, to so many innocent persons being thus reduced, yet as God was still the same as he was in the days of Job, he trusted, that notwithstanding his own unworthiness, he would help them out of their distress. This confidence of our Saint was amply recompensed, for not long after our Lord restored him by one means or other, twice as much as he had lost, the whole of which he employed in comforting and assisting more abundantly than ever the poor and distressed.

The Saint being informed that one of his servants had laboured under a pressing necessity, gave him privately with his own hand the weight of two pounds in gold; and when the man, confounded at the excess of his goodness towards him, told him he did not know he should be ab'e to look him any more in the face: "Brother," replied the Saint, " I have not yet shed my blood for you, as Christ our common Master and God has done for us all, and has commanded us to do for our brethren."

One of the citizens being closely pressed to pay a debt, which he had not at that time the means to discharge, addressed himself to a rich nobleman, begging he would lend him fifty pounds of gold upon proper security. He assured him he would, but delayed to put his promise in execution, whilst the other, still closely watched by his creditor, apprehending he would proceed to extremities, had recourse to the holy patriarch whose heart and hand were ever open to relieve the necessities of all. No sooner had he told him his case, but the Saint replied: " My son, if your necessity required it, I would even give you the clothes off my back," and without further hesitation he lent him the whole sum. The following night the nobleman saw in a dream a person standing upon an altar, to whom many others approached to make their offerings, and for every offering they laid upon the altar they received a hundred fold in return. He seemed also to observe the holy patriarch come in immediately after him, and that there lay a sum of money upon a bench before him, which one of the bystanders bid him take up and offer upon the altar, that he might receive a hundred

fold.; but as he hesitated and was dilatory in doing as
he was desired, the patriarch, who stood behind him,
stept forward, took up the offering, and putting it upon
the altar, presently afterwards received a hundred fold.
The next morning the nobleman having sent for the man,
offered to let him have the money he wanted; but he
replied, that his lordship's delays to fulfil his promise had
obliged him to have recourse to the holy patriarch, by
whom he was immediately relieved; upon which the
other related the vision he had seen, and severely condemned himself for having lost, by his want of diligence
in doing good, that great reward wherewith God recom-
penses those works which are done for his sake.

Amongst the many others who, on seeing the boundless charities of the Saint, brought their money to him to
be disposed of at his discretion for the relief of the poor,
a man who had an only son aged fifteen years, came one
day and presented him the weight of seven pounds and
a half of gold, assuring him it was all he had, and only
besought him to pray for his son, whom he had sent in
a ship to the coast of Africa, that God would protect
him and conduct him back in safety with his vessel to
the haven. The Saint did not only pray himself, but
also earnestly recommended the welfare of the youth and
the vessel to the prayers of his clergy, as the man had
desired; when behold, before the expiration of thirty
days, the boy being taken ill died, and shortly after the
ship, in which was also the uncle of the youth, on returning home, was cast away near the port of Alexandria,
and nothing whatever saved but the lives of the persons on board, and the boat which conveyed them on
shore. The melancholy news of the loss of his son and
his ship arriving so rapidly one after the other, caused
the most inexpressible affliction to the poor man. The
holy patriarch was also exceedingly affected with it,
more especially on account of the death of his only son;
wherefore not knowing what else to do, he besought the

Father of mercies, and God of all consolation, to comfort the afflicted parent. Then sending a messenger to the man, as he had not the courage to see or speak to himself in person, he desired him not to lose his confidence in God, whose judgments, though inscrutable, are nevertheless just, and according to what he knows is best for us, though we do not; and therefore cautioned him against any want of resignation on this occasion, lest he should bereave himself of the immense reward which God had prepared to recompense his faith and charity, manifested in the offering he had made to God. This message was followed by a dream or vision the ensuing night, in which the man of God appeared to the afflicted parent while asleep, and said to him, " Why do you afflict yourself, dear brother, and suffer yourself to be thus oppressed with grief? Did not you desire me to pray to God to save your son, and behold he has saved him. For I can assure you, that had he lived he would have become a very lewd man; and as for your ship, had not God been moved to mercy, by the good work you did in addressing your charity to me, it would have been utterly lost, together with every person on board, so that you would have lost your brother also. Arise, then, and return thanks to God not only for preserving the life of your brother, but also for having saved your son, by taking him to himself before he became corrupted by the wicked maxims and vanities of the world." Having awoke and found himself wonderfully comforted, he went early in the morning to the patriarch, to return thanks to God and to him, and related to him the vision he had seen. The holy man having glorified God, for his infinite goodness, desired the other not to attribute any thing of what happened to his prayers, but to God alone, and the faith he had placed in God; for the blessed prelate had always the meanest opinion of himself, as was ever apparent from all his words and whole com-

portment, as he would never suffer any thing of good to
be ascribed to him.

One of the principal men of the city, observing that
the Saint, who was so liberal to others, allowed himself
only a poor little bed on the floor, with an old tattered
blanket for a covering for his lodging, sent him in one
day a rich coverlet that cost six and thirty pieces of silver, conjuring him to make use of it for his sake. The
servant of God, yielding to his importunity, used it for
one night; but as they that lay in the same chamber observed, that instead of sleeping he spent the whole night
in reproaching himself in the following manner with lying beneath such a rich covering, whilst the brethren of
Jesus Christ, as he called the poor, lay starving with hunger and cold, and destitute of all the commodities of life:
" and thou who aspirest after the joys of a happy eternity," he said to himself, " thou who drinkest wine, eatest
good fish, art well lodged, and, like one of the children
of this wicked world, art also warmly covered, and liest
at thy ease under a coverlet that cost six-and-thirty pieces
of silver; surely living in so unmortified a manner, instead
of expecting the joys of heaven hereafter, thou hast rather
cause to apprehend that sentence pronounced on the rich
man will fall to thy lot, to whom it was said, Luke xvi.
*Thou hast received good things in thy life time, whilst
the poor received evil things: and therefore they are now
comforted, and thou art tormented.*" The result of
these reflections was, that he resolved to get rid of this
rich piece of furniture the next morning, and sell it for
the benefit of the poor, which he did without any delay.
When the gentleman saw his present exposed for sale,
he purchased it, and sent it to him again, entreating him
to make use of it: he sold it a second time, and again,
in like manner a third time, giving the price of it to the
poor, and telling his friends, with a pleasant countenance,
" we shall now see which of " us shall be first wearied
out." This gentleman being very rich, and one from

whom the Saint received many things, which he gave to the poor, upon these and similar occasions the Saint used to say, it was no harm to get all he could from the rich for the service of the poor, since by so doing he served both the one and the other; the poor, by relieving their wants, and the rich, by affording them the occasion to purchase heaven by their alms.

Amongst other exercises and lessons of charity which the Saint inculcated to his people, we must not pass over his sentiments with regard to the manner in which masters ought to treat their servants. Attend to the manner in which he expressed himself one day on this subject, to one who was cruel and inhuman to his slaves: "My son," said he, with the utmost meekness, "I understand that by the temptation of the enemy, you are apt to treat your servants ill; let me entreat of you, for the time to come, to stop till your passion is passed over before you offer to correct them. For God has given them to us in order that they may serve us, but not that we should beat and abuse them; nay, perhaps he may have given them more with a view of exercising our patience, in supporting their faults and defects, than for any other service they can do. But tell me, Sir, with what price could you buy any one of these who has the honour to have been created, no less than yourself, after the image and likeness of God; for, though you are his master, what have you either in body or soul that he has not? Give ear to St. Paul, Gal. iii. *All you that have been baptized in Christ, have put on Christ; there is no distinction of Jew or Gentile, bond or free,—you are all one in Christ Jesus.* Jesus Christ then, by taking upon himself the form of a servant, has taught us that we ought not to lift ourselves by pride over those whom he had made our servants: for as the prophet teaches us, Ps. 112, there is but one great Master and Lord of the universe, *who is high above all nations, and his glory is above the heavens: and who looketh down upon the low things, in* heaven and in earth; he does not say *on the high things,* but *on the low things.* How then can we pretend to domineer over those who have been redeemed, no less than ourselves, with the blood of our God and Master, for whose service he has made the heavens, the sun, the stars, the earth, the sea, and all the things therein;—for whose protection he employs his angels, and for whom the Son of God has subjected himself to all the humiliations and torments of his passion?—Can you, I say, Sir, treat with contempt this man whom God treats with honour? Shall you strike him as you would a beast, or as if he were not of the same nature as yourself? Tell me whether you be willing that every time you offend God he should punish you the same moment? I am certain you would not. How then can you say daily to God, *forgive us our trespasses, as we forgive them that trespass against us?* Do you do as you would be done by?"

This charity which the Saint inculcated to others he ever practised himself, without excepting his very enemies. Instead of being offended against those who had injured or wronged him, he, on the contrary, conferred on them greater favours, that he might overcome evil with good; nay, he even humbled himself sometimes to impenitent sinners, by casting himself at their feet, and begging their pardon, although the fault was wholly on their side, that by these means he might bring them to a reconciliation with God and his Church.

One day a beggar having asked an alms of the holy patriarch, he ordered them that accompanied him to give him ten pieces of brass. The man, who expected more, instead of thanks returned him very abusive language, and treated him in a most insolent manner. Those that were present, being moved to indignation, would have punished the wretch upon the spot, had not the Saint severely reproved them, saying, " Let him finish what he has a mind to say; for why should not I, my brethren, suffer this small injury from a poor man, I who, for these sixty years, have been continually offending and injuring my God by my sins?"

Amongst other charities, the Saint also founded several hospitals; and whilst a great mortality raged at Alexandria, he was very assiduous in attending such as were at the point of death, and in assisting them in their agony. He was also very diligent, not only in providing himself, but in ordering prayers to be offered in behalf of the souls of the faithful departed. In recommendation of this charity, and as a proof of the efficacy of such prayers, he related what had happened not long before to one of his countrymen, who had been carried away captive by the Persians, and cast into a prison called Lethe, or Oblivion. His friends having heard that he was dead, procured prayers to be said three several times every year, for the repose of his soul; at each of which (as he assures them, when after four years he made his escape out of prison, and returned home) he was always visited and comforted by a person shining like the sun, and was delivered on those occasions from his chains for the whole day.

The Saint recommended very much to his people the remembrance of death, as a most wholesome meditation for all men; and having been told, that on the day of the coronation of the emperor, several pieces of different sorts of marble were presented to him, in order that he might choose the kind of which he would have his tomb made, that being ever mindful of his mortality and speedy return to dust, he might not suffer himself to be puffed up with pride, but take care to live and govern in such a manner, as to be always prepared for his last end; he also, with the same intention, gave orders to have a sepulchre prepared for himself amongst the tombs of the patriarchs his predecessors, but that it should not be finished till his death; in the mean time he desired that the workmen, upon certain solemn days, should come and tell him, in presence of all his clergy: "My lord, your tomb remains unfinished, give orders, if you please, that it may be completed, since you know not the hour, as the scripture says, when the thief shall come." He also often entertained his friends that came to visit him with this same subject, of the continual thought we ought to have of death, and of that separation which shall then take place between the soul and body. "I am of opinion," said he, "that the means to work out our salvation is, to be always thinking with sorrow on the hour of our death, and to consider well that we shall have no one to share with us the pains and conflicts we must then go through—that at that hour the whole world shall forsake us, our good works excepted, which will never abandon us :--to think how great our astonishment and affliction must be, if at our departure hence we are not prepared for our trial :—to reflect that it will be in vain then to ask for a little more time wherein to do penance when we shall be reproached for having had so much, and made such ill use of it. "And how," said he, "shall poor John, (for so he commonly called himself) escape the claws of these cruel beasts that shall watch to catch him at his departure hence ? What can he do when he shall see before him those bands of evil spirits, who shall strictly examine him, and charge home upon him all the evil he had done ?" Which, he said, alluding to a vision in which St. Simon Stylites had seen in spirit, how, at the time of the separation of the soul from the body, when she would willingly fly up towards heaven, she meets with devils in her way, divided into different companies, according to the different vices which they usually suggest; and that the demons of pride examine the soul upon the sins committed in that kind :—those of impurity examine her upon all her carnal sins and impure delectations :—those of detraction, upon every word that has proceeded out of her mouth against her neighbour ; and so of all her other sins. Our Saint had this vision often

22

in mind; as also that passage of the life of St. Hilarion, of the fear and apprehension he had, and the words he spoke to his soul, when he was upon the point of death; and therefore he would often be saying to himself: "If so great a Saint, who had served our Lord for such a number of years, who had wrought so many miracles, and even raised the dead to life, yet apprehended so much that dreadful hour, what shalt thou be able to say or do, when thou shalt find thyself encompassed by those cruel and unmerciful examiners of all thy actions? What shalt thou be able to answer to such of these unhappy spirits as shall examine thee with regard to thy lies, thy detraction, thy hardheartedness, thy avarice, thy remembrance of injuries, or thy ill-will, &c. O merciful God, may thy almighty hand defend me at that hour from all the efforts of these enemies of my salvation! May thy goodness send thy angels to guide and conduct me safe in this last great and dangerous journey from time to eternity!" Such were the sentiments of our Saint, in his entertainments upon this most interesting subject, of the soul's passage out of this world into the other.

St. John had now illustrated the church of Alexandria for ten years as *a burning and a shining light,* when the time drawing near in which our Lord designed to take him to himself, he resigned his patriarchal see, and retired into his native country, Cyprus, in order to prepare himself for eternity. As soon as he arrived at Amathus, the place of his nativity, having a foreknowledge, by revelation, of his approaching death, he made his last will and testament in words to this effect: "I John, who was born a slave to sin, but have been made a free man by the grace of God, who, without any deserts of mine, has raised me to the priestly dignity, return thee most humble thanks, O Lord, that thou hast vouchsafed to hear the prayer I have made to thee, that I should not possess at my death any more than one small piece of money; and that whereas when I was made bishop I had great treasures at my disposal, and have received since immense sums from thy servants, thou hast always made me sensible that all this store was thine, and hast done me the favor ever to give back to thee without delay what belonged to thee; therefore, as this piece of money which remains belongs also to thee no less than all the rest, I desire it may be likewise returned to thee, by putting it into the hands of the poor."

St. John the Almoner departed to our Lord in the sixty-fourth year of his age, anno 616. His body was interred in the church of Amathus, in the chapel of St. Tychon, formerly bishop of that see, where many miracles were afterwards wrought through his intercession. His name is recorded in the Roman Martyrology on the twenty-third of January.

ST. SYNCLETICA.

From her ancient Life, by a Writer of the same Age, believed by many to have been St. Athanasius.

ST. SYNCLETICA was born at Alexandria, about the latter part of the third century, of noble and wealthy christian parents, whom God had blessed with four children, two sons and two daughters. One of the sons died very young, the other, having attained to the age of twenty-five, when, at the desire of his parents, he was contracted to a young lady, and when all things were prepared for solemnizing the marriage, he was suddenly carried off by death into another region, where *they neither marry nor are given in marriage.* Syncletica, the eldest of the two daughters, from her tender years consecrated her heart to the love of Christ, and accustomed herself to the exercises of christian piety and solid devotion, taking always far more care of the soul than of the body. As she advanced in age she increased in virtue and in the love of purity, which determined her to choose no other spouse but Jesus Christ. For the love of him she rejected the most advantageous worldly offers that could be made her; and instead of the outward ornaments of the body, which those of her age and quality are usually so fond of, she diligently procured the better ornaments of the interior house of her soul, where she desired to entertain the King of kings, who is beautiful above the sons of men. Hence she carefully shunned all dangerous worldly diversions and unprofitable recreations, seeking always the conversation of such as entertained her with godly discourses and exhortations to piety, to whom she hearkened with the most diligent attention, laying up their words in her memory, and meditating frequently upon them. In the mean time she was exceeding temperate, and mortified in her eating and drinking, looking upon this virtue as the best preservative of purity; and though by her fasting and other austerities, her countenance became both pale and meagre, yet she regarded it not, being not so desirous to please the eyes of men as those of God; and finding by experience that what weakened the body served to invigorate the soul. However, she was always discreet in these corporal mortifications, and took all possible care to conceal them, from being either seen or observed by others.

Her parents dying, left her mistress of all their worldly substance; so that now finding herself at full liberty to follow the call of God, and to retire altogether from the world, after having made a sufficient trial of herself, by way of preparation for those austerities she designed to embrace, she disposed of all her wealth in favour of the poor; and cutting off her hair, in token of her renouncing the world and all its superfluities, she withdrew herself from the town, and chose a sepulchre, or monument, in the neighbourhood, for her dwelling place, during the remainder of the days of her mortality, taking also along with her her youngest sister, who was also desirous of following the same kind of life. Here she lived separated in a manner from the conversation either of men or women, in the exercises of mortification, penance, and continual prayer.——Her food was coarse bread made of bran;——her ordinary drink was water, and her bed the bare ground; and as the watchful enemy plied her with frequent and troublesome temptations, she opposed to all his assaults the buckler of faith, with the helmet of hope and confidence in our Lord, to whom she had continual recourse; and on these occasions she redoubled her austerities, in order to keep the flesh in subjection, yet so as still to have an eye upon the *salt* of prudence and discretion, wherewith our Lord wills that all the *sacrifices* we offer to him should be *seasoned,* Levit. ii. 13. Far from conceiving a good opinion of herself for having quitted her worldly goods, she kept herself always humble; by thinking she was still at a very great distance from what she ought to be; and instead of contenting herself with that voluntary poverty which she had embraced when she renounced all exterior possessions, she made it her chiefest labour to purify her soul, as well from all desires and affections to any thing created, as from all those spiritual vices that are apt to lurk secretly in the interior.

Notwithstanding her utmost endeavours to hide her eminent virtues from the eyes of others, and to avoid, as much as possible, all commerce with the world, yet, as the Almighty had so ordered it for his own greater glory, and the good of a great number of souls, she could not keep herself so closely concealed as to prevent the sweet odour of her sanctity from breaking forth from her sepulchre, and spreading herself by degrees over the

22

whole neighbourhood. Hence many devout virgins came to visit her, desiring to profit by her heavenly conversation, and to learn from her lips the lessons of religious perfection and of a truly christian life. At first humility would not suffer her to converse with them, or give them the instructions they desired; but when they pressed her to speak on divine matters, she contented herself with edifying them by her silence, sighs, and tears, till at length charity prevailing over humility, she yielded to their importunity, and gave them many excellent lessons for the regulating of their lives, set down at large by our author in her life, as a rule for such holy virgins as aspire after religious perfection, of whom she is generally considered the mother and foundress.

She begins by inculcating to them as her principal lesson, to have always before their eyes, and to imprint deeply in their hearts the two principal commandments : *thou shalt love the Lord thy God with thy whole heart,* &c. *and thy neighbour as thyself :* which she tells them are an abridgment of the whole divine law, and comprise all the perfection God desires from us.——That in the exercise of this divine love, those who desire to dedicate themselves to God, must fix no bounds to themselves, but endeavour always to advance :——that they must not content themselves with being the land that bringeth forth only *thirty fold,* but must labour to bring forth *sixty,* and a *hundred fold :*——that as it would be infinitely dangerous to fall from a higher to a lower degree of virtue, from bringing forth sixty, to bring forth only thirty fold, it being so natural when we once begin to sink downwards, to fall lower and lower, till we fall headlong down the precipice, so we must never think of standing still in the way of God, which would in effect be going backwards; but as the apostle admonishes, Philip. iii. 13, 14, *forgetting the things that are behind, and stretching forth to those that are before, we should still press forward towards the mark, to the prize of the high calling of God in Christ Jesus.*

In the next place she tells them, that in order to preserve and maintain the purity of their souls and bodies,
they must exercise themselves in the mortification of their
sensual appetite, not only with regard to eating and
drinking, but also with respect to the guard they ought
to keep upon their eyes, their ears, their tongue, &c.
lest the angels of darkness, who are the robbers and
murderers that are always endeavouring to do us as
much mischief as they can, should steal into our soul by
any avenue that should be left unguarded : therefore she
recommends a spirit of recollection and retirement, and
to have as little communication as possible with the
world; for how, says she, can a house surrounded on all
sides by smoke, escape being sullied and made black within, if the doors and windows are always open ? She
adds, that they must, according to our Lord's prescription, be ever *wise as serpents, and innocent as doves,* wisely
watching against all the deceits and assaults of the wicked one, who is ever besieging them within and without;
and in all their actions keep close to God, by purity and
simplicity, both in their intention and affection ; and that
the arms they must continually make use of in this warfare, are the exercises of a spiritual life, more especially
fasting and fervent prayer.

She proceeds in the next place to treat of the advantages of voluntary poverty, and of quitting all things for
Christ, by shewing that nothing can be of greater service to a soul that has, by the exercise of other virtues,
and the custom of mortifying herself in eating, drinking,
hard lodging, &c. first to learn to be content with little,
and cheerfully sacrifice her own will, inclinations, and
pleasures to God ; for no sooner do we renounce the
perishable goods of the earth, than we easily learn to
turn our eyes towards heaven; to seek that hidden treasure which alone is able to make us rich for eternity, in
the happy possession of God himself. Oh! what a shame,
would she say, that we should not be ready to undergo

all kinds of labours and sufferings for acquiring so invaluable a treasure, when we daily behold the children of this world expose themselves to far greater labours, sufferings, and dangers, for the sake of a little worldly dirt.

She also warns them against making a parade of their virtues, or publishing their good actions, by making them the subject of their conversation with others; for as a treasure that lies exposed to the public is quickly taken away and lost to its owner, so virtue presently fades and evaporates, when we make a shew of it, or publish it to the world. Praise and applause are ever apt to weaken the vigour of the soul; whilst, on the other hand, it commonly receives an additional increase of strength from affronts, reproaches and injuries. She therefore exhorted them to rejoice under sufferings, and endeavor, by prayer and spiritual canticles, to banish sadness in general away from them as an enemy, that wholesome sorrow only excepted, *which is according to God*, by which we grieve for having offended him.

She goes on by strenuously recommending a constant watchfulness over their hearts, that they be ever fearful and diffident of their own strength, and never think themselves secure in this life. Upon which occasion she treats at large on the excellence and necessity of self-knowledge and humility, and warns them against the pernicious consequences of pride, self-conceit, and presumption, which she tells them are the most heinous of all sins, as well as against the passions of anger, resentment, remembrance of injuries, envy, and detraction, the daughters of pride, which being spiritual sins, frequently overlooked and neglected, are apt to leave mortal wounds behind them in the most noble parts of the soul;—wounds the more hard to be cured, as they are generally less apprehended.

The Saint also gave her spiritual daughters many other excellent lessons, inserted by the author of her life at large, who assures us, that what she taught them by words, she continually enforced by her example; and that no tougue was capable of expressing the spiritual advantages, that those who were so happy as to hear her, received from her heavenly conversation, and the incredible fruits which her instructions produced in many souls.

Syncletica continued her regular exercises of devotion and penance, advancing daily more and more in the love of God, till she arrived at the age of fourscore years; at which time our Lord was pleased to permit her to be afflicted by the most violent interior pains and diseases, joined with as horrible temptations as if Satan had obtained permission from God to put her patience to as severe a trial, and torment her as much as he did Job, with a complication of the most severe sufferings. She passed through this course of penance for the space of three years and a half, with an incredible patience and courage, to the great edification of all that approached her, to whom she ceased not to preach both by word and example. Towards the latter part of this time, a cancer in her mouth was added to the rest of her sufferings, which spread itself so far as to consume a great part of her face, and which, besides the pain and the insupportable stench it caused, prevented her from being able either to eat or to speak. In this condition she remained suffering, like a martyr, for the space of three months, supported only by divine grace, till the end of her life approaching, she was favoured with a rapt, or ecstacy, in which she beheld the glory and light of the heavenly mansions that were prepared for her, with troops of angels and holy virgins, who invited her to come and join their happy company. Returning to herself, she found herself able to give her last instructions to the virgins that surrounded her; exhorting them particularly to constancy, courage, and perseverance in their holy undertaking, and telling them, that within three days, at an hour which she named, she should be taken away from them. Accordingly when that hour arrived, her pure soul took its flight from this vale of tears, and went to take possession of the kingdom of her heavenly Bridegroom. Her name stands recorded in the Roman Martyrology on the fifth of January.

ST. THAIS THE PENITENT.

From an ancient Greek Writer

THAIS was a native of Egypt, who being exceedingly beautiful, was so unhappy as to be betrayed and prostituted by her own mother to infamy and sin. Having followed a most wicked course of life for a long time, she, on account of her extraordinary beauty, became the ruin of many, who spent their fortunes on her, and frequently quarrelled so much about her, that murders were sometimes committed on her account. There happened to live at this time in a neighbouring desert a holy abbot, called Paphnucius, who, on hearing of the wretched life she led, and of the havoc which Satan by her means had made amongst the youth of that part of Egypt, became inspired with a desire to attempt her conversion. For this purpose, procuring a secular habit, and taking some money with him, he went to the place where she lived, and desiring to speak to her in private, was introduced by her into a chamber richly furnished. Having asked her if she had not some more retired apartment? she replied she had : but added, what can you be afraid of? for as for men, I assure you, no mortal can see us, or dare to come into the room where we are ; and as for God, he would equally see us wherever we went. "O!" said he, " dost thou then believe there is a God, whose all-seeing eye is always upon us." " Yes, Sir," replied she, I do believe there is an all-seeing God ; and what is more, I do believe there is a heaven, where the good shall be rewarded with never-ending bliss ; and also a hell, where the wicked shall be tormented for all eternity."

Paphnucius rejoicing interiorly to hear her make this profession of her faith began to represent to her the dismal state of her soul, and the dreadful account she must one day give for the souls of so many others whom she had seduced into sin, in so pathetic a manner, and with such powerful unction of divine grace, that perceiving him to be a man of God, she cast herself at his feet, and poured forth torrents of tears, gave herself up to be directed by him, offering, without a moment's delay, to undergo whatsoever penance he should think proper to appoint, and in what place he pleased ; hoping, as she said, that through his prayers God would shew her mercy. Paphnucius having mentioned the place where she should come to him, departed, whilst she immediately prepared herself to follow him. But first gathering what she had acquired by sin, viz. all the rich presents of her lovers, together in one heap, she made a bonfire of them in the midst of the street, in the sight of all the people, and of those who had been accomplices in her crimes, declaring publicly an abhorrence of every thing that contributed to detain her in that way of life. Having made this first sacrifice, she repaired to the place appointed by Paphnucius, who conducted her from thence to a monastery of nuns, where he shut her up in a cell by herself, and stopped up the door, leaving only a small aperture, or window, to which he desired the sisters to convey to her a little bread and water every day, which was to be her whole allowance for the remainder of her life.

Before he departed from her, she asked him what prayers he would recommend to her, and in what manner he would have her address herself to God in prayer? "Thou art not worthy," said he, "either to invoke the sacred name of God with thy polluted lips, nor to stretch forth thy hands, or lift up thy eyes towards heaven, after so many abominations ; let it suffice then for thee to sit turned towards the East, and frequently to repeat these words : *Thou that hast made me, have mercy on me.*"

She continued this course of penance, in her solitary enclosure, for the space of three years, till at length Paphnucius, having compassion on her, went to consult the great St. Antony, at that time the oracle of Egypt, to learn whether God had accepted her penance and pardoned her sins. St. Antony having assembled his disciples together, and exhorted them to pray that God would be pleased to let them know what Paphnucius so earnestly required. St. Paul the Simple saw that very night in a vision, a glorious throne, or bed of state, in heaven, surrounded by three virgins, glittering with beams of heavenly light ; and whilst he was thinking within himself that this throne could be designed for no other than St. Antony, he was answered by a voice : "It is not for thy father Antony, but for Thais the harlot." This vision being notified to Paphnucius, he concluded it was the will of God that Thais should be released from her confinement, and therefore let her out, whilst she, on her part desired to remain where she was, but at length humbly submitted to the will of her holy director. Having told her that God had forgiven her sins, she assured him, that from the time she first entered into her cell, she had collected them together as it were into one heap, and placing them before her eyes, never ceased to think on and bewail them.

"It is on beholding your contrition," said Paphnucius, "that God has shewn you mercy, and not "on account of the rigour of your penance." She lived no longer than fifteen days after she had been released from her penitential enclosure, when she was called to see *the good things of our Lord in the land of the living.*

ST. PELAGIA THE PENITENT.

From her Life by James the Deacon, her Contemporary.

PELAGIA was a famous actress in the city of Antioch, at that time the capital of Syria, and of the whole East. Her extraordinary beauty drew many lovers after her, and so unhappy was she as to yield herself up to a very sinful course of life, without the least restraint, although she professed herself a Christian, and had been formerly admitted into the number of Catechumens who were under instruction for baptism, but had now left off her attendance at church for that purpose. It happened at this time, viz. about the beginning of the fifth century, that several bishops, and others of the clergy, were assembled at Antioch upon some ecclesiastical affairs ; amongst whom was the holy prelate Nonnus, who, from a monk of the monastery of Tabenna, was, on account of his admirable virtue and wisdom, raised to the see of Heliopolis. These prelates were lodged in the neighbourhood of the church of St. Julian the martyr, where they met together to treat upon the business that had called them to Antioch. One day, whilst they were sitting before the church with St. Nonnus, who was then entertaining them with a spiritual conference, to their great edification, Pelagia passed before them in great pomp, decked with gold, pearls, and precious stones, accompanied by a numerous train of young men and women. Her beauty with the lustre of her jewels, and her rich attire, drew the eyes of all the fond admirers of these empty toys upon her; but whilst the prelates turned away their faces aside, because having no veil over her head, and her very sholders being uncovered, they were offended at the immodesty of her dress, Nonnus only seemed to take notice of her, and to consider her with great attention. After she had passed by, turning

23

to his fellow-bishops, he said to them, with many sighs and tears: " I fear God will one day bring this woman to confront us before the throne of his justice, in order to condemn our negligence and tepidity [in his service, and in the discharge of our duty to the flock he has committed to our care. For how many hours do you think she has employed this very day in her chamber in washing and cleansing herself, in dressing, adorning, and embellishing her whole person to the best advantage, with a view to exhibit her beauty to please the eyes of the world, and particularly her unhappy lovers, who, though alive to-day, may possibly be dead to-morrow? Whereas we, who have an Almighty Father, an immortal Spouse, in heaven, to whose love and service we have consecrated ourselves;—we,—to whom the immense and eternal treasures of heaven are promised as the reward of our short labours upo earth, are far from taking as much pains to wash and purify our souls from their stains, and procure for them those bright ornaments of virtue and sanctity, which alone can render them truly agreeable in the eyes of God." Having spoken to this effect, he rose up and returned home, where, prostrating himself on the floor, he bitterly lamented his misery, [in having suffered himself to be thus outdone by a sinful woman, and implored the divine mercy for the forgiveness of his negligence and tepidity.

The next day, being Sunday, all the bishops assembled in the great church where the patriarch of Antioch celebrated mass. After the gospel was read, he presented the book to St. Nonnus, and desired him to make an exhortation to the people. The holy prelate obeyed, and made a most pathetic discourse, full of the unction of the spirit of God, on the subject of the last judgment, and of the world to come, which drew tears from the eyes of his whole auditory, amongst whom was Pelagia, who had not been within a church for a long time before, and his sermon made so deep an impression on her soul, that she could not refrain the whole time from sighing, and sobbing, and pouring out floods of tears, through the deep sense she conceived of her sins. As soon as the divine service was over, she sent a letter to the holy prelate to this effect.

To the holy disciple of Jesus Christ, from a sinful wretch, a scholar of the devil.

I have learnt that the God whom you worship came down from heaven to the earth, not for the sake of the just, but to save poor sinners, and that he humbled himself so far as to suffer publicans to come to him, and did not disdain to speak with the sinful Samaritan woman at the well; wherefore, as I understand, that though you never have seen him with your mortal eyes, you are nevertheless a follower of his, and have served him faithfully for many years, I conjure you, for his sake, to shew yourself to be his true disciple, by suffering a poor sinner to come to you, and not despise the extreme desire I have to approach to him through your assistance." The Saint sent her word, that if she was sincere in her desires of instruction and conversion, she might come to him to the church of Julian, where he would speak to her in the presence of the other bishops, not thinking it proper to converse with her in private.

No sooner had Pelagia received this permission than she ran with all possible speed to the church, and cast herself at the feet of the holy prelate, earnestly beseeching him, through the example of his great Master, to receive the worst of sinners, and cleanse her from the filth and abomination of her crimes, in the fountain of baptism. The Saint told her, that by the discipline of the Church, persons who like her had been a long time engaged in criminal habits, could not be admitted to baptism without first producing proper sureties who should answer for her returning no more to their sinful ways; but she not being able to bear the enormous weight of her sins, or to continue any longer contaminated by their filth, would hear of no delay, wherefore embracing the feet of the servant of God, and washing them with floods of tears, she conjured them to baptize her upon the spot, in order to a new life, that she might instantly be presented without spot or blemish to Jesus Christ : this petition she urged with so much fervour, such demonstrations of a lively faith, [and so ardent a desire of saving her soul, that the prelates were unanimously of opinion, that as the hand of God minifested itself in her favour in so extraordinary a manner, her request ought to be admitted. They therefore sent to acquaint the patriarch with all that had passed, who approving of her being baptized, sent the lady Romana, the chief of the widows that were in the service of the great church, to attend her as godmother on the occasion. This good lady found her still bewailing her sins at the feet of the Saint, from which she could not be prevailed to remove, till he commanded her to rise, in order to proceed to the exorcisms and prayers as used by the Church before baptism. After making a public confession and detestation of all her crimes, he baptized her ; and then, according to the custom of the Church in those days, administered to her the sacraments of confirmation and of the body of our Lord.

The same day, as our author relates, who being deacon to St. Nonnus was himself present, whilst the holy bishop and he sat at table together, rejoicing with the angels upon the conversion of so great a sinner, they heard distinctly before the door a voice as of one bitterly complaining in these or the like words : " Alas ! alas ! must I be continually tormented by thee in this manner ? Not satisfied with having robbed me heretofore of no less than thirty thousand souls of the nation of the Saracens, which thou hast presented to thy God ; not content to have also snatched the city of Heliopolis out of my hands, where all the people worshipped me, must thou also bereave me of the greatest hope I had left ? or dost thou think I can any longer bear with thee, or support the persecutions thou makest me suffer ?" In this manner did Satan express his grief at the loss of his prey, and his rage against the holy prelate, who took no notice of him, but armed his convert against all the efforts and temptations of this enemy, and taught her to drive him away by a confidence in her Saviour, and the sign of his cross.

The third day after baptism, Pelagia having taken an inventory of all her plate, jewels, rich clothes, and other goods, put it into the hands of St. Nonnus, saying : " My Lord, here is the whole of the goods I have acquired from the devil ; I give them all up to your disposal ; give such orders concerning them as you judge to be for the best. As to my part I desire, no riches for the ti me to come but those of my Saviour Jesus Christ." The h oly prelate sent immediately for the treasurer of the chur ch, and delivering the inventory into his hands, charged hm, as he would answer for it before God, not to apply any part of her goods either to the service of the bishop or the church, but to distribute the whole to poor widows and orphans, and such like objects ;—that as they had been ill gotten, they might now at least be well app lied. On the same day Pelagia set all her slaves, both men and women at liberty, earnestly exhorting them, at the same time, to shake off that yoke of servitude by whi ch they had, as well as herself, been slaves to a corrupt and sinful world ; that passing over with her to the true liberty of the children of God, they might one day arrive with her at the enjoyment of that true and eternal life which knows neither sin nor sorrow.

On the eighth day, when those that had been baptized, according to the ancient custom of the Church, put off the white garment they received at their baptism, Pelagia rising privately in the night, exchanged her baptismal robe for a habit of haircloth, and an old mantle which she had received from St. Nonnus, and without communica-

23*

ting her design to any one but him, she withdrew from Antioch, and going into the Holy Land, took up her habitation for life in a narrow cell upon mount Olivet, where she lived as an anchoret, shut up in such a manner as to have only a small window through which she might receive the necessaries of life, and spending her whole time with our Lord in fasting and prayer. The other religious inhabitants of this holy mountain were so perfectly ignorant who she was, as not even to know whether she was a woman, so effectually had she concealed her sex, calling herself by the name of *Pelagius ;* but they all admired the great abstraction, austerity, and sanctity of her life.

Some years after this, our author, James the deacon, made a pilgrimage of devotion to visit the sepulchre of our Lord at Jerusalem. Upon this occasion his holy bishop recommended to him to enquire after a servant of God named Pelagius, that led an anchoretical life upon mount Olivet. He executed his commission, little thinking that this anchoret was the famous Pelagia whom he had seen baptized, and who presently after disappeared and was no more heard of. But though he readily found out the cell, by enquiring of the religious who dwelt in the neighbourhood, and went and spoke to her through the window, yet being much altered by her austerities, he knew her not. He told her he came by the desire of Bishop Nonnus to enquire after her. Nonnus, said she, is a great Saint, and I beg that he will pray for me. With that she shut the window and began to sing Tierce, or the third hour of the divine office, whilst the deacon was praying without, much comforted with having seen so holy a person. Afterwards visiting the monasteries round about, and finding that all the servants of God, wherever he came, conspired in giving testimony to the wonderful sanctity of Pelagius, he resolved to return and visit this holy anchoret once more before he left the country, in order to receive some wholesome instruction from him. When he came to her cell and knocked at the window, no one opened it to him, and when he called no one answered;—so that having continued for some time knocking and calling aloud, he began to think the anchoret was gone away. At length having forced open the window, he looked in and perceived the Saint to be dead. Having conveyed the news of her death to the neighbouring religious, they immediately came, and opening the cell took out the body, in order to its being interred with all the honour due to so great a servant of God. The secret of her sex being now discovered and noised abroad all the holy virgins that dwelt in the monasteries of Jericho and on the banks of the Jordan, in the place where our Lord was baptized, came out with lighted tapers in their hands, singing hymns and psalms, to meet the corpse of the Saint. which they conducted to their church, and there deposited it as a rich treasure.

Her name is recorded in the Roman Martyrology on the eighth of October, and the name of St. Nonnus on the second of December.

ST. MARY OF EGYPT.

From her Life, written by St. Sophronius, Patriarch of Jerusalem.

THERE was in a monastery of Palestine, a holy priest name Zosimus, who had from his childhood dedicated himself to the love of God, and spent fifty-three years in that community in the exercises of a monastic life, with such perfection as to be respected and admired by all who knew him. This good father being one day tempted with a thought that nothing more was now wanting in him, and that he had already arrived, as he imagined, at the top of the hill of religious perfection, was admonished by one appearing to him in the shape of a man, of his error, and directed by this messenger of heaven to another monastery more remote from all conversation with the world, situated in a solitary place on the banks of the river Jordan, in order to learn still higher lessons in the school of religion. In this place he found a company of angels rather than men, so great was their fervour in all that related to the service of God. They sang his divine praises every hour of the night; and in the day, whilst their hands were employed in manual labour, the psalms were always in their mouths and hearts. Here was no room for any unprofitable conversation, having made it their whole business not only absolutely to forget the world, but even every thing in the world, and to live as men quite dead to all things but the *one thing necessary*. Their thoughts were continually occupied on heavenly truths;—the emptiness and vanity of all such things as pass away with time, and the greatness of things eternal, were the subjects of their constant meditation. Their greatest dainties for their corporal sustenance were bread and water, whilst their souls continually feasted on the word of God and prayer.

It was the custom of these religious every year on the first Sunday of Lent, after assisting at the divine mysteries, and receiving the precious body and blood of our Lord, to go forth into the vast wilderness beyond the river, there to spend that holy season in perfect solitude. They eat but very seldom, and then only a few figs or dates, which they carried, or such herbs as grew wild in the desert, frequently singing psalms, and praying without ceasing. After spending the greatest part of Lent in this manner, they all returned back again to the monastery, to celebrate the passion and resurrection of our Lord, contriving always to meet there against Palm-Sunday. The holy man, Zosimus, according to the custom of the others, when Lent came, crossed the river, designing to penetrate as far as he could into the heart of the desert, in hopes, as he afterwards said, of meeting with some Saint from whom he might receive instruction and edification. He took with him but slender provisions, and never eat but when necessity compelled him. When night found him, there he lay down on the ground to take a little rest; and as soon as the daylight permitted, he hastened forward, as if he had been making the best of his way towards some person of his acquaintance, halting only at certain times of the day, to sing some psalms standing, and to spend some time in prayer on his knees.

He continued his journey after this manner till about mid-lent, when one day stopping at the sixth hour, and performing his usual prayers, turned towards the East, he perceived on his right the shadow, as it were, of a human body; but when he had finished his devotion, turning his eyes that way he plainly saw a person walking hastily towards the West, whose naked body had grown quite black with the heat of the sun, and whose hair was turned white as wool. Upon this sight Zosimus was overjoyed, hoping he had now found what he sought, and therefore he began to run with all his strength, in order to overtake the person whom he perceived to fly from him, and through his earnest desire of coming up to her, he continually gained ground of her, till coming within hearing, he cried out, "Servant of God, why dost thou fly from a sinner, and a poor old man? Whoever thou art, I conjure thee, by that God, for whose sake thou spendest thy days in this frightful desert, to let me come near thee. I beg of thee to stop a little, and not to refuse thy blessing and prayers to one who entreats thee in the name of that God who has never cast off any man that desired to come to him." Whilst he was thus calling after her, she arrived at a place that had been made hollow by the water of a torrent, but which was now dried up; and when she had passed over to the other side, whither he not being able to follow her, she cried, " Father Zosimus, I beseech you, for God's sake, excuse my turning about to speak to you, because I am a woman and quite naked; but if you are willing to favour a poor sinner with your blessing, fling over your mantle that I may cover myself with it, and then turn towards you and receive your benediction."

The holy man, struck with astonishment to hear her call him by his name, which he was convinced she could not know but by revelation, readily complied with her desire, and threw his mantle over; turning his back towards her till she had covered herself therewith; which when she had done, she asked him, what had brought him so far to see such a wretched sinner as she was? or what could he expect to know or learn from her? Having already conceived a high opinion of her sanctity, he instead of answering her, prostrated himself upon the ground, and, according to the custom of the religious when they visited one another, craved her blessing. No, father, said she, falling down upon her face, it is your part to bless and to pray for me, since you are a priest, and having for so many years served the altar, are admitted to a greater grace and light of God, and to the sacred mysteries of Jesus Christ. The amazement of Zosimus was inconceivable when he heard her speak of his being a priest, and therefore venerating the spirit of God within her, insisted the more upon her giving him her blessing first; nor would he rise from the ground till she had so far condescended as to bless him in the following manner: " *Blessed be the Lord, that worketh the salvation of souls ;*" to which he answered, *Amen.* When they both rose up, she began to enquire concerning the state of christendom ;—whether the Church enjoyed peace ;—and how the faithful behaved in their respective stations? Zosimus answered, that God had doubtless heard her prayers and granted peace to the

Church; but, added he, I beseech you, in his name, not to refuse a poor unworthy monk the comfort he asks for the love of Jesus Christ; which is, that you would offer up your prayers to him for the world in general, and for me, a poor sinner, in particular, that the long and painful journey I have taken through this vast wilderness may not prove unprofitable to me. She replied, that it belonged rather to his function to pray both for her and the world; however, as obedience was a duty incumbent on her, should comply with his command.

Then turning towards the East, with hands and eyes lifted up to heaven, she prayed for a long time in silence, whilst Zosimus stood without saying a word with his eyes cast down on the ground. But finding that she continued very long in her prayer, he looked up a little, and saw that she was raised a cubit from the earth, and prayed in that manner suspended in the air, for the truth of which he afterwards called God to witness. This sight filled his soul with so much surprise and apprehension, that he cast himself upon the ground bathed in a sweat, crying out, *Lord have mercy upon me.* His amazement was succeeded by a thought, that perhaps all he had seen might be an illusion, and that this appearance of a woman might be some evil spirit that only pretended to pray. In the mean time she turned towards him, and answering this thought which he had conceived of her, she assured him she was no spirit, but a poor sinful woman, composed of flesh and blood, dirt and corruption, adding that she had been baptized and was a Christian; in testimony whereof, making the sign of the cross upon her forehead, her eyes, her lips, and her stomach, she said, "God deliver us, father, from the evil spirit, and from all his snares and suggestions; for we know that he bears us an implacable hatred."

Hereupon Zosimus entreated her to tell him who she was,—whence she came,—when, and why she retired into this desert;—and, in a word, all that concerned her life since she came thither, as well for the glory of God as for his instruction and edification, not doubting, as he told her, but that God had brought him into that desert, and enabled him, notwithstanding his great age and weakness, to make so long a journey in so short a space of time, with no other design than that the wonders which his divine grace had wrought in her might be made manifest to the greater glory of his name. He added, that she need not apprehend any vain-glory in the recital of her life, since her motive would be no other than the glory of God and the comfort and instruction of a poor sinner. She answered, that with respect to her life, there was indeed no room for her taking any vanity in the relating the history of it, since she had been a vessel of election, not of God, but of the devil; that she was even ready to die with shame and confusion to think of declaring all her infamous crimes. and that she apprehended he would fly from her as from a serpent when he began to hear her history. However, she was resolved to be quite sincere with him, and to declare the particulars of her infamous life, in hopes that he would never cease to pray to God that she might find mercy at the last day.

Here she began to relate the history of her life, saying, that she was a native of Egypt, and had run away from her parents when she was but twelve years old, and went to Alexandria, where, falling into bad company, she quickly lost her honour, and afterwards abandoned herself to all kinds of lewdness, as a public prostitute, for the space of seventeen years. That at the end of this time, seeing a great many persons flock towards the sea-shore in order to embark for the Holy Land, to celebrate the feast of the Exaltation of the Cross in Jerusalem, she had impudently thrust herself into their company; and both during the voyage and after her arrival at Jerusalem had made herself the devil's instrument, introducing many into a partnership in her abominations. That when the day of the feast was come, she attempted to enter with the rest of the faithful into the church of the Holy Cross, but was repulsed by an invisible power; and though she saw all the people about her go in with ease, and had striven on her part with all her might to enter in along with them, yet she could never advance further than the threshold, but always found herself still thrust back again into the portico. "This happening to me," said she, "three or four times, I began to consider what might be the reason that I was thus debarred the sight of the life-giving wood of the holy cross, when a salutary thought striking my mind, and opening the eyes of my soul, I concluded that it was the filthiness of my life that prevented me from entering the temple of God. Then bathed in tears and in the utmost consternation of mind, I knocked my breast, and sighing ready to break my heart, I cried, lamented and mourned at my wretched condition, till at length perceiving over my head in the place where I stood the image of the holy mother of God, I immediately addressed myself to her, and with my eyes steadfastly fixed on her picture, I said, O sacred virgin, who hast brought forth God according to the flesh, I acknowledge myself unworthy to venerate or even to look at thy image with eyes so much defiled by uncleanness as mine have been. As thou art a pure unspotted virgin both in soul and body, it is but just that thy incomparable beauty should abominate, and drive away from thee so filthy a creature as I am: nevertheless, having been taught that the God whom thou wast worthy to bring forth was made man, in order to call sinners to repentance, I beseech thee to assist me, who am here left alone destitute of all assistance. O receive the confession I here make of my sins, and permit me to enter into the church, that I may not be so unhappy as to be deprived of the sight of that precious wood to which that God-man was fastened, who was born of thee, without any

24

prejudice to thy virginity, and on which he spilt his blood for my redemption. Ordain, O blessed Lady, that the door may be open unto me, though most unworthy, that I may salute that divine cross; and be thou responsible to Christ thy Son, that I shall never more defile myself with any of my former detestable uncleannesses, whilst I, for my part, as soon as I shall have seen the tree on which thy son vouchsafed to die, promise absolutely to renounce the world with all its wicked ways, and to depart immediately to the place to which thou, my surety and my guide, shall be pleased to conduct me." So far her prayer to the blessed Virgin.

Then proceeding to her narrative, she declared that after having made this prayer and promise, on attempting again to enter into the church she found no manner of obstacle, but went in with the utmost ease, and penetrated, notwithstanding the great crowd, as far as the sanctuary, and there had the happiness not only to see and venerate the precious and life-giving wood, consecrated with the blood of our Redeemer, but also to be sensibly affected with the experience she now felt of the inconceivable excess of God's mercy in his readiness to forgive penitent sinners. Full of these sentiments she prostrated herself upon the ground, and having kissed the sacred pavement of the sanctuary, she then ran out to the place where she had made her solemn promise to the blessed Virgin, where kneeling down before her image, after giving thanks for the goodness and charity she had already experienced, she offered herself ready to fulfil the promise she had made, and begged of our blessed Lady to direct her now to the place to which she would have her to go to do penance for her sins. Upon which she heard a voice as of one crying out at a distance: *Go beyond the Jordan, and there thou shalt find rest.* Conceiving these words addressed to herself, and begging of our blessed Lady not to forsake her, she arose in haste to follow this call. As she was going she met with a stranger, who gave her three pieces of money, with which she immediately went and bought three loaves; and having enquired of the baker the way that led to the river Jordan, she set forward immediately without stopping, till she arrived at the church of St. John the baptist upon the banks of the river. Here she performed her devotions, and received the blessed sacrament; eating during her short stay there the half of one of her loaves, drinking of the water of the river, and using no other bed but the bare ground. On the morning after her communion she passed over to the other side of the river: " and then," continued she, " having again prayed to the blessed Virgin, my guide, to conduct me to whatever place she pleased, I came into this desert, and from that time to this day, which I compute to be seven and forty years, I have, according to the psalmist, *kept myself far off flying away* from all company, *and have abode in solitude*, Ps. 54, looking for the mercy of my God, who saves both little and great who are converted to him."

Zosimus then enquired what she had lived upon all that time? She answered, that the two loaves and a half which she had brought with her were for a long time her only food, though they soon grew as hard as stones, so that she could eat but very little of them at a time, and that after they were consumed she lived upon what few herbs she could find in the desert. That as for clothes, those which she had brought over with her being quite worn out, she had been without any for the greatest part of the time, and had laboured under inexpressible difficulties for the want of them, being broiled with excessive heat in the summer, and suffering the extremity of cold in the winter; but that under all these hardships and necessities, together with a multitude and variety of temptations which she had to struggle with, she continued to experience to that very day the power and the goodness of God in the various ways whereby he had still preserved her poor soul and body. So that when she called to mind from how many evils the Lord had delivered her, she felt herself nourished and supported with a never-failing food, and found a banquet which satisfied her whole appetite in the hopes she entertained of her eternal salvation.

Zosimus desiring also to learn more particulars from her with relation to the conflicts she must have sustained, more especially upon her first entering on this new kind of life, she acknowledged that for the first seventeen years she was in a manner under perpetual temptations; --that she suffered much from hunger and thirst, and was frequently attacked with vehement desires of returning to partake of the flesh-pots of Egypt ;—that she longed for wine which she formerly loved and drank to excess, whereas now she could not even come at a drop of water ;—that the lascivious songs she had formerly been accustomed to sing were often recurring to her mind, and other impure suggestions disturbing her soul, and violently moving her to lust ; but that upon perceiving any of these assaults, it was her custom to strike her breast, shed many tears, and remembering the solemn engagement she had made before she came into the wilderness, to place herself in spirit before the image of the blessed Virgin, whom she had desired to be her surety, and ceased not to weep and lament, and to beg of her protectress to drive away from her those wicked thoughts which troubled her poor soul, till after long and earnest prayer, accompanied with floods of tears, and with the bruising of her body with blows, she used to perceive a light to shine round about her, and a heavenly calm restored to her soul. "Thus," continued she, "I had always the eyes of my heart lifted up without ceasing to her that was my surety, beseeching her to stand by me in my solitude and penance ; and I always experienced the help and assistance of her who brought forth the Author of all purity, and so I passed safely through the many conflicts and dangers of those seventeen years; and from that time till now, the blessed mother of God has never forsaken me, but always, and in all things, has assisted and directed me."

Zosimus hearkened with great attention to all that she said, and taking notice that she had in her relation of her life made use of passages taken out of the psalms and other parts of the scripture, he asked her if she had ever learnt the psalms, or read any part of the holy scripture? She told him she could not read, nor had even so much as ever heard any person read or sing the psalms, or ever seen either man or beast from her coming into the desert till that day. "But," said she, "the Word of God, which is living and effectual, interiorly teaches the understanding of man; wherefore, as you have now heard all that relates to me, I conjure you by the incarnation of the Eternal Word, to pray for me, who, as you see, have been so vile a sinner."

When she had finished her narrative, Zosimus cast himself on his knees, and with a loud voice magnified the Lord for the wonders of his goodness and mercy to those who fear and seek him; whilst she, on her part, begged of him, for the sake of our Lord and Saviour Jesus Christ, not to speak of the things she had related to him to any one living, till God should deliver her out of the prison of the body: and, said she, "about this time twelvemonth, by God's grace, you shall again see me; I beg of you therefore, for our Lord's sake, that when the holy time of Lent shall return next year, you would not come over the Jordan, according to the custom of your monastery, but remain at home during that time (but indeed you shall not be able to go out, if you would) and on the most sacred evening of our Lord's last supper, bring out for me, in a holy vessel worthy of so great a mystery, the divine body and life-giving blood of our Saviour, and wait for me on that side of the river which you inhabit, and I shall come and receive those precious

24*

gifs that are the life of the soul, at the very hour in which our Lord imparted that divine supper to his disciples." Having said this, and once more begged the holy father to pray for her, she hastened away into the remoter parts of the wilderness; whilst Zosimus, after casting himself down upon the ground, and kissing the earth upon which she had stood, returned through the desert the same way he came, and arrived in due time at the monastery.

During the following year he kept all that he had seen and heard a secret to himself, longing for the return of Lent, that he might be once more blessed with the sight and conversation of one whom he justly held in the highest veneration. But when the holy fast of Lent was come, he was visited with a fever, which as the Saint had foretold, was attended by no other consequence than that of preventing him from going abroad into the desert with the rest of the brethren; wherefore, on Maunday-Thursday evening, in compliance with her desire, he carried out the body and blood of our Lord Jesus Christ in a small pix or chalice, to the bank of the river, and there waited, looking attentively towards the desert, in expectation of what he had so great a desire of seeing, but not without some apprehension, as it was a long time before she came, that she might have been there already, and not finding him had returned back again. Another perplexing thought also occurred to his mind, viz. how in case of her coming, she should be able to pass over the river to him, as there was neither bridge nor boat near that place. Whilst the holy old man was revolving these difficulties in his mind, he discovered the Saint on the opposite bank of the Jordan, by the light of the moon, which was then at the full, and saw her making the sign of the cross upon the river, and presently after walking towards him upon the water, as if it had been firm ground, with which sight he was so much astonished, that he was going to cast himself upon his knees, had she not stopped him by crying out—"Father, what are you about ? Recollect you are a priest of God, and that you carry with you the divine mysteries."

Having now passed over the river, she craved his blessing, and after desiring him to recite the creed and the Lord's prayer, she received the blessed sacrament from his hands ; after which, lifting up her hands to heaven, sighing and weeping, she cried out : *Now dost thou dismiss thy servant, O Lord, according to thy word, in peace ; because my eyes have seen thy salvation.* Then turning to Zosimus, she begged pardon for the trouble she had given him, and requested he would for the present return to the monastery, but on the following lent he would not fail to come to the place where she had first spoken to him, and that there he should see her again in the manner God should be pleased to ordain. The good old man desired her to eat something, having brought a basket of figs and dates, with some lentiles steeped in water, with him for that purpose. She took a few grains of the lentiles, saying she had no occasion for any more; for that the grace of the spirit was sufficient to preserve the soul in its purity. Then begging of him again for God's sake to pray for her, and never to forget her miseries, whilst he, on his part, recommended himself and the whole church to her prayers, she took leave of him, and making the sign of the cross upon the river, crossed it again in the same manner as she came to him, walking upon the waters.

The next year Zosimus going out in Lent, according to the custom of the monastery, into the desert, made the best of his way towards the place where he had first seen the Saint, in hopes of being still more edified by her sight and heavenly conversation, and of learning also her name, which he regretted not having enquired after when he last saw her. After a long and painful journey, when he arrived at the dry torrent, he found in the higher part of that concavity the dead body of the Saint extended decently on the ground, with her hands crossed, and her face turned towards the east.   Hereupon he fell down at the feet of the holy corpse, which he washed with his tears, and then began to sing the psalms and recite the prayers for the burial of the dead, when behold he perceived on the ground these words written in the sand: "Father Zosimus, bury the body of poor Mary; render to the earth what belongs to the earth; and in the name of God pray for me on the *ninth day of April*, the day of the passion of our Lord, after the communion of the divine supper."*   The old man, reading these words, could not conceive by whom they were wrote, as the Saint had assured him she could neither read nor write. He was however not only pleased to have found out her name, but also astonished to think how quickly she had been brought back in the space of one night after receiving the holy communion, over as large a tract of ground as had taken him twenty days travelling without ceasing.   Hence it appears that after her return her blessed soul had left her body, and taken its flight to heaven.

But now his greatest solicitude was how he should contrive to bury her body, as he had no proper instrument to open the earth, or dig a grave.   But he was not long under this perplexity before he perceived a great lion standing by the body of the Saint, and licking her feet. To recover himself from the terror excited by the sight of so tremendous an animal, he made the sign of the cross, trusting that God and her holy body would protect him from all dangers, when behold he found the lion began to fawn upon him, as if he proffered him his service! So that being convinced that God had sent the beast to make a grave for his servant, he commanded him in the name of God to set about that work with his claws.

* The anniversary of her happy death, viz. the day immediately following that on which Zosimus had, the year before, administered to her the blessed eucharist.

The lion obeyed, and presently made a sufficient grave, in which Zosimus interred the body of the Saint, covering it only with the mantle she had received of him, and with many tears, having recommended both himself and the whole world to her prayers, he departed praising God, whilst the lion, like a tame lamb, went his way into the remoter parts of the desert. Zosimus, at his return home, related to his brethren the whole history of the life of the Saint from the beginning, to their great edification, concealing no part of what he had seen or heard. After which he still continued serving and glorifying God in that monastery, till he was a hundred years old, with such perfection as to be enrolled after his death amongst the Saints. His name occurs in the Roman Martyrology on the fourth of April, and that of St. Mary of Egypt on the second of the same month.

APPENDIX;

CONTAINING

A COLLECTION OF REMARKABLE ANECDOTES, APHORISMS AND EXAMPLES,

OF THE

EASTERN SOLITARIES:

Extracted from Ancient Ecclesiastical Writers.

From the Third Book of the Lives of the Fathers, by Rufinus.

1. An ancient father said one day to his disciples, brethren, if we hate the repose of the present life, the pleasures of the body, the gratification of its appetites, and seek not the honour that is from man, the Lord Jesus will then give us the honour and glory of heaven, the repose of eternal life, {and never ending joys with his angels.

2. An ancient father, who had many years led an anchoretical life in the heart of the wilderness, in the practice of extraordinary abstinences and continual labours, being one day visited by some of his brethren, after admiring his patience and perseverance, they asked him how he was able to endure so many trials and great sufferings as he was obliged to undergo in that dry and frightful solitude ? " O brethren," said he, " all the labours and sufferings of the many years I have been here are not comparable to one hour of suffering in the flames of hell; wherefore, in order to escape them, we must cheerfully undergo the hardships and labours of the short time of our mortal life. We must mortify ourselves here, that we may find never-ending rest hereafter in the happy mansions of the world to come."

3. The emperor Theodosius having heard that a certain religious hermit lived a recluse and penitential life in a small cell near the suburbs of Constantinople, and being desirous to see this servant of God, he went one day alone to his cell and knocked at the door. The hermit having let him in, they, according to the custom of the religious in their visits, first made their prayer together, and then sat down. The emperor enquired of him concerning the employment and manner of living of the holy fathers in Egypt. They all pray, said the hermit, for your salvation. Theodosius looked about to see what he had in his cell, and discovering nothing but some dry bread in a basket, he said : father, give me your benediction, and let us refresh ourselves together. The hermit put some salt into water, and then soaked the dry bread in it, of which they made their meals together, and when they had done, he presented the emperor with a cup of water. Theodosius said to him: Do you know who I am ? God knows who you are, said the hermit. "I am Theodosius the emperor," said he, "and I came hither to be edified by you. O how happy are you solitaries, who being altogether free and desengaged from wordly cares and occupations, enjoy a calm and quiet life, having no other solicitude but for the salvation of your souls, nor any other thoughts but how to make yourselves worthy of the heavenly rewards of that life, and kingdom to come, that knows no end. But I, though born to the purple, and seated on the imperial throne, declare to you in truth, that I never sit down to my meals without having some cares upon my mind." Having said this, and testified a great deal of honour and esteem for the servant of God, he returned home. But the hermit suspecting, that in consequence of this visit from the emperor, a great number of all conditions, not excepting even the courtiers and senators, would be frequently coming to interrupt his devotion; and being also apprehensive lest he should come at length to take a complacency in their visits, and in the honours they would shew him, and thus fall, by degrees, into the nets of Satan, by pride and vain-glory, in order to secure himself from the danger, he departed that very night, and made the best of his way into Egypt, where he associated himself with the holy fathers of the Egyptian deserts.

4. Amongst the many holy inhabitants of the Egyptian deserts, there was an ancient anchoret named Agatho, who was much admired for his extraordinary patience and humility. Some of the brethren, with the design of putting his virtue to a trial, went one day to his cell and complained of the scandal his pride and self-conceit had given by his contempt of others, setting them at nought, and taking the liberty to censure and detract them, and all this, said they, because, being yourself ...ious and given to lewdness, you think to disguise you...o.vn vices by charging them upon others. The holy man heard all they said without discovering the least emotion or disturbance of soul, or denying any part of the charge; on the contrary, casting himself at their feet, he confessed himself to be indeed a most grievous sinner, and begged they would be so charitable as to intercede to our Lord for a poor miserable wretch, loaded as he was with so many crimes, to the end he might obtain mercy and forgiveness for them through the assistance of their prayers. But, said they, we must tell you moreover, that some people say you are also a heretic. O no, said the Saint, however wretched I am in other respects, or how guilty soever I may be of innumerable other sins, I am not so great a wretch as to forfeit my share in Jesus Christ by heresy; far be this thought from my soul! The brethren hereupon casting themselves at his feet, desired to know why he, who had suffered so many other false accusations, without the least emotion or resistance, shewed so much horror and so great a repugnance at being accused of heresy? The man of God answered, that as to the other accusations, it was the part of humility to love to be despised, and be willing to pass for a grievous sinner; to bear also with reproaches and calumnies, after the example of Jesus Christ himself, who suffered in silence such treatment as this from the Jews for our instruction; but that there was a particular enormity and malignity in *heresy*, which is an obstinate opposition to the revealed truths of God, by means whereof the *soul* is separated in such manner from Jesus Christ, as to destroy *faith*, the very foundation of its salvation, and is given up as it were to the devil, without reserve; therefore, as no one ought to be willing to pass for an obstinate enemy of Jesus Christ, or of any of his revealed truths, so no one ought to be willing to pass for a heretic.

25

5. There was in a certain monastery of Egypt a monk named Eulalius, endued in an extraordinary degree with the grace of humility. As there were not wanting in that numerous community several lukewarm brethren, who had been guilty of frequent faults and negligences, particularly in breaking or destroying the earthen vessels and other utensils of the monastery, they were accustomed to lay all upon Eulalius, whom they found ever ready to bear the blame. On these occasions the superiors often took him to task, whilst he, instead of pleading *not guilty*, prostrated himself before them, and begged pardon for his faults and negligences. The rule of the monastery enjoined penances for these faults, which he cheerfully underwent, even to the passing often two or three days together without eating. But as fresh accusations still were brought against him, the ancient religious, who were ignorant that he endured all this for the sake of Christ, and for the exercise of his patience and humility, represented to the abbot, that as they found no amendment in Eulalius, it became necessary to think of taking some other course with him, since by his negligences most of the utensils of the house were already destroyed, and that there would be no keeping any thing whole in the monastery so long as he remained amongst them. The abbot desired some time to consider on the manner, and in the mean while begging light of heaven to direct him, he learnt from God in prayer the extraordinary merit, patience, and humility of Eulalius, which his divine Majesty was also pleased, not long after, to declare by a miracle, in the presence of all the religious. Upon this the brethren began to esteem him as a saint, and to honour and praise him as such on all occasions, which became so sensible a mortification to this humble servant of God, that he heavily complained of his misfortune in having now lost as he said, the treasure of humility, which by the grace of Christ he had for so long a time been labouring to acquire. At length, to fly from all this honour and esteem, he withdrew himself privately by night from the monastery into a desert, where he might be unknown to all men, and there chose a lonesome cave for his habitation, in which he spent the remainder of the days of his mortality, in order to guard his humility from those dangers to which it was before exposed in the midst of applause and esteem.

6. A certain solitary having come one day to the monastery of abbot Sylvanus, on mount Sinai, and finding the brethren all at work, said to them : *Why do you labour for the meat that perisheth?* did not *Mary choose the better part?* The abbot turning to his disciple Zacharias, bid him hand that brother a book, and conduct him to an empty cell. When the hour came at which the monks were accustomed to take their meal, viz. about three in the afternoon, the stranger was incessantly looking out, in expectation that the abbot would send for him to the refectory ; but finding that the hour had passed, and no one came to call him, he went and asked the abbot if the monks did not dine that day? He told him, yes, they had dined ; but that, as for his part, they had not sent for him, because they understood he was a *spiritual* man, and had no need of *the meat that perisheth ;* whereas they, being carnal, and standing in need of food, were under a necessity of labouring for it; but you have, said he, *with Mary, chosen the better part* by reading the whole day long, without requiring this *perishable* food. The brother having begged pardon, and acknowledged his error, the abbot desired him to remember, that as Martha wanted the assistance of Mary, so Mary could not do alone, without the help of Martha.

7. Abbot Moses was accustomed to say, that as when a general besieges a city he endeavours to prevent any provisions being brought to the besieged, in order that through hunger and want the enemy may be obliged to deliver up their city ; so the man that desires to overcome his carnal passions, must starve them out by fasting and abstinence.

8. A certain religious man having received an injury from another, came to complain of it to one of the ancient fathers. The old man bid him, on this and the like occasions, to think with himself that the injury or affront was not levelled at him, but at his sins ; and advised him to sit down contented, and to say, *all this is for my sins.*

9. Another good brother, when any person affronted him, scoffed at him, or injured him, used to rejoice and to say : these are my friends who are giving me an opportunity of advancing in virtue ; whereas they that extol and applaud us are rather our enemies according to

that of Isaiah, iii. 12.: *O my people, they that call thee blessed, the same deceive thee, and destroy the way of thy steps.*

10. A brother having asked an ancient father to give him some short prescription by the observance of which he might be saved. The father told him the best prescription he could give for the security of his soul, was to overcome himself so far as to bear the greatest injuries and reproaches with meekness and silence.

11. St. Macarius used to say, " *He that overcomes himself in all things is a monk indeed.* For if a person, whilst he corrects or rebukes another for his faults, suffers himself to be moved to anger, he is only gratifying his own passion. No one ought to run the risk of losing his own soul, whilst he pretends to save that of another.

12. The abbot Sylvanus, being asked by certain brethren to speak something for their edification, desired his disciple Zacharias to give them a lesson. The disciple taking off his outward habit, laid it upon the ground, and stamped with his feet upon it, saying: "No one can be a truly religious man who is not willing to be trodden under foot in this manner."

13. Some of the brethren having extolled, in the hearing of St. Antony, the *virtues* of one of the monks the Saint *putting him to a trial*, found that he could not bear an *injury ;* whereupon the man of God told him, that he resembled a building which had a beautiful front, but which lay open behind to thieves and robbers.

14. It was observed by one of the fathers, that all the labours of a monk are vain without humility ; for since humility, said he, is the forerunner of charity, as John the Baptist was the precursor of Christ, drawing all to him, so in like manner humility draws men to charity, that is, to God himself; *for God is charity,* 1 John iv.

15. St. Antony having seen one day in a vision the whole earth as a large field, covered on every side with the nets and snares of the enemy ; whereupon sighing. he cried out, who shall be able to pass over them, or escape them? and immediately he heard a voice answering, *Humility alone can pass secure.*

16. A monk in a certain monastery having committed a fault, for which he was severely rebuked by the rest of the brethren, went away to St. Antony. The brethren having followed him thither in order to bring him back, they warmly upbraided him with his faults, in the presence of the Saint, which he, on his part, as warmly denied. The holy abbot Paphnucius, surnamed Cephala, happening to be present, put a stop to the contention, by the means of a parable: "Whilst I stood one day on the banks of a river, I saw a man sunk into the mire up to his knees, when behold there came other men stretching out their hands, endeavouring to help him out; but instead of succeeding in their attempt, they pushed him further in, even up to the neck." St. Antony hearing the parable, and approving of the moral lesson it conveyed, said of St. Paphnucius: "Behold a man who has the right notion of the way of reclaiming the faulty, and of saving their souls." The brethren presently took the hint, and begging pardon for their heat, received the brother in the tender bowels of the mercy of Jesus Christ.

17. St. Pemen, alias Pastor, gave it as an invariable rule to his disciples: "Never to do their own will, but rather humble themselves to do the will of their neighbours."

18. A certain anchoret, who dwelt in a cave not far distant from a religious community in great abstinence and sanctity of life, being one day visited by some of the monks, they prevailed on him to eat before his usual time, and then asked him if it was no pain or trouble to him to be put out of his way, by eating contrary to his custom? "No," replied he, "nothing gives me pain or trouble but following my own will."

19. The holy abbot Agatho coming one day into the neighbouring city to sell his work, found a certain stranger lying in a bye corner very sick, without any one to take care of him; the servant of God, on beholding so great an object of charity, instead of returning back to the wilderness, hired a lodging in the city, to which he carried the sick man, and attended on him for the space of four months, working in the mean time with his own hands, in order to procure for him all necessaries, aid, and comfort; after which, the sick man being now

25*

perfectly recovered, the Saint returned back again to his cell.

20. An ancient servant of God, on seeing his disciple sick, bid him be of good comfort, and return thanks to God for this visitation: "For," said he, "if thou art but iron, the *fire* will serve to take the rust away from thee; and if thou art gold, it will refine thee, and purify thee. Resign thyself then, my dear brother; for since it hath pleased God to send thee this sickness, who art thou that thou shouldest grieve or repine at the accomplishment of his will? O rather suffer all with patience and resignation, and let thy only prayer be, that God would deal with thee according to his pleasure."

21. An ancient religious, who was accustomed to be visited with sickness, happening to pass one whole year without any illness, he wept and grieved exceedingly, saying: "Lord, thou hast forsaken me, for thou hast not once visited me this year." O what a just notion he must have had of the inestimable value of patient sufferings.

22. When the holy abbot Agatho was drawing near to his end, and had lain for the space of three days with his eyes fixed, in silence, some of the brethren touching him, said: "Father, where are you now?" He answered, "I am standing before the judgment seat of God."— "Why then," said they, "are you afraid?" "According to the utmost of my power," replied he, "I have always endeavoured to keep the commandments of my God; but being a poor frail mortal, how do I know whether my works are pleasing to him or not?" "But do you not trust," said they, "that they are pleasing to him?" "I dare not trust to my works," said he." "in his sight; for the judgment of God is very different from the judgment of men."

23. A certain brother having asked one of the fathers how the soul might attain to perfect humility: he answered, "by thinking only on her own evils, and not on those of others."

21. Nothing gives so much pleasure to the enemy, said the abbot Pemen, as when a person will not discover his temptations to his superior or director.

25. A certain father observed, that as the flies cannot come near a pot that is boiling hot, but only rest on such things as are neither hot nor cold, and there deposit their maggots; so the devils are kept at a distance by such religious as are quite fervent in the love and service of God, but have so great a power over such as are but lukewarm, as to defile and corrupt them with sin.

26. An ancient father gave the following lesson to his disciple: "Think every day," said he, "that the hour of thy death is at hand, and as if thou wert already shut up in thy tomb, be not solicitous about this world. Let the fear of God continually abide with thee. Believe thyself to be inferior to every one. Speak no evil of any one because God knows all things; and be at peace with all men, and the Lord shall at all times give rest to thy soul."

27. Abbot John used to say, that a religious in his cell ought to resemble one sitting under a tree; for as the latter, on seeing any wild beast or serpent coming towards him, climbs up the tree, that he may get out of their reach; so the former, on perceiving any evil thoughts approaching, ought to ascend up to God by the tree of prayer.

28. Some of the brethren coming one day to visit the holy abbot Lucius, he enquired of them what kind of work they followed? They answered; they did not work, but, according to the Apostle, *prayed without ceasing.* "But do you not eat and sleep, said the father, "and who prays for you then?" To which having made no reply, "Now, I will tell you," said he, "the manner in which I endeavour to *pray without ceasing*, and yet never fail to work with my hands. Whilst I am making baskets, or cords, or the like, I say to my God: Have mercy on me, O God, *according to thy great mercies; and according to the multitude of thy tender mercies blot out my iniquity.* Thus, when I have finished my work, I am enabled to give some part of the price of it to the poor servants of Christ, to engage them thereby to pray for the forgiveness of my sins, even whilst I am eating or sleeping; and thus they by praying for me, help to make my prayer continual, and without ceasing."

29. A certain young man, desirous to embrace a mo-

nastic life, was prevented from so doing for some time by his mother; but as he still persevered in begging her to let him go, by often repeating that he was resolved to save his soul, she at length consented to his entering into a monastery. Being admitted to the habit, although an utter stranger to the spirit of religion, he led for many years a very tepid and negligent course of life. His mother having in the mean time died, and he soon after falling grievously sick, lay for some time in a trance, as if dead, in which he seemed to be carried before the judgment seat of God, where he met his mother amongst others expecting their sentence. "How now, my son," said she to him, "art thou also brought hither, to receive with us the sentence of damnation? What is become of that specious determination of thine, which thou so often repeatedst, that thou wast *resolved* to save thy soul?" The horror and confusion that oppressed him, upon hearing this reproach from his mother, was so inexpressible, that he seemed to himself to stand, as it were, upon the brink of hell, till he heard a voice, ordering that he should be sent back again, as not being the person called for, and that such another of a neighbouring monastery, that was of the same name, should be brought thither. Hereupon, having come to himself, he related to those about him all he had seen and heard, and desired that one of them would instantly go to the neighbouring monastery and enquire whether the brother alluded to was departed this life, and being informed that he was just then dead, they were confirmed in their belief of the truth of what he had related. As to this young monk, no sooner was he recovered from his sickness, than he shut himself up in his cell, and applied himself with such diligence to the care of his salvation, as to think now of nothing else, but to weep night and day, and do penance for his former negligences and sins; and although some of the brethren advised him to be more moderate in his tears and other penances, lest the excess of his compunction might prove prejudicial to his health, he nevertheless persevered in his penitential labours to the end, telling them upon these occasions: "If I could not bear the reproach which I heard from my mother, how shall I be able to endure the reproaches of Christ and his angels at the day of judgment?"

30. A certain monk in the deserts of Egypt, having

had a sister that followed a wicked course of life in the city, where she enticed many into sin, his brethren persuaded him to go in search of her, in order to reclaim her from her wickedness, and rescue her soul, as well as the souls of many others who were ensnared by her beauty, from the paths that lead to eternal perdition. When he came near the place where she dwelt, one who knew him, ran and told her that her brother was come from the desert to see her. Upon hearing this she immediately left her company, and going out with joy to meet him, offered to salute him; but he keeping at a distance, earnestly besought her to have pity on her soul, expatiating on the dreadful state of life in which she was engaged, and the dismal consequences she had to apprehend for eternity, if she did not immediately return to God. This exhortation he delivered in so nervous and pathetic a manner, that, seized with dread and horror, she asked him, trembling, whether there remained any hopes of salvation for her, and whether it was not now too late for her to think of returning to God? He assured her it was not, provided she would be quite in earnest in her application to the throne of divine mercy, by the practice of true penance. Hereupon, casting herself at his feet, she begged that he would take her along with him into the desert, where she might do penance for her sins. Go then, said he and cover your head (for she had run forth to meet him bareheaded), and then come along with me. O brother, said she, let us make no delay; is it not better for me to suffer the disgrace of going bareheaded, than to enter any more into a house that has been the shop of my iniquities? They therefore departed with speed towards the desert, the brother preaching penance to her on their way thither; till observing some of the brethren coming towards them, he desired her to step aside, and keep at some distance, for fear of any one's taking scandal at seeing him in the company of a woman; for every one, said he, don't know that you are my sister. She did so: and as soon as the brethren had passed by, he went in search of her, and found her lying dead on the ground, with her feet all bloody, for she had walked the whole way barefoot. Having lamented her death, he went and related all that had happened to the ancient religious. Whilst these servants of God were at a loss what judgment they should make with regard to her soul, dying as she did, so shortly after so sinful a life, without any time to do penance, one of them learnt by revelation, that as she had forsaken all she had in the world, and been solicitous for nothing but the healing of the wounds of her soul, in a word, as she had so bitterly wept, and grievously lamented her sins, the divine goodness had accepted her penance, and shewn her mercy.

From the fifth Book of the Lives of the Fathers, translated from the Greek of an ancient ecclesiastical Writer into Latin, by Pelagius, *Deacon of Rome, who was made Pope, Anno 558.*

31. WHEN the holy abbot John, surnamed the Dwarf, drew near his end, his disciples entreated him to leave them, by way of legacy, some short wholesome lesson of christian perfection, he sighed and said to them : "I never followed my own will, nor did I ever teach any other what I had not first practised myself.

32. Abbot Sisois being asked which was the best way to obtain peace and rest for the soul, he replied : "Be contemptible in your own eyes—cast pleasures behind your back—be free from all earthly cares, and you shall assuredly find rest."

33. Another holy man prescribed for this end the following precepts : "Pray incessantly to God that he would grant you compunction and humility ;—think always on your own sins, and do not presume to judge others ;—be subject and obedient to all ;—avoid familiarity with women, boys, or heretics ;—place no confidence whatever in yourselves ;—restrain your tongue and your sensual appetite ;—contend with no man ;—contradict no one in discourse, and your mind shall be at peace."

34. A certain brother came to visit abbot Moses in the desert of Scete, in order to learn of him the way to perfection, "Go, said the Saint, and keep thyself retired

and recollected in thy cell, and thy cell shall teach thee all things."

35. Some brethren going from Scete to visit St. Antony, entered into a boat that was to convey them part of the way up the Nile, in which they found a strange old man, who was also going to St. Antony. Whilst they were entertaining each other, during their passage, with discourses upon different subjects, the old man sat by himself in silence and recollection. Finding, when they came to land, that the old man was also going to St. Antony, they went along with him. St. Antony, on their arrival, told them they had met with a good companion in that servant of God; and you, said he, father, addressing himself to the old man, have found them good company. "I believe," replied he, "that they are good; but having no door to their dwelling, whoever pleases goes into the stable, and takes out the beast to ride upon it;" alluding to their want of recollection, and setting no guard upon their tongue, but uttering whatever came uppermost in their mind.

36. An ancient religious seeing another laugh, said— "How can you laugh, since we must by and by appear before the great Lord of heaven an earth, to give a strict account of our whole lives?"

37. A certain gentleman came one day to the church of the wilderness of Scete with a bag of money, which he desired the priest, the superior, to distribute amongst the brethren. The priest told him they did not want it; but as the gentleman became very pressing, and would not be content except he would receive it, he put the money into a basket, and setting it in the entrance of the church cried out to the brethren: *if any one wants, let him here take what he wants*: but so far from touching it, some of them would not so much as look on it. The superior then addressing the gentleman, said: "our Lord, Sir has accepted of your offering, go now and give it to the poor; and thus he dismissed him, much edified with their disinterestedness."

38. Another brought a sum of money to a brother, who was a leper, saying: keep this for your own use, because you are old and infirm. The old man answered: "would you then deprive me, Sir, of my nursing father,

who has fed me threescore years? Behold for so long a
time, notwithstanding my infirmity, I have never been
in want; for God has always provided for me, therefore
I cannot distrust him now."

39. The brethren having desired one of the ancient
fathers to remit something of his great labours and austerities, he answered: " believe me, my children, I am
of opinion, that Abraham himself when he saw the
greatness of the eternal rewards of heaven, was sorry
he had not laboured more than he did whilst he remained
here upon earth."

40. As a certain hermit, who dwelt in a cell near the
wilderness, at the distance of twelve miles from any water, was one day going for water, he found him self so
much exhausted and tired with the journey, that he began to blame himself for taking so much unnecessary
pains, and to think of changing his abode, and building
himself a cell near the spring. Whilst he had this
thought in his mind, he heard one behind him number-
ing his steps; and turning about, he saw an angel, who
told him he was commissioned from heaven to take an
exact account of his laborious steps, which should all
be hereafter rewarded. This vision encouraged the good
old man, and made him not only give up his design of
fixing his habitation near the water, but also determined him to remove his cell to a still further distance, since
the divine goodness was pleased to reward all his steps
in so bountiful a manner.

41. There was an ancient hermit in Thebais, who
dwelt in a cave, together with a virtuous young man,
his disciple. It was his custom to deliver an exhortation to the young hermit every evening for his instruction, direction, and progress in virtue and piety, and
after spending some time together in prayer, the old
man gave him his blessing, and sent him to bed. It
happened one day, when the servants of God had entertained some visitors with discourses of piety till a late
hour, that after their departure, whilst he was making
his exhortation, as usual, to his disciple, he fell fast
asleep. The brother waited in expectation of the father's
awaking, that they might make their prayer, according
to custom, before he went to bed: but the old man slept
on so sound, as not to awake till after midnight. In the

mean time the young man, finding he slept so long, and being wearied and sleepy himself, was strongly tempted to leave him and retire to bed : but he resisted the temptation, and continued to remain with him. Shortly after the temptation returned, and became very troublesome to him ; but he again got the better of it, and drove it away : and in this manner was he violently assaulted seven different times, but still overcame the temptation, and forced himself to stay till his master awaked. After midnight the father awaking, and finding the young disciple with him, asked him why he did not go to bed ? Because, replied he, you did not discharge me. Why then, said the father did you not awake me? I could not presume, said he, to disturb you. Wherefore, it being now midnight rising up, they began their matins together, and when they had finished, the father sent him to take his rest. Whilst the old man was sitting afterwards by himself, he fell into a trance or ecstasy, when a stranger pointed out to him a glorious palace, in which was placed a throne, and over the throne seven crowns, telling him that they were destined by our Lord as a reward for the virtue and piety of his disciple; and that as to the seven crowns, he had purchased them that very night. The father having asked him in the morning what he had done in the night? he answered, nothing particular ; but as he insisted upon his telling him all that had passed, even to his very thoughts, he at length assured him he knew of nothing whatever, except that he had been seven times strongly tempted to leave him whilst he continued asleep, and to retire to bed; but as he had not discharged him, according to custom, he had forced himself to stay : hence the father was given to understand, that every victory over one's self purchases a crown from God, and how much it imports to overcome ourselves, even in small matters.

42. St. Antony being told one day of a young religious man who had been already so far favored with miraculous gifts, that the very wild beasts of the desert obeyed him. The Saint, apprehending some ostentation and pride in the manner of his proceeding, said, he seems to resemble a ship richly laden, which is in danger of being shipwrecked before it reaches the haven. Not long after, the Saint being in company with some of his disciples, began all on a sudden to weep and la-

26

ment, and being asked the reason, he exclaimed, Oh! a great pillar of the church is just now fallen; go ye and look after such a one, naming the young religious man. They went and found him in a most melancholy way, for having just then committed a mortal sin; but he begged they would desire their holy father to obtain for him by his prayers, a reprieve of ten days, that in that time he might make satisfaction for his crime. But this was not granted him, for within five days he was called out of this life.

43. When a certain brother came one day to visit the holy abbot Serapion, he begged of him, according to the custom of the ancient religious in their visits, to give out the prayer which was to be made when they first met; which he refused, saying he was a poor sinner, and unworthy to wear the religious habit. In like manner, when the Saint offered to wash his feet, according to the custom, he would not permit him, still alleging his great unworthiness. The holy man, after having entertained him at table with what his cell could afford, dismissed him with this charitable advice: "My son, if you desire to make due progress in religion, return to your cell, and there, attending to God and yourself, employ yourself in working with your hands; for coming abroad in this manner is not so good for you as it would be to remain at home." The brother on hearing these words was so much disturbed and offended, as to discover his displeasure and resentment by the change of his countenance; which the holy abbot observing, said to him: A little while ago you said you was a poor sinner, and accused yourself as one who were not worthy to tread upon the earth, how comes it then that you are so much disturbed at the charitable admonition I have given you? If you have a real desire to be humble, you must learn to bear patiently the things that others lay upon you, and not be ever saying reproachful things of yourself which you would not be willing another should believe of you." The brother having acknowledged his fault departed, highly edified with the lessons he received from the Saint.

44. When the holy abbot Moses being told that the judge of the province, who had heard of his eminent sanctity, was coming to visit him in his cell in the desert of Scete, the man of God to shun this visit left his cell,

and retired towards the marsh. In his way he met the judge with his train, who not knowing him, enquired of him where the cell of the abbot Moses was? Why do you enquire, said he, after that worthless wretch? He is one that is void both of sense and religion. Whereupon the judge went to the church, and told the clergy that he came into the desert on purpose to visit abbot Moses, and to be edified by his conversation, but that he had met with an old man who had given him a vile character. Pray, Sir, said they, what sort of a person was he who gave so bad a character of that holy man? A tall black man, said the judge, with his habit very much worn. It was abbot Moses himself, said they, who spoke thus of himself, to avoid being visited and honoured by you. Upon hearing of which the judge departed very much edified with the Saint's humility. This was that same Moses who had formerly been a captain of a band of robbers, but who after his conversion became not only an illustrious penitent, but so eminent in all virtue and sanctity as to be raised to the dignity of a priest, and superior of the holy monastery of Scete, and after his death to be enrolled amongst the Saints. See the Roman Martyrology, August 28.

45. A brother having committed a fault for which he was expelled the convent of Abbot Elias, went to Saint Antony on his mountain, and after remaining a while with him he sent him back to the convent, but the brethren refusing to receive him, he returned again to Saint Antony. The Saint sent him back again the second time with this message: "A ship that was cast away at sea had lost all its cargo, but with much ado the empty vessel has been drawn to the shore; and would you, my brethren, after it has been thus brought to land go and sink it entirely?" The brethren understanding the meaning of the Saint presently complied, and received the brother again into their congregation.

46. Another brother had fallen into some sin, on account of which the priest bid him go out of the church; whereupon the abbot Besarion, who was present, rose up, and went out with him, saying: I also am a sinner as well as he." This was the great Besarion, of whose extraordinary sanctity and wonderful miracles frequent mention is made in ancient monuments, whose name is recorded in the Roman Martyrology amongst the Saints on the seventeenth of June.

47. A certain priest was accustomed to come from time to time to the cell of a hermit who lived in the wilderness, to celebrate mass and to administer to him the blessed sacrament, till at length it happened that the man of God heard an ill report concerning the priest, and accordingly the next time he came he shut the door against him and sent him away; but he had no sooner dismissed him than he heard a voice saying: *"Men have taken away the judgment that belongs to me, and have arrogated it to themselves."* After which he was rapt in a kind of ecstacy or trance, in which he saw a golden well full of most clear and excellent water, with a chain and bucket of the same precious metal, and a leper drawing up some of this water, and pouring it out of the golden bucket into a clean vessel. Now he seemed extremely desirous to drink of it, and was only prevented by the repugnance he felt at seeing it drawn up by the leper.— Whereupon he thought he heard a voice which said to him: "Why dost thou not drink? What harm has he done who has drawn the water, since he has done no more than filled the bucket, and then poured it out into the vessel?" The hermit upon this returned to himself, and having reflected on the vision, called back the priest, and desired him to celebrate and consecrate for him as usual.

48. Some of the brethren went one day to consult St. Antony whether they ought to pay any regard to their dreams when they found them followed by the event, or to despise them as illusions of the devil? Now having had an ass with them who died by the way, as soon as they came to the Saint he was before hand with them, and asked them how their ass happened to die? How, father, said they, how did you know of the death of the ass? The devils, said he, shewed it me in a dream. Upon this they told him the occasion of their coming, for that they had also often dreams which came to pass, and for fear of being deluded they desired his opinion concerning these matters. The Saint gave them full satisfaction on this head, assuring them by the example of the ass, that dreams being only tricks of the enemy to fill the mind with superstition, are by no means to be regarded.

49. The holy abbot Agatho being asked whether the mortification of the flesh by corporal labours and aus-

terities, or the keeping a guard upon the inward man was of greater importance in a spiritual life, he answered, that man was like a tree, of which corporal labours and austerities were the leaves, but the regularity of the interior was the fruit: wherefore, as our principal care must be about the fruit, because it is written, that *every tree, which doth not bring forth good fruit, shall be cut up, and shall be cast into the fire,* our chief solicitude must be about the interior, yet we must not neglect the leaves of corporal exercises, since they are both an ornament and a covering to protect the fruit.

50. The same holy abbot used to say, that a man who does not restrain the passion of anger, though he were even to raise the dead to life, cannot be pleasing to God.

51. The holy abbot Pemen used to say, "Evil cannot be cast out by evil; wherefore if any one doth evil to you do you good to him, that you may overcome his evil by your good." He was also accustomed to say: "He that is quarrelsome, or apt to murmur and complain, is no monk;—he that renders evil for evil is no monk;—he that is passionate is no monk."

52. The same Saint said, self-will stands as a wall of brass between man and God; wherefore he that renounces his own will, may say with the Psalmist, Ps. xvii. 30. *Through my God I shall go over the wall,* and may arrive at the justice of God; concerning which it is written in the following verse, *as to my God his way is undefiled.*

53. Abbot Abraham, who had been a disciple of St. Agatho, having asked St. Pemen, "How it came to pass that the devils were always assaulting him? The devils, replied the Saint, don't oppose those who do their own wills; for our own wills are devils with respect to us, because they are always tempting us to follow them. But it is such, as like Moses and other saints, have got the better of their own wills that the devils impugn."

54. A certain brother complained to St. Pambo, that the wicked spirits would not suffer him to do good to his neighbours. Don't say so, said the Saint lest you charge our Lord with not being true to his word, for he has told us, Luke x. *Behold I have given you power to tread upon serpents and scorpions, and upon all the power of the enemy.* 'Tis then your want of a good will, and not the wicked

26*

spirits which you ought to accuse on this occasion, for why don't you resist them, and tread them under your feet ?

55. One having asked abbot Sisois, what can be the meaning, father, that these passions will not depart from me ? The abbot answered, because by your irregular affections you keep within you what belongs to them ; but if you give up all that is theirs, by mortifying your disorderly affections, they shall have no controul over you, but shall depart from you.

56. An ancient father being asked, which was that *strait and narrow way that leads to life*, as is spoken of Matt. vii.? answered, to do violence to our own thoughts and inclinations, and to sacrifice our own will to the will of God, and that such as do this may say with the apostles, Matt. xix. *behold we have left all things, and have followed thee.*

57. One of the brothers said to the abbot Sisois: "I desire to keep a guard upon my heart ;" he replied, "how can you guard your heart, and preserve it from dangers, if you suffer the gate of the tongue to be always open?" The same holy abbot used to say : " That the great business of our pilgrimage is to keep a guard upon our mouths.''

58. Abbot Allois said : " Except a religious man think in his heart that there is no one in the world but God and himself, he will never enjoy true rest."

59. One of the ancients said : " As no one presumes to offer violence to a person whilst he is at the side of the emperor, so neither can Satan do any hurt to a soul whilst it sticks close to God ; for it is written ; *Draw nigh to God, and he will draw nigh unto you.* James iv. But because the poor soul is frequently dissipated and forgets her God, the enemy has power to drag her away into shameful passions.''

60. One of the brothers told an ancient religious, that he was not sensible of any conflict or war in his soul.— " O," said the father, "it is because your soul is like an open place, where every one comes in and goes out at his pleasure without meeting with any resistance on your part, or your ever taking any notice of them ; but if

you kept the door shut, by guarding against evil thoughts, you would quickly become sensible of the war they would wage against you."

61. Another ancient father said, that Satan had three precursors who usually prepared the way for him, and helped to introduce sin into the soul, viz. *forgetfulness of God, negligence,* and *concupiscence.*

62. When the patriarch Theophilus visited the religious of mount Nitria, he asked the superior what was the most important thing he had found out in that way of life? The father answered: *to accuse and reprehend myself without ceasing.* The prelate replied, *there can be no way more safe.*

63. Abbot Mathois said, the nearer a man draws towards God, the more he perceives himself to be a sinner; thus when the prophet Isaias saw the Lord, chap. vi. he immediately exclaimed, *Wo is me,—because I am a man of unclean lips—and have seen with my eyes, the King, the Lord of Hosts.*

64. St. Arsenius related as of another though it was thought himself was the person, that whilst one of the ancient religious was sitting alone in his cell he was called out by a voice that said to him: "Come, and I will shew thee the works of men." The person that called him out, brought him first to a place where he saw a negro cutting wood, and making a large bundle, which he tried to carry, but found it too heavy; whereupon instead of lessening the bundle he went to cut more wood, and still continued to add to his burden, without offering to take anything away from a load which even at the first was more than he could carry. Having gone a little further, he perceived a man standing by a lake drawing water and pouring it into a vessel full of holes, through which the water ran again into the lake. Afterwards he was brought to another place where he saw a building like a temple, with two men on horseback marching abreast, and carrying a long pole together on their shoulders, with which they endeavoured to go into the temple, but as they would not be put out of their way, nor stop, nor turn the pole, so that one might pass in before the other, they were both of them kept out, because the length of the pole, and the manner they carried it, would not suffer them to enter within the gate of the tem-

ple. The person that shewed him these things told him, that these two men resembled such as pretend to carry the yoke of religion without renouncing their pride; and if they are not reclaimed, so as to walk humbly in the way of Christ, they shall assuredly be excluded from God's eternal temple. He also told him, that the man whom they saw cutting the wood, represented worldlings loaded with sins, who instead of doing penance, or turning from their evil ways, were, by adding sin to sin, continually increasing their burden; and that the man who poured the water into the vessel full of holes, resembled such as do many good works, but lose the fruit of them by mingling with them many that are evil. Wherefore every one ought to be watchful with regard to the purity and perfection of his works, that he may not be found hereafter to have laboured in vain.

65. St. Arsensius also informs us, that there was in the wilderness a certain old man, who was wonderful in his actions, but simple in faith, so that being ignorant, he had an erroneous opinion with respect to the holy eucharist. saying, that the bread which we receive is not really the body of Christ, but only the figure of his body. Two of the ancient fathers, on hearing this, went to beg of him to lay aside so erroneous an opinion, and to believe with them and the universal church, that the eucharistic bread was indeed the body of Christ, and the chalice his blood, according to the truth, and not according to figure; because Christ himself had assured us, saying, *this is my body*, &c. But as the old man did not appear satisfied with what they said on this subject, it was agreed upon between them, that they should all three earnestly pray to God during the week with relation to the mystery, that the truth might be made manifest to him. On the following Sunday, having placed themselves together in the church, at the time of celebrating the sacred mysteries, there appeared to them a little child as it were lying upon the altar, and when the priest was going to divide the sacramental bread, they saw an angel with a knife dividing the body of the child, and receiving his blood in the chalice; and when they went up to communion, whilst the other two received the blessed sacrament in its usual form, the particle that was given the old man appeared to be bloody flesh, at which he he was frightened, and exclaimed: " *I believe, O Lord,*

that the consecrated bread is thy body, and the chalice thy blood," immediately what he was going to receive returned to the shape of bread according to the mystery. Whereupon they all returned thanks, and blessed God for his wonderful goodness, in not suffering his servant to lose, by incredulity, the fruit of so many years labor.

Out of the Book of the Virtues and Miracles of the Religious of their own Times, published under the Title of " The Spiritual Meadow," by that holy man John Moschus, sirnamed Eviratus, and his intimate, friend and individual companion, St. Sophronius.

66. An ancient religious, who dwelt in the monastery of the towers of Palestine, was so eminent in that virtue, that all the monks were desirous of choosing him for their abbot; but the old man begged to be excused, saying : " Pardon me, reverend fathers, and suffer me to bewail my sins, I am not worthy to be intrusted with the care of souls; that is an office only fit for such men as an Antony, Pachomius, or Theodore, and not for such a. wretch as I am." But as the brethren still importuned him to accept of the superiority, and would hear of no excuse, he at length told them : " Let me pray for three days, that I may know the will of God; and whatever he ordains that will I do." This he said on the Friday, and the Sunday morning following our Lord took him to himself.

67. Another religious man of the same monastery, an eminent servant of God, having died in the hospital of Jericho, when the brethren took his body from thence, and carried it to be buried in his own monastery, they perceived a bright star over his head, which accompanied them the whole way, and continued to be visible till the body was interred.

68. Another monk of the same monastery, whose name was Myrogones, who, by the austerity of his life, had fallen into a dropsy, when the brethren came to visit and comfort him under his sufferings, used to say to them :—

" Good fathers, pray for me, that the inward man may not fall into a dropsy ; for as to this exterior infirmity, I make it my prayer to God that it may continue with me." The Patriarch of Jerusalem, Eustochius, hearing of this holy man, desired to be at the charges of furnishing him with all necessaries, but the servant of God declined accepting his charitable offer, and only begged that he would pray for him, that he might be delivered from the everlasting sufferings of the world to come.

69. A brother having desired the abbot Olympius, priest of the monastery of St. Gerasimus, to give him a word of instruction : " Fly," said he, " the conversation of heretics ; put a restraint upon thy tongue, and thy sensual appetite, and whersoever thou art, say always to thyself—I am a stranger and a pilgrim."

70. One of the fathers of the laura of Cupatha related, as what he had heard from the person himself to whom it happened, that when there was a war in Africa, between the Romans and Moors, and the latter, in a certain engagement, had defeated the former, and slain many of them, one of the Roman soldiers in the flight, being closely pursued by a barbarian, whose spear almost touched his back, prayed earnestly to our Lord to deliver him, as he had delivered St. Thecla out of the hands of her enemies, and promised, if he escaped with his life, he would presently retire into the desert, and dedicate himself wholly to the love and service of God ; when behold, looking back, he could neither see the barbarian that pursued him, nor any other enemy. Wherefore, to fulfil his promise, he presently repaired to the laura of Cupatha, and had already passed five and thirty years alone in a neighboring cave, in devotion and penance.

71. When John and Sophronius came to the monastery called Philoxene, near the town of Dade in Cyprus, they found there a monk, a native of Melitine, named Isidore, who passed his whole time in weeping and mourning. The brethren often desired that he would desist from his lamentations, and allow himself some rest and ease : but he would not hear of it, alledging that he was the most enormous sinner that ever had been since the creation. His history, which we had from his own mouth, was briefly to the following effect. Whilst

he lived a married man in the world, both himself and his wife were followers of the heresy of Severus the Eutychian; but one day his wife visiting a catholic woman, her neighbour, went with her to receive the catholic communion. The husband being informed thereof, made what haste he could in pursuit of her, to prevent her so doing; but when he arrived he found she had just communicated. Upon which, in a great rage, he seized her by the throat, and obliged her to cast up the consecrated species, which he let fall into the dirt; when presently he perceived the sacred particle which he had abused, shining with brilliant rays of light. Two days after he saw a deformed black fellow, who said to him : "You and I are condemned to suffer the same punishment together;" and having asked him who he was, he answered : "I am the wretch who struck the Lord Jesus, the Maker of all things. on his cheek at the time of his passion." For this reason, said Isidore, I can never leave off weeping. And now you have heard my history, I hope you will be pleased to pray for me.

72. Two ancient religious, travelling from Æga, in Cilicia, to Tarsus, were obliged, by the heat of the day, to go into an inn, where they found three young men with a harlot in their company. The two religious went and sat down by themselves; and when one of them took out the holy gospel, and began to read, the woman left her company, and came and sat down by his side to hear him. The servant of God, in order to drive her away, asked her how she could be so impudent as to come and sit by them? It is true, replied she, I am a wretched sinner; but as our God and Saviour Jesus Christ did not prevent a sinful woman from coming to him, why should you cast me off? The woman that came to our Saviour, rejoined the holy father, renounced her wicked way of life, and was no longer a harlot. And I, said she, trust in Jesus Christ, that from this very instant, by his divine grace, I shall quit this sinful way, and never more be guilty of the like sins. Firm in her resolution, she instantly quitted the world with all she possessed, and went to the nunnery near Æga, to which the two old men recommended her; "where," says my author, "I saw her, being now an old woman of great prudence, and learnt these things from her own mouth." Her name was Mary.

73. A certain comedian of Tarsus in Cilicia, named Babylas, who led a very wicked life and kept two concubines, one called Cometa, and the other Nicosa, one day hearing in the church those words of the gospel; *do penance, for the kingdom of God is at hand,* (Matth. iii.) was so suddenly touched with an extraordinary compunction for his sins, that he resolved upon the spot to quit the world entirely, and to dedicate the remainder of his days to devotion and penance. This resolution, as soon as he returned home, he imparted to the two women, telling them that they might, if they pleased, divide his whole substance between them; but as for his part he was resolved to provide for the salvation of his soul, by renouncing the world from that very instant, and entering into religion. Both being greatly moved by his words, told him with one voice, and an abundance of tears, that as they had been partners with him in his sinful ways, and had borne him company whilst he was walking in the broad road to perdition, so they were also determined to accompany him in his conversion to God, and to enter with him upon the narrow way of eternal life; for why should you, said they, choose the better part for yourself, and leave us in the lurch? Wherefore Babylas went and shut himself up in one of the towers belonging to the walls of the city; and the two women, after selling all their substance, and giving the price to the poor, made themselves also a cell in the neighbourhood, where they dedicated themselves to a recluse and penitential life. This man, says our author, I myself have seen, and was very much edified by his conversation; for he was exceedingly humble, mild, and charitable.

74. One of the fathers related a remarkable anecdote to us concerning St. Ephrem, the patriarch of Antioch: —that being very zealous and fervent in faith, he attempted the conversion of a famous monk who lived on a pillar in the neighbourhood of Hierapolis, who had been tampered with by the Eutychian heretics, and seduced into their errors. This Stylite being obstinate against the remonstrances of the holy patriarch, to shew how confident he was of the truth of his religion, made a proposal that a great fire should be kindled into which he and the patriarch should go together, and that they should abide by the faith of him who should come out

of the flames without hurt. St. Ephrem told him, that although he had proposed a thing that far exceeded the strength of such a poor sinner as he acknowledged himself to be, however, that confiding in the mercies of his Saviour, and hoping by this means to bring about the salvation of a soul in error, he would agree to the proposal, and immediately he ordered a great quantity of wood to be piled up, which he himself set on fire, and then he desired the monk to come down from his pillar, that they might go hand in hand into the flames. But the heretic, who thought to have frightened the patriarch with his proposal, being dismayed at his courage and resolution, would not come down. The Saint then going up to the fire, and taking off his stole, prayed to our Lord Jesus Christ, who was pleased to be incarnate for the love of us, to make manifest on this occasion his divine truth; and when he had ended his prayer, he cast his stole into the midst of the flames, where it remained for the space of three hours, till all the wood was consumed, and then it was taken out whole and entire, without having been so much as singed by the fire. The Stylite, astonished at so evident a miracle, gave glory to God, and was converted upon the spot to the Catholic Church, and was admitted by St. Ephrem to receive the holy communion from his own hands.

75. St. Ephrem, who, before he was patriarch, was count or governor of all the eastern district of which Antioch was the capital, was very illustrious for his alms deeds and works of mercy. In his time, the city of Antioch was destroyed by an earthquake, which calamity, amongst many other occasions of exercising his charity, furnished him with that of employing a number of workmen and labourers in repairing the public buildings of that city. Now one of the fathers related to us, says our author, that on this occasion a certain bishop privately withdrawing himself from his see, and putting on a poor labourer's frock, came to Antioch, and there hired himself to serve the masons. After some time the governor, in a vision by night, saw this labourer lying asleep, and over his head a pillar of fire, which reached even up to the firmament. He was the more astonished at the sight, because he perceived nothing in the whole garb, or person of the man, but what appeared mean and contemptible; however, as he continued for many

27

nights to see the same thing, he sent for the laborer, and asked him who or what he was? He answered he was a poor man, who endeavoured to gain his little livelihood by his work. The count, not satisfied with this answer, told him plainly he should not depart from him till he had discovered the whole truth, and continued to conjure him in so pressing a manner to give him a more particular account of himself, that at length, after requiring a solemn promise of secrecy, at least till he should be dead, he told him: "I am a bishop, who have for God's sake resigned my bishopric, and am come hither as to a strange place, where no one might know me; to mortify my flesh, employ myself in labour, and by the work of my hands to earn myself a little bread. Ask not my name, for that I must and will conceal; but take care to multiply thy alms-deeds and good works as much as possible, for before it be long God will promote thee to the apostolic see of this city, to feed the flock which Christ our true God has purchased with his own blood. Therefore, as I said, be diligent in all the works of mercy, and always stand up zealously, and contend earnestly for the orthodox faith; for with such sacrifices as these God is best pleased." St. Ephrem hearing all this, glorified our Lord, who has many hidden servants in the world, known to himself alone.

76. The abbot Stephen related to us, that a certain monk, named Cyriacus, of the monastery of our holy father St. Sabas, being one day visited by his worldly friends, when they knocked at the door of his cell, he prayed to God that he might not be seen by them; then opening the door, he went out without their perceiving him, and remained abroad in the desert till he understood they were gone away.

77. The same abbot Stephen related to us the following extraordinary anecdote concerning father Julian the Stylite, who was illustrious for many miracles: the servant of God understanding that there was in his neighborhood a lion that did much mischief, called one day to his disciple Pancratius, and bid him go two miles to the south, and there, said he, thou shalt find the lion, to whom thou shalt say: "Julian, the poor servant of Jesus Christ, commands thee, in the name of the same Jesus Christ, the Son of God, who gives life to all things, to depart from this country." Pancratius having found

out the lion, and spoken to it as the saint had ordered, the beast immediately obeyed, and was seen no more in that province.

78. Father Peter, a priest of the same monastery of St. Sabas, told us of another holy man, named Thaleleus, of the province of Cicilia, who had spent three score years in religion, in such perpetual compunction and devotion as never to cease from weeping, and saying: " this present time is allowed us by divine mercy for repentance, and penance, and O what a terrible account shall we have to give if we do not make good use of it!"

79. Three ancient religious men came one day to the cell of the holy abbot Stephen, priest of the monastery of the Æliotæ, to be edified by his conversation; but he keeping silence whilst they conversed on different subjects of piety, Father, said they, we came to you, in hopes of learning something, why don't you say something to us? " I beg your pardon," said he, "I really did not take notice of what you were speaking; for, to tell you the truth, I have nothing before my eyes, night or day, but our Lord Jesus Christ crucified." With this answer they departed not a little edified.

80. Abbot John, surnamed Molybius, related to us concerning the same holy priest Stephen, that being in his last illness obliged by his physicians to eat meat, a brother of his, a secular, but a very virtuous man, was shocked, and exceedingly grieved, that he who had lived so many years in such extreme abstinence and mortification, should, at the end of his life, fall to the eating of flesh meat. In the midst of these thoughts he fell into an ecstacy, and saw in spirit one standing by reprehending him for being scandalized without cause at what his brother did through necessity, and by obedience. "But, (said he) if you desire to know the merit and glory of your brother, turn and see him." Upon which, turning about, he saw his brother fastened to the cross with our Lord: " Behold," said the person that appeared to him, " the happy state of your brother, and learn to glorify him who glorifies, in this manner, those that love him in truth."

81. Abbot Theodosius related of himself, that in his younger days, before he embraced a solitary life, he

saw one day in an ecstacy, a person shining brighter than the sun, who took him by the hand, and said :— " Come along with me ; for thou must wrestle and fight for a crown." Whereupon he led him into a theatre that appeared immensely wide, and full of people ; one part of whom were clothed in white, the other in black, and placed him in the centre. And here he saw a filthy negro of a gigantic size and strength, standing before him, with whom he was told he was to wrestle. He strove to excuse himself, alleging that no strength upon earth could be able to stand against such a monster ; but the person that brought him thither said, you must wrestle with him. " Advance then courageously and attack him, and I will stand by and assist thee, and give thee the crown of victory." Upon this encouragement Theodosius seemed to himself to have entered the lists, and with the help of his friend to have overthrown his adversary, and received the crown ; to the great joy of those that were clothed in white, who gave praise and glory to him who had given his servant the victory, whilst the others in black were all confounded, and put to flight. The same abbot Theodosius, as we learnt from his disciple, the abbot Cyriacus, spent thirty-five years in solitude, eating but once in two days, and observing a perpetual silence. Of this, says John Moschus, I was for some time an eye-witness, having lived during ten years with him in the monastery.

82. When Sophronius and I, said John Moschus, were at Alexandria, we went to visit abbot Palladius, a true servant of God, superior of the monastery in Lithosomenon, to learn of him some lessons of edification. " My children," said he, " our time here is very short ; let us then fight during this short time ; let us labour in earnest for the immortal goods of a happy eternity. Behold the martyrs ; look upon those champions of heaven, and see how bravely they have fought and conquered ; what cruel torments they have sustained ; with what ardor of faith they have gone through all the sufferings of the present life, and thereby purchased an eternal and immense weight of glory. To labour, therefore, to suffer, and to overcome, with the help of our Lord, the tribulations of this life, is the way to prove ourselves true lovers of God. In the mean time he himself will remain with us ; he will fight and conquer in and

for as; he will alleviate by his divine grace all our labours and sufferings. Patience and penitence must then be our exercises during the short time that is allowed us here, that so we may arrive at the honor and dignity of being the eternal temples of God." He added, that we should always set before our eyes him who *had not*, during his mortal life, *whereon to lay his head:* and that we should remember that the suffering of *tribulation*, according to St. Paul, Rom. v. *worketh patience, and patience trial, and trial hope, and hope confoundeth not*, &c.; so that this is indeed the true way to dispose our souls for the kingdom of heaven. Wherefore, *my children*, said he, *let us not love the world, nor the things that are in the world*, 1 John ii. but let us keep a constant guard upon our thoughts, by recollection of spirit, which is the medicine of salvation.

83. We asked this holy man what had been the first occasion of his call to this monastic life? Upon which he related to us the following history: "There was," said he, "in my country (Thessalonica in Macedonia) an ancient religious man, named David, a native of Mesopotamia, who lived during the space of fourscore years shut up in a little cell by himself, at the distance of about three furlongs without the walls of the city, in great sanctity and abstinence. Now it happened, on account of the inroads of the barbarians, that soldiers were placed round the walls of the city to guard it at night from the attack of the enemy. These guards observed one night flames of fire issuing forth from the windows of the cell of the servant of God, from whence they concluded that the barbarians had been there, and had set fire to his cell; but to their great astonishment, when they went out the next morning to see what mischief had been done, they found the old man safe and sound, and no mark of fire in his cell. The following night they saw the same fire again, which from that time continued to be seen every night for a long time after, even till the death of the holy anchoret; and many of the citizens often passed the night upon the wall on purpose to see it. This I myself saw, not once, or twice, but many times; upon which I said to myself, if God gives so much 'glory to his servants in this world, how much, thinkest thou, has he reserved for them in the world to come; where *the just shall shine like the sun in the king-*

27*

dom of their Father. This was the first occasion of my resolving upon taking the monastic habit, and entering upon a religious course of life."

84. The same holy abbot told us of a soldier in Alexandria, named John, who constantly observed the following rule and order of life. Every day he came early in the morning to the monastery, and sitting down alone, clothed in hair-cloth, at the steps of the chapel of Saint Peter, employed himself in making baskets in silence and recollection, till the ninth hour of the day. In the mean time he used no other vocal prayer but this:— "*From my secret sins cleanse me, O Lord*, that when I pray I may not be confounded." This he repeated seven times in the day, and after each time continued recollected and silent for a whole hour. At the ninth hour he put off his hair cloth, and put on his military habit, and went to his station amongst the soldiers. With this man, said the father, I lived for eight years, and was much edified with his silence and his whole manner of life.

85. The same holy man told us one day, that the source of all heresies and schisms in the church was loving God too little, and ourselves too much.

86. He also related to us the history of a certain merchant of Alexandria, a very religious, charitable, and hospitable man, who had a wife that was also a very pious humble Christian, and a little daughter six years old. This man being called away by his affairs to Constantinople, was asked by his wife, at parting, to whose care and protection he would recommend her and her child during his absence? He answered, I recommend you to our blessed Lady, the mother of God. Having left behind with them only one servant man, a slave, the wretch, by the instigation of the devil, conceived the design of murdering his mistress and her little daughter, and after rifling the house, to decamp with the spoils. To put his diabolical plan in execution, taking the kitchen knife with him, he attempted to go into the parlour where his mistress, with her little girl, was sitting at her work ; but no sooner had he come to the door than he was struck blind, and withheld in such manner that he could neither go forward nor backward. At length he called to his mistress to come out to him, whilst she, ig-

norant of his case, replied, that if he wanted anything he might come in; and although he called aloud again and again, still she would not come, until at length, in a fit of rage and despair, he stabbed himself.—His mistress hearing him fall, and seeing what he had done, called in the neighbours, with whom came in also some of the officers of justice, and finding him not quite dead, they learnt from his own mouth the particulars here mentioned, and glorified our Lord, who had in so miraculous a manner preserved the life both of the mother and the child, who were thus recommended to the care of his Virgin Mother.

87. The same Palladius related also to us another remarkable history, which he learnt from a master of a ship, to the truth whereof himself was a witness. A widow, named Mary, had made away with two of her own children, in order to recommend herself to a man with whom she was in love, but who refused to marry her on account of her children. But when she had secretly perpetrated this crime, and had signified to the man that her children were now removed out of the way, he conceived so great a horror for her, that he declared, with a solemn oath, he would never marry her on any account whatsoever. Being thus disappointed, and apprehending lest her guilt being divulged, she should fall into the hands of justice, and be put to death, to withdraw herself as far as possible from the danger, she went on board the vessel belonging to the captain above mentioned. But although she thus fled from the justice of man, she could not escape the justice of God; for when they had set sail, and were advanced into the deep, the ship all on a sudden stood still, so that for many days they could neither go forward nor backward, though they saw other ships, not far distant from them, sailing various courses, and going on with prosperous gales. All were in the utmost consternation at seeing themselves stand thus immovable in the midst of the sea, (for there were many passengers on board), but particularly the master of the ship, whose all was at stake, being in the greatest perplexity of mind, with the utmost fervour begged that God would send them a deliverance. At length in his prayer he heard a voice, saying: "Put Mary out of the vessel, and you shall have a good voyage." As he did not comprehend what the meaning of

this could be, nor knew who this Mary was, and therefore was dubious what was to be done, the voice said to him again: "Put Mary, I say, out of your ship, and all shall go well with you." Upon this he called out *Mary, Mary*; and upon her answering to her name, he desired to speak to her apart, and told her he was afraid, that on account of his sins, they were all going to perish. O no, Sir, said she, fetching a deep sigh, it is rather on account of my sins; for there is no crime of which I have not been guilty, and immediately told him the history of the murder of the children. He then proposed to her, as it were in order to know whether it was for his own, or for her sins, that the ship was stopped in her course, that the boat should be let down, and that he should first descend into the boat to see whether the ship would then advance, and if not, then he should return into the ship, and she should go down into the boat. The captain went down first, according to his proposal into the boat, but still the ship and boat remained immoveable; but no sooner had he come back, and she gone down out of the ship, than the boat immediately turning round five times, went down with her to the bottom and was never seen more. Immediately the ship sprang forward, and continued to advance with such unusual speed, as to sail in three days and a half a voyage which otherwise must have cost them fifteen days.

88. As another instance of the justice of God often overtaking the wicked even on this side of eternity, our author relates how he and Sophronius, sheltering themselves one day at noon from the violence of the heat of the sun, under the shade of a place called Tetrapylon, where the Alexandrians say the bones of the prophet Jeremias were deposited, they found there three blind men sitting, and heard them relating to each other the manner how they became blind. The first said, that being a sailor, he was struck blind by lightning at sea: the second, that he had lost his eyes by the fire, working in a glass-house; but the third made a sincere confession, that being an idle young fellow, and averse to labour, he begun to take to pilfering; and that seeing one day a man carried to be buried in rich clothes, and deposited in a monument behind St. John's church, he had watched his opportunity, and going into the monument, stripped the corpse of the clothes; but that when he was

about to take away the linen which was next to the body, the corpse, by some supernatural power, sat up, and fixing its nails in his eyes, plucked them out: "And thus," concluded he, "wretched I, in great anguish and desolation, quitting all that I had taken, fled out of the monument; and this is the true history of my blindness." This account which these two servants of God heard from the mouth of the blind man himself they committed to writing, as a warning to sinners not to think, even in their most private sins, to escape the notice of the justice of God.

89. No less remarkable in this kind is the history which the same holy men learnt from abbot John, superior of a monastery near Antioch, with relation to a young man who had presumed to strip the dead corpse of a maiden gentlewoman. When he was going out of the monument laden with the spoil, she held him fast, and would not suffer him to stir, till he had restored all he had taken. Hereupon he made a solemn promise to renounce his wicked course of life, and to enter forthwith into religion; and being as good as his word, he went immediately to abbot John, and with the greatest marks of compunction besought him, for the love of God, to receive him into his monastery. When the abbot enquired into the cause of that excessive grief and anguish wherein he saw him, he related to him the whole matter of fact as above. The abbot after having comforted him, received him into the monastic habit, and appointed a cavern in the mountain for his cell, where, at the very time my authors heard from him this history, which happened but a little while before, the young man was actually doing penance for his sins, and serving our Lord with great fervor and piety.

90. Sophronius and John Moschus having one day visited a holy anchoret, who had his cell at the distance of eighteen miles from Alexandria, they begged of him to give them some lessons for their instruction and edification. "My children," said he, "you do well in renouncing the world, in order to secure your salvation. Go then and remain in your cells;—be sober and watchful; keep yourselves quiet;—be silent and pray without ceasing, and I trust in God that he will there enlighten your souls, and instruct you in the science of the Saints." He

said again, " My children, if you desire to be safe, flee from the company of men, and be not of the number of those that run gadding about from house to house, or from place to place, for the sake of worldly interest or empty glory, and thus fill their souls with nothing but vanity. Let us flee, my children, let us flee, for the time is near at hand." Again he said; " Alas, alas ! how bitterly shall we repent our not being sincere penitents now? Our misery is so great, that when we are praised we are puffed up, and when we are dispraised we are quite dejected : the former suggests to us poor wretches, pride and vain glory ; the latter depresses us with sadness and anguish. Now there can no good be found where either sadness or vain glory resides." He said again, " the devils make it their business, when they have drawn a soul into sin, to strive to cast her headlong into dejection and despair, that so they may complete her ruin. They are always plotting against the poor soul, and saying, *when shall she die, and her name perish ?* but let the soul that is sober reply with confidence in God, *I shall not die, but live, and declare the works of the Lord.* And if they should say to her again, *Get thee away from hence to the mountain like a sparrow*, let her reply, behold *my God and my Saviour, he is my protector, I will not go hence.*" He also said : " keep a guard at the gate of your hearts, and let no stranger in, but diligently enquire, *Art thou one of ours, or of our adversaries ?*" Jos. v.

91. We went also to the abbot John of Petra, and desired a word of instruction from him. This good father recommended continual mortification and poverty of spirit to us, in such a manner as to love to be stript of all earthly things ; and to this purpose he related to us that when he was a young man, and abode in the desert of Scete, one of the religious of that place being ill, had occasion for a small quantity of vinegar, but that so great was their poverty and abstinence, that a single drop could not be found in all the four monasteries, although they contained at that time no less than three thousand five hundred fathers.

92. John the Cilician, abbot of Raithu, used to inculcate the following lessons to his brethren : " My children, as we have fled from the world, by entering into religion, let as also flee from the flesh, and all its passi-

ons and concupiscences. Let us walk in the steps of our fathers and holy founders who first inhabited this place, and led such strict and mortified lives with so much silence and recollection. O, my children, let us not be so unhappy as to defile this place by our sins, which our fathers have taken so much pains to cleanse and purify from the evil spirits and their works of darkness." He also told them for their encouragement, that when he came thither first he found aged monks who had spent seventy years in that place, living the whole time upon nothing but herbs and dates; and that for his own part he had now been seventy-six years there, and had gone through many a conflict, and a great variety of molestations and temptations from the spirit of darkness. This was the same abbot of Raithu to whom Saint John Climacus dedicated his *Ladder of Paradise.*

93. We went also to visit abbot John the Persian, who recounted to us the following anecdote concerning Gregory the great, the most blessed bishop of Rome. "When I went," said he, "to Rome to venerate the sepulchres of the holy apostles Peter and Paul, and was one day standing in the midst of the city, they told me that the Pope was about to pass that way. Upon which I thought I would stop and cast myself at his feet, to shew reverence to him and crave his blessing; but when he came near and saw me ready to pay him that veneration, I call God to witness that he first prostrated himself upon the ground before me, and would not rise again till he saw me get up: then saluting me with a wonderful humility, he put three pieces of money into my hand, and gave orders to his people that I should be supplied with every necessary, which gave me occasion to glorify God for the exceeding great humility, mercy, and unbounded charity, which he had bestowed upon this his servant."

94. Abbot Andrew, superior of a monastery near Alexandria, related to us, that whilst in his youth he was going from Alexandria into Palestine, with nine others in his company, one of the number who was a Jew, named Theodore, was taken ill with a violent fever in the desert through which they were obliged to pass. The rest of the company pitying his case, afforded him what comfort they could, and led him forward in hopes of being able to reach some town or village where he might

meet with refreshment, but the vehement heat of the sun, joined with the fatigue of the journey, and the excessive thirst he endured, would not suffer him to go any farther: in a word, he was brought to that extremity of weakness and debility, that there were now no hopes left of his life, so that his companions fearing lest the same should be their own case if they did not make the best of their way out of the burning desert, thought of leaving him, since they could no longer be of any service to him. Seeing them about to depart from him, he conjured them for Christ's sake not to suffer him to die without baptism, since he ardently desired to die a Christian. They answered, that there was not one amongst them who could baptize him, as this sacrament could not by any means be administered without water, which could not possibly be had in those burning sands; but as he still persevered in begging and praying with many tears, that they would not be so cruel as to suffer him to die without making him a Christian, one of the company, inspired as we may believe from heaven, desired the rest to lift and hold him up, for he was not able to stand by himself, when filling both his hands with sand, he poured it upon his head at three effusions, repeating at the same time the form of words used by the Church in the administration of baptism, to which all the company answered, *Amen.* When behold, "As God is my witness, brethren," said the abbot to us, "the man who was dying before was so suddenly and perfectly healed, and strengthened by Christ our Lord, that there remained in him not the least signs of illness, or weakness, or of having suffered any thing whatsoever; but, on the contrary, he appeared to possess a sound, strong, and florid countenance, and performed the remainder of the journey through the desert with such wonderful alacrity, as to be always the foremost of the company." The abbot also related, how that as soon as they entered into Palestine and came to the city of Ascalon, they carried the convert to the holy bishop Dionysius, recounting to him all that had happened, and his miraculous cure upon his being baptized with the sand. The good prelate glorified our Lord for his goodness and mercy shewn on this occasion; but after consulting with his clergy, he concluded that as neither scripture nor tradition allow of the administering baptism otherwise than in water, the man ought to be baptized in water as the

Church prescribes; and for greater solemnity he sent him away to the banks of the Jordan, that he might be baptized in the same font wherein our Lord himself was baptized.

95. When we were in the isle of Samos, Lady Mary, the venerable and charitable matron, mother of the courtier Paul, related to us that whilst she resided at Nisibis in Mesopotamia, there lived in that city a very pious christian woman who was married to a pagan husband, but a well-meaning simple man. Being low in their circumstances, they had only a small sum of about fifty pieces of silver by them, which the husband designed to put out to use. The wife told him the best way he could put his money out was to give it to Jesus Christ, the God of the Christians, for that no one gave such good interest for money as he did, for that he would even return the principal double. Having asked her where he could find this God of the Christians, that he might put out his money into his hands, she led him to the church porch, and there shewing him a number of poor people, told him that whatever was given to the poor the God of the Christians would accept of as given to himself, and repay it with interest; whereupon without hesitation he cheerfully distributed the whole sum amongst the poor. After a lapse of three months, finding himself in some straits, he told his wife that the God of the Christians seemed not to take any notice of the debt, now that he stood in want of money; but she, strong in faith, bid him go to the place where he had lent him the money, and no doubt he should be paid. Accordingly he went to the church, where he saw the poor to whom he had given the money, but met with no one that offered to reimburse what he had lent them, or pay him any interest. At length, whilst he was considering within himself what he should do, or to whom he was to address himself, he saw a piece of silver lying at his feet, which he took up, and having carried it home, his wife told him that the God of the Christians, who, without being seen by us, disposes of all things, and provides for the whole world, had sent him that piece of money, and desired him to go and buy with it what they wanted for that day, assuring him that he would not fail to provide for them also for the time to come. Having gone to market with the money, he bought some bread and wine, and a fish,

which he gave to his wife to dress for their dinner, when
behold upon opening the fish she found in its entrails a
precious stone of admirable beauty, which she shewed
to her husband, and he, without knowing the value of
it, carried it to a jeweller to sell. The jeweller at first
sight bid him five pieces of silver for it. "What," says
he to himself, "so much as that?" supposing the man
not to be serious. The jeweller then bid him ten pieces;
but he still thinking him to be in jest, as he had no idea
of the value of the stone, stood silent; but when he offered him twenty, then thirty, and afterwards forty, and
had at length rose to fifty pieces of silver, he began to
be convinced that the jewel was worth a great deal more,
and stood out for a higher price. The jeweller advancing gradually, at last offered him three hundred pieces
of silver, which he agreed to take, and carried the money home to his wife. From thence she took occasion
to represent to him how liberally he had been dealt with
by the God of the Christians, and how kind and how
bountiful he must be, who for the fifty pieces of silver
he had lent to him three months before, had returned
him in so short a space of time, three hundred. This
wonderful event was immediately followed by the conversion of the man, who ceased not afterwards to glorify God for his infinite goodness, and to hold himself
highly indebted to the wisdom and piety of his religious
wife, who had been the happy instrument by which he
was brought to the knowledge of the saving religion of
Jesus Christ.

96. When we were at Alexandria, in the days of the
holy patriarch Eulogius, the cotemporary and intimate
friend of St. Gregory the Great, we met with Leontius of
Apamea, a most religious and faithful man, who lived for
many years at Cyrene, and came to be consecrated bishop
of that see, from whom we heard the following history:
In the days of the patriarch Theophilus, a famous philosopher, called Synesius, was made bishop of Cyrene, who
had an intimate friend, a philosopher also, whose name
was Evagrius. This man, being a pagan, was very
averse to the christian religion, to which the holy prelate
would gladly have brought him over; he particularly
objected against the articles of the resurrection of the
dead, and of the eternal rewards and punishments of the
world to come. Synesius, however, was not discourag-

ed with the resistance he met with, and did not desist from using all the means in his power for the conversion of his old friend, till the grace of God blessing his endeavours, Evagrius at length determined to embrace the christian faith, and was baptised with his whole family. Some time after he brought a bag of three hundred pieces of gold to the bishop, and put it in his hands for the use of the poor, desiring he would be pleased to give him a note under his own hand, that Christ would repay him in the world to come, with which proposal Synesius readily complied. Evagrius some years after fell ill of a distemper, of which he died; and being near his end, he gave the bishop's note of hand to his sons, desiring it might be buried with him. The sons, according to his desire, put the note into the hand of the father's corpse, and buried him with it. Three nights after Evagrius appeared to Synesius in his sleep, and bid him go to the monument where his body lay, in order to receive back his note, for that the whole had been repaid to him; and that in testimony thereof, he should find an acquittance, written by his (Evagrius's) own hand. The bishop next morning sent for the young men, asked them if they had not buried some paper with their father? They acknowledged that at his request they had, but that no one besides themselves knew any thing of the matter. Then taking them along with him, together with his clergy, and the principal men of the city, he ordered the tomb to be opened in their presence, where they found the philosopher lying, with the paper in his hand, which when they had taken from thence and opened, they saw at the bottom an acquittance, which appeared to be newly written, in Evagrius's own hand, whereby he acknowledged that he had received the contents, and was fully satisfied for the whole sum which he had given by the hands of Synesius to Jesus Christ our God and Saviour. This note and acquittance, as the same Leontius assured us, is kept to this day in the treasury of the church of Cyrene, and is always, in a special manner, recommended to the care of the treasurer of that cathedral.

97. One of the fathers related to us, that being at Constantinople upon some necessary business, whilst he was sitting one day in the church, a gentleman of condition came up, and saluting him, desired to sit down by his

side to hear from him some lessons for the good of his soul. The father told him that if he made a good use of the things of the earth, it would be a great means to bring him to heavenly goods. "Father," said he, "you are in the right; and that man is truly happy who places his confidence in God, and commits himself wholly to his providence. My father, who was a gentleman of distinction and opulence, but a great alms-giver, who distributed large sums of money to the poor, asked me one day, after giving me an account of all his worldly wealth, whether I chose that he should reserve it to bequeath wholly to me at his death, or whether he should dispose of it in the manner he had begun, by giving it to Christ by the hands of the poor, and to leave me Christ for my guardian and trustee. I told him I was very well satisfied with his disposing of his worldly substance in charity, and that I chose Christ before all worldly riches, which quickly pass away; they are with us to day and gone to morrow, but Christ remains for ever. After this, my father became so liberal in his alms, that at his death he left me very poor, but not without the utmost confidence in Christ, to whose care he had committed me. There happened to be at this time another gentleman of distinction in the city, exceeding rich, who was married to a very pious christian lady, who greatly feared our Lord. This worthy couple had one only daughter to inherit all their substance; and as she was now marriageable, the wife proposed to her husband, that instead of giving her in marriage to some rich nobleman, who, if he were not a servant of God, might make her miserable, they should rather look out for some virtuous humble man that feared God, and would both love and cherish her, and go hand in hand with her to heaven; for riches they wanted none for her, having a large fortune to give her; and therefore virtue and happiness was all they had to seek for. The husband being of the same way of thinking, bid her go to church and recommend the matter earnestly to God; and after praying, with all possible fervour, then address herself to the first person whom God should send into the church, as to the man designed by providence to be the husband of their daughter. Having accordingly gone to church, after she had finished her prayers, she sat down; and, as providence had ordered it, I was the first that entered. As soon as she perceived me, she sent her servant to call me, and having enquired of me who or whence I was? I told her I was a native of this city, and the son of such a one. What, said she, of that gentleman who gave away all his estate in alms? Yes, replied I, of the same. Are you married, said she? I answered, no; and told her all my father had said, when he left me Christ for my guardian and trustee. Hereupon she glorified God, and told me that my good guardian had provided both a wife and a plentiful estate for me, and wished me to use them both with the fear of God. Thus I received both her daughter and all her worldly substance; and I pray God that I may walk to the end of my life in the footsteps of my father."

98. Another of the fathers related to us concerning a certain lady of the first quality, who, after visiting the holy places, and performing other devotions in Jerusalem, went down to Cesarea to fix her abode in that city. Here she desired the bishop to place some religious woman with her, who might teach her humility and the fear of God. The bishop made choice of a virtuous humble maid, whom he recommended to her for that purpose. After some time he asked her how she liked the companion he had placed with her? She is good, said she, but is of no great service to my soul; for she is so exceedingly humble, that she lets me do whatever I please, and never contradicts me. Upon this the bishop sent a woman of a more rough and untowardly disposition to her, who failed not to afford the good lady frequent opportunities of exercising her patience, as well as her humility and charity, in bearing with her sour temper, her unruly tongue, her perpetual contradictions and reproaches. After some time the bishop again desired to know how she liked her new companion? She answered, that she had reason to be contented with her, because she was of essential service to her soul, by teaching her patience, meekness, and humility, which are best learnt in the school of reproaches and contradictions.

99. Another told us, that there happened to be a dispute between two neighbouring bishops upon affairs relating to their respective dioceses, which was like to turn out very much to the prejudice of the weaker of the two, because his antagonist was a politic man, and one that had great power and interest. Wherefore,

28*

being sensible of his danger, he assembled one day all his clergy, and told them he had found out an expedient, by means of which, through the grace of Christ, he made no doubt but they should gain their cause and overcome their adversary. They could not comprehend how this could possibly be, considering the power and the craft of the man with whom they had to contend. Well, said he, stop a little, and you shall see the goodness of God. On such a day they celebrate the feast of the holy martyrs with great solemnity in that diocese, therefore you shall accompany me thither, and provided you imitate me in whatever I shall then do, we shall certainly carry our cause. Having assured him they would, on the day appointed they all followed him to the neighbouring city, although ignorant of the means whereby he intended to overcome his adversary. At their arrival they found the whole people assembled, with their bishop and his clergy; when, without a moment's hesitation, the humble prelate advanced, his clergy all following him, and, together with them, prostrated himself at the feet of the other bishop, saying: *Forgive us, my good lord, we are all of us your servants.* The other, struck with astonishment at such profound humility, and at the same time touched with compunction, God changing his heart, fell also down upon his face, and taking hold of the feet of his fellow bishop, cried out: *it is you that are both my Lord and my father:* and from that moment their dispute was happily terminated, and they ever after lived in perfect concord and mutual charity. Thus the good prelate, by his humility, gained both his cause and the heart of his adversary, and told his clergy upon the occasion, that this was the true way to overcome their enemies.

100. A certain brother being assaulted with sadness, applied to one of the fathers, asking what he should do to prevent his thoughts from continually suggesting to him, that he was but losing his time in religion, and could never be saved? "Brother," said the father, "whatever you do, never think of going back to the world which you have renounced. If we cannot arrive at the land of promise, it is better for us to die in the wilderness, than to return into Egypt."

101. Gregory, the Governor of the province of Africa, a good Christian and great lover of the poor and the re-

ligious, related to us the following history which happened in our times in his native country, the district of Apamea in Syria. There is in that part of the world a place called Gonagus, forty miles distant from the city of Apamea, in the neighbourhood of which some country boys, by the way of play took upon themselves to mimic the sacrifice of the mass and the holy communion, according to what they had seen done by the priests in the church. For this purpose they appointed one of their number to officiate as priest, and two others to assist as deacon and sub-deacon; and making a large stone, in the middle of the field, serve for an altar, they placed some bread and some wine in an earthen cup upon it. Then he that personated the priest, having his two ministers on each hand of him, recited the words of the sacred oblation and consecration, which he had learnt by heart, by being near the altar, as in some places the priests recited them aloud, and proceeded in the mass till towards the end of the canon; but before they came to the breaking of the bread and the communion, a fire descended from heaven, which instantaneously consumed both all they had set upon their altar, and the stone itself, so as to leave no mark or trace of them remaining. Upon which they all fell to the ground, half dead with the fright, and for some time could neither recover speech or motion. In this condition they were found by their friends and carried home; to whom, as soon as they were able to speak, they recounted all that had happened, whilst the marks of the fire, in the place where it fell, plainly demonstrated the truth of what they related. The bishop of Apamea, on hearing of this extraordinary event, came out with all his clergy, and took cognizance of the whole matter upon the spot, by first examining the boys, and then viewing the footsteps of the fire, and in the conclusion caused a monastery to be built and a church erected in the field, the altar of which he fixed in the very spot where the fire had fallen. As to the boys, he placed them all in religious houses, one of whom afterwards became a monk in the said monastery, where Gregory, the governor, who related to us this wonderful history, saw him, and knew him.

F I N I S.

CONTENTS.